DIVORCE AND SECOND MARRIAGE

MARRIAGE

Facing the Challenge

New and expanded edition

KEVIN T. KELLY

GEOFFREY
CHAPMAN

Geoffrey Chapman Pastoral Studies Series

Making RCIA work, handling the management of change and loss, parish evangelization, diocesan renewal, moral theology at the end of the twentieth century, the challenges raised by *Christifideles Laici*, reconciliation, these are all issues to be covered in the Geoffrey Chapman Pastoral Studies series.

For the clergy, pastoral workers and interested lay people, the series is based on experience, and provides a comprehensive introduction to the issues involved.

The authors are recognized authorities on their subjects and bring their considerable experience and expertise to bear on the series.

Geoffrey Chapman
An imprint of Cassell Publishers Limited
Wellington House
125 Strand
London
WC2R 0BB

127 West 24th Street
New York, NY 10011

First published by Collins in 1982.
This new and expanded edition published by
Geoffrey Chapman, 1996.
Additional material for Appendix 2 used with permission
of authors/publishers.

British Library Cataloguing-in-Publication Data.
A catalogue record for this book is available from the British Library.

ISBN 0–225–66820–3

Typeset by Keystroke, Jacaranda Lodge, Wolverhampton.
Printed and bound in Great Britain by Biddles Ltd, Guildford
and King's Lynn.

CONTENTS

PREFACE TO THE NEW EDITION

This book was first published in 1982. Since then the divorce rate for England and Wales has risen by fourteen per cent and the divorce figures for 1993 show an all time high of 160,000. Four in ten new marriages can now be expected to end in divorce. That is the highest divorce rate in the European Union. Translating those figures into children affected by divorce, there were 176,000 children aged under sixteen whose parents were divorced in 1993 alone. If this trend continues, around one in four children will experience divorce in their family before reaching the age of sixteen. It is no wonder that Cardinal Hume writes: 'It is hardly surprising that the *Catechism of the Catholic Church* does not mince its words, describing divorce as "truly a plague on society"' (*The Tablet*, 20 January 1996, p. 68). The Policy Studies Institute study, *Britain 2010*, even predicts that by the year 2010 the normal pattern will be cohabitation, marriage, divorce and remarriage. The frequency of remarriage after divorce helps to explain why today over 2.5 million children and young people are part of a stepfamily. This, in turn, is one of the main reasons why in 1983 it was found necessary to establish a new charity, STEPFAMILY (The National Stepfamily Association) specifically to provide support, advice and information for all members of stepfamilies and those who work with them.

In the light of all the above, it might seem singularly inappropriate to be publishing a new edition of a book which argues in favour of a more open pastoral policy in the Roman Catholic Church towards remarriage after divorce. Surely that would only be encouraging this 'plague on society'! In the current situation, a moral theologian would be better employed trying to bring home to people the social harmfulness of this unhealthy trend in society. What would seem to be needed is writing which would help to strengthen people's belief in and commitment to the permanence of their solemn marriage vows.

It cannot be denied that a major focus for the Church must be to do all it can to help couples achieve what they want more than anything else, namely, a marriage in which their love grows and deepens and remains faithful to death. Cardinal Hume stresses this in his article in *The Tablet*. As well as highlighting the important role of the Church 'both in marriage preparation and support for existing marriages', he also insists that 'a comprehensive family policy is needed to ensure that a range of government policies, including employment, housing and the tax and benefit system become more helpful to families' (p. 70). Here the Cardinal is simply summarizing part of the final paragraph of the November 1995 bishops' conference statement. It is worth giving the full text of their statement:

> The bishops of England and Wales urge the Government and Parliament to take account of the following three needs whatever reforms are proposed in respect of the divorce law.
>
> a. Marriage needs to be strengthened, and the likelihood of divorce lessened by making adequate resources available to increase education for marriage and to bring about a change of people's attitudes and expectations regarding marital relationships and the bringing up of children. This must include helping young people to acquire the necessary social skills of communication, to deal sensibly and maturely with conflicts, and to develop an understanding of what commitment means in terms of changing and adapting within the marital relationship as the couple grow and change.
>
> b. Provision needs to be made for the generous funding of marriage counselling services and other organisations supportive of marriage and family life, so that access to such services is available, especially when difficulties begin to arise in marital relationships.
>
> c. Realistic support for marriage and the family requires a comprehensive family policy. This will have to deal with the support of families, including single parent families, through the tax and benefit system, access to adequate housing and employment, and child care facilities. A constructive debate must concentrate on all the elements required for an effective family policy (*Briefing*, 21 December 1995, p. 7).

A report in *The Guardian* (23 August 1995) also noted the belief of marriage guidance counsellors that 'the recession should take some blame for the divorce rate reaching an all time high'. Perhaps the *Catechism of the Catholic Church* might also have said that divorce is a symptom of a sick society. If that is true, many people whose marriages break down are tragic victims of this social sickness more than fearsome carriers of a social plague.

Cardinal Hume concludes his article with the statement:

If our society is to recover a healthier family life, it requires us to become more aware of the extraordinary potential for human fulfilment within marriages which, although they may not be perfect, are nonetheless good enough. There is a clear need to bring about a change in people's attitudes and expectations regarding marital relationships and the bringing up of children. This requires not so much a change in the law as a change of heart (p. 70).

I fully agree with that statement. However, the need for a change of heart is not confined to married couples or those entering marriages. It is true that people's expectations can be unrealistic and that the longing for a 'perfect marriage' can be destructive of the 'good enough' marriage with its 'extraordinary potential for human fulfilment'. However, as the Cardinal notes, all sorts of social policies can have a major impact on marriages and seriously affect their potential for survival and growth. The 'change of heart' he refers to is also needed among politicians, economists, business managers, civil servants, housing departments, health authorities, insurance companies, educationalists etc. I have never forgotten an experience I had in my early days as a priest in a Liverpool city parish. I had called to visit a young couple who were living in rented accommodation in a multiple occupancy house. They had four children under five, including twins, and lived and slept in one room, sharing a common kitchen, bathroom and toilet with six other families. I rang the housing authorities to see what could be done to help them. The response I got was a dismissive laugh along with the comment, 'If you think that is bad, you've got a lot to learn.' I have no idea whether that couple are still together. If they are, it is a miracle. On the surface, social factors outside their control meant that, humanly speaking, their marriage never had a chance. I do not believe that it is the couple who need a 'change of heart' in a situation like that. The 'change of heart' called for by the Cardinal must be far more wide-ranging.

I believe that the line of argument put forward in this book contributes, in its own way, to this 'change of heart'. In no way is this book meant to be an apology for divorce. In fact, it is based on the belief that marriage breakdown is the occasion of great suffering and harm for all concerned, couples, children and their relatives. In that sense, it can truly be described as an 'evil'. It is the very opposite to the human good that couples set their hearts on when they commit themselves to each other in marriage.

The 'change of heart' I am arguing for in my book is a recognition that the covenant-relationship paradigm of marriage which was canonized at Vatican II has far-reaching implications for our theology of marriage and the pastoral practice flowing from this. It implies that couples cannot take the indissolubility of their marriage for granted. To give their marriage a realistic hope of being indissoluble, they need to prepare themselves properly before they undertake such an awesome commitment. And they need to keep working at their relationship as each new challenging phase of their marriage presents itself. In a very real sense, they themselves have to create and fashion the indissolubility of their own marriage. Moreover, they need help if they are to achieve this. Ideally, that help begins with the example of their own parents' married and family life. However, for a variety of reasons couples may not find that their own parents' relationship offers them a helpful role model for marriage today. Their education at school should also make an important contribution, enabling them to develop the skills needed to communicate their feelings and listen to the feelings of others. They also need help in learning how to handle conflict creatively in their relationship. How real forgiveness and reconciliation operates is another field of human interaction where they can learn from the experience and wisdom of others. All that is relevant to the 'change of heart' I am arguing for in my book. How to help couples achieve real indissolubility in their marriage is a challenge facing all of us in the Church. The bishops have clearly recognized that challenge in their November 1995 statement quoted earlier.

This pastoral challenge retains its validity even though some readers may not accept the philosophical/theological interpretation of indissolubility which I argue on pages 16–24. As I point out in those pages, that section of the book is offered as a theological exploration. In no way am I claiming that it represents the Church's *teaching* on indissolubility. I am merely suggesting that it might offer a helpful way of understanding indissolubility in the light of the Church's acceptance of the covenant-relationship paradigm of marriage. Disappointingly, there has been little discussion of that section of my book. Even James Provost's masterly survey of recent Catholic writings on divorce-remarriage, 'Intolerable Marriage Situations: A Second Decade' (*The Jurist*, 1990, pp. 575–612), though it frequently refers to my book, does not record any major theological discussion of this precise point over the past ten years.

There is another dimension of the 'change of heart' theme which I put forward in this book. A parallel example might help to illustrate it. Through CAFOD I have been drawn into the HIV/AIDS scene, especially insofar as the pandemic is affecting people in the developing countries. HIV/AIDS is wreaking havoc in some countries and the suffering and loss caused to many people, especially women and children, is devastating. Two major priorities stand out. The first is to find an antidote or cure. The second is to prevent the virus spreading. These two priorities concern respectively the fields of medical research and the social dynamics of behaviour change. However, concern for these two priorities does not eliminate our obligation to care for those actually suffering as a result of HIV/AIDS, whether because they are sero-positive or because they are AIDS orphans.

Something similar must be said with regard to divorce and remarriage. As well as giving high priority to remote and proximate marriage preparation and to on-going support for married couples, we must not ignore the fact that those whose marriages have broken down also have a legitimate claim on the Church's pastoral care. They and their children have already suffered intensely through the shattering experience of their marriage disintegrating and their family life falling apart. Though it is the 'social plague of divorce' which has devastated their lives, what they need now is help towards healing, not condemnation. In recent years the Association of Separated and Divorced Catholics, and Rainbow groups have played an important role in helping to provide this healing ministry. It must be acknowledged that Marriage Tribunals have also, in many cases, helped people to find healing and wholeness.

However, we know that many divorced partners enter a second marriage. As mentioned earlier, over a third of marriages involve a previously married partner. In fact, three-quarters of all divorcees eventually remarry. A fact-sheet from the Marriage and Partnership Charity, One plus One, offers this information:

> In the last twenty years the number of remarriages has increased, with remarriages of divorced people more than doubling: from 15% in 1971 to 34% in 1991. More men than women remarry (1990: 80,300 remarriages for divorced men; 78,000 for divorced women). After divorce, men have greater social freedom – only rarely will they have custody of any children of the previous marriage. It is common for them to marry women younger than themselves, meaning that they are less restricted than women in their choice of new partners.

Second marriages are more likely to be preceded by a period of cohabitation.

A quarter of all divorces involve marriages where at least one partner has been divorced before. Remarriages involving divorcees are more likely to break down than marriages of those where neither partner has been divorced. One of the reasons for this may be that unresolved issues from a former marriage have an impact on the new partnership.

Thankfully, the Church has not buried its head in the sand and pretended that all this is not happening. At different levels of the Church, a lot of thought and effort has gone into trying to formulate and implement a much more positive pastoral approach to couples in a second marriage. The bishops of England and Wales have certainly made this an important item on their pastoral agenda. Papal and Vatican statements, too, have urged priests and laity to adopt a positive pastoral attitude towards the divorced-remarried and not to treat them as though they were outcasts from the Church.

One of the problems is trying to discern how far this 'positive attitude' can go. Some Catholics might consider that the republication of this book is going too far. For instance, a good friend of mine, a priest whose wisdom I respect, keeps telling me that statistically, compared with first marriages, remarriages after divorce stand a higher chance of ending in divorce themselves. Hence, he would suggest that it is a false kindness to be too positive towards the possibility of a second marriage itself, since that is likely to bring yet more pain on the partners themselves and their children. That is an objection which I take very seriously. It has led me to look further into the statistical evidence on this point and also to reflect pastorally on its practical implications.

It is true that the statistical data present a picture which does not offer very optimistic prospects for a divorced man or woman entering a second marriage. This has been brought out very clearly by John Haskey, an eminent researcher for the Population Statistics Division of the Office of Population Censuses and Surveys (OPCS). In his article, *Marital status before marriage and age at marriage: their influence on the chance of divorce*, working on the assumption that the divorce rates for different groups of spouses would continue at the levels observed in 1980–81, he states as one of his conclusions:

The chance that the marriage of a divorced man would again end in divorce is one and a half times that of a single man who marries at the same age. Analogously, a divorced woman who remarries is approximately twice as likely to divorce as a single woman who marries at the same age (in *Population Trends*, 32, Summer 1983, p. 14).

For anyone involved in the marriage and family life field of pastoral care, this is a very disturbing picture. Of course, it would be misleading to conclude from this that a previous divorce is the only factor of significance which is likely to have a bearing on the duration of a marriage. It is well known that age at marriage is also an important factor – the older the age at marriage, the greater the stability of the marriage, other things being equal. It is noteworthy that in the quotation above John Haskey is very careful to make his comparisons between individuals 'at the same age'. In fact, his data about grooms between the ages of 20 and 40 actually show that, statistically, the likelihood of a second divorce drops, the older the divorced groom is within the age range studied. Hence, the likelihood of marriage ending in divorce is actually less, statistically, for a divorced groom aged 35–39 at marriage than for a bachelor groom aged 20–24 at marriage, and only marginally higher than for a bachelor groom aged 25–29 at marriage. That can help us bear in mind that a previous divorce is not the only factor affecting marriage duration which should be of concern to pastoral theology.

Nevertheless, the picture is still very disturbing from a pastoral point of view. A divorced partner entering a second marriage is likely to start off yet another cycle of marriage breakdown with all the attendant trauma and suffering for the various parties involved, including any children of this or the previous marriage. Some people would argue that this is an added reason why the Church should keep well away from remarriages since they are likely to be a recipe for further disaster.

That is one possible pastoral conclusion that could be drawn from the above very disturbing statistical data. Whether it is the only, let alone the best, pastoral conclusion is open to question. After all, there must be some reason why the remarriage of a divorced person is more at risk in this way. The One plus One fact-sheet, *Remarriage and stepfamilies*, suggests that 'one of the reasons for this may be that unresolved issues from a former marriage have an impact on the new partnership.' If there is any truth in this, it could be argued that, by refusing to give any help to couples contemplating a remarriage after divorce, we as a Church are laying ourselves open to the accusation that we are denying help to wounded people who are in great need of pastoral care. The high risk of failure would seem to suggest that divorced people who remarry are in even greater need of help in preparing for marriage, even though their needs might be of a very special kind. Moreover, if the person they are marrying is single, that adds a further complication to the help needed. It might even increase its urgency. People claim that one of the advantages of the Roman Catholic marriage tribunal system is that the process, if handled sensitively, offers a divorced person the opportunity to deal with some of the unfinished business of the previous marriage. An interesting piece of research might be to explore whether there is an equally high level of risk of breakdown in the case of second marriages involving someone whose first marriage has been declared null following the full matrimonial tribunal process. Paradoxically, it is possible that the experience of marriage tribunals might even be able to provide some helpful guidance in preparing divorced people for a second marriage!

Nevertheless, with regard to pastoral care of the divorced-remarried, admission to the sacraments still remains a stumbling block. That comes out in Cardinal Hume's article in *The Tablet* to which I have already made reference. Cardinal Hume is very strong on compassion for all who have been through the tragedy of marriage breakdown and insists that those who have re-married must not be excluded from that compassion. I suspect that it must have been with some sadness that he felt constrained to note that admission to the sacraments could not be included in that ministry of compassion:

> Nor must we forget that the Church's role always includes the care and support of those who have suffered the pain of separation and divorce, whether it is their fault or not. What should be the attitude of bishops and priests towards those who have been divorced? We must first remind them that the fact of being divorced does not debar a person from the sacraments; Remarriage by the divorced does. But even towards those who have divorced and then remarried, pastors must show understanding and compassion, without compromising the Church's teaching on the latter. For example, even when the sacraments are excluded, pastors must nonetheless give what spiritual help they can to those who have remarried, reminding them, of course, that they remain members of the Church. The Church is strict in respect of principles but very compassionate towards those whose marriages have broken down.

On this matter of non-admission to the sacraments of the divorced-remarried, the position in the Church remains the same as it was when my book was first published in 1982. That is why I believe that Chapters 3 and 4 are as relevant today as when they were first written. Admittedly, there have been some developments since then. The most notable has come from the three bishops of the German province of the Upper Rhine: Bishop Karl Lehmann of Mainz, president of the German bishops' conference; Archbishop Oskar Saier of Freiburg, vice-president of the bishops' conference; and Bishop Walter Kasper of Ruttenburg-Stuttgart, one of the most respected theologians in the Roman Catholic Church. On 10 July 1993 these bishops published a pastoral letter on the pastoral care of the divorced-remarried. Along with this letter, they published a document giving 'Principles of Pastoral Care' for the divorced-remarried. The aim of these principles was to help priests engage in dialogue with parishioners remarried after divorce with a view to enabling them to arrive at a conscientious assessment of their situation. This would include discerning whether or not they could feel justified in presenting themselves for the sacraments. These principles were formulated with great care and were certainly not intended to encourage indiscriminate admission to the sacraments. Nonetheless, they recognized the possibility that a person in this situation might arrive at a genuinely conscientious decision to receive the sacraments and that a priest-counsellor might have a role to play in their reaching such a decision.

Because these bishops held positions of major responsibility in the Church, their letter and statement of principles attracted widespread attention. In Appendix 2 I have included the full text of their document, with the doctrinal argumentation which underpins it. As far as I know, this is the first time the latter has appeared in its entirety in English. The Congregation of the Doctrine of the Faith (CDF) stepped in quickly and summoned the three bishops to Rome to explain the situation. The world-renowned Jesuit canon lawyer and theologian, Ladislas Örsy, discussed the German bishops' letter and the Vatican reaction to it in an article in *The Tablet*, 18 June 1994, p. 787. Noting the report that the bishops had been called to Rome to 'discuss their point of view', Örsy remarks, perhaps somewhat impishly: 'One hopes that the significance of this invitation is that those who by their offices are called to legislate for the universal Church are anxious to be enriched by the experience and the insights of the bishops who have the direct care of souls.' Actually, that would have been close to what I suggest about the need for pastoral practice to develop initially at grass roots level rather than by edict from on high (cf. pp. 81–82).

The CDF response to this pastoral initiative by the German bishops came in the form of a letter addressed to all the bishops of the world. Without mentioning the German bishops by name, it stated quite bluntly that the present teaching and practice must be strictly adhered to.

Soon after, the three German bishops issued a letter for their people in which they explained where matters now stood after their discussions with the Congregation and in the light of the CDF's letter to the bishops of the world. On a first somewhat hasty reading of this letter, it struck me that the German bishops were withdrawing completely from their earlier position. However, after a more careful reading of their text, I formed the impression that they are openly acknowledging the concerns expressed by the CDF, concerns which they themselves share. However, they are also recognizing that they still have their own pastoral concerns and responsibilities as local bishops towards their people. Included among those responsibilities is the task of guiding their priests in their ministry of helping the divorced-remarried form their consciences with honesty and integrity before God. I would suggest that it is not helpful to read this second letter as though it were the bishops' reply to the CDF. This letter is written to their own priests and people. It is a further exercise of their pastoral responsibility. It should be read as a supplement to their original statement of pastoral principles. I do not believe it is simply a withdrawal from those principles.

In an article in *The Tablet* (29 October 1994, pp. 1374–1375), I noted that the CDF letter did not add any new theological insights to the discussion of this pastoral issue. It says nothing which the Pope had not said in his 1981 post-synodal Apostolic Exhortation, *Familiaris Consortio*, which carries much more authority than the CDF letter. I thus concluded that the CDF letter did not substantially change the situation. For the very same reason, I believe that the line of argument developed in my book retains its force, despite the subsequent publication of the CDF letter.

I have included all the above documentation in Section A of Appendix 2. I also thought it would be helpful to the reader to have available some other recent official church texts. Consequently, I have included the two sections of *The Catechism of the Catholic Church* which deal with divorce and remarriage and also the relevant paragraphs of n. 34 of the 1984 post-synodal

Apostolic Exhortation of John Paul II, *Reconciliatio et Paenitentia*. The new Code of Canon Law contains no canon explicitly forbidding admission to the sacraments to the divorced-remarried. Canonists seem to think that such a prohibition is implicit in canon 915. However, the way different canonists interpret this canon suggests that it leaves room for considerable flexibility in pastoral practice. I have also included in Section B of Appendix 2 the interpretations of canon 915 found in the two major English-language commentaries on the new code. For good measure I have also included the much fuller discussion of this canon found in James Provost's extremely thorough article, 'Intolerable Marriage Situations: A Second Decade', in *The Jurist*, 1990, pp. 575–612 (at pp. 590–596). His conclusion is worth noting:

> What is remarkable is that neither code (i.e. Latin and Eastern rite) explicitly excludes divorced and remarried Catholics from the Eucharist, despite the attention given to this topic in the process of revising at the least the Latin code, and in two apostolic exhortations by the pope who promulgated both codes. It is difficult to determine the significance of this silence with accuracy, but it can at least be observed that where the law leaves room for nuance, it is not inappropriate for those who interpret or apply the law to leave room for nuance also (p. 596).

Section C of Appendix 2 contains nine pieces of writing published since my book first appeared in 1982. These articles or excerpts throw further light on the discussion. Readers might find them helpful at the level of deepening their theological understanding or reflecting further on pastoral practice.

My book revisited

I must confess that it was only when Ruth McCurry of Geoffrey Chapman took up the suggestion of a number of people that this book should be republished that I found time to re-read it again from cover to cover. I approached that exercise with some apprehension. How would I react to what I had written nearly fourteen years ago? I must confess that I was pleasantly surprised. Not only did I find that I still agreed with almost everything I had written, I also felt that for the most part I could not improve on the way I had expressed my thoughts. Is that arrogance on my part or a sign that my thinking has not moved on at all? I hope not! I think it is simply due to the fact that there has been little or no movement in pastoral practice since my book was published and so there has been little stimulus for further reflection among pastoral theologians. I hope, therefore, that the book's republication will help to kick-start the discussion of this issue anew or, at least, bring it out more into the open.

I would like to conclude this Preface by sharing with the reader some of my reactions on re-reading this book. I will do this under two general headings.

Some alterations to the text or reservations regarding content

There were a few passages which I felt I could not leave without comment either because of subsequent developments or because I now saw things in a somewhat different light.

1. On p. 35 I mentioned a 1958 Roman Rota decision stating that 'consummation can be had independently of consciousness and free consent of the will'. Readers who, like me, were appalled by that decision will welcome the fact that the new Code of Canon Law adopts a more personalist approach to consummation in canon 1061, §1, which states that a marriage is consummated 'if the spouses have *in a human manner* engaged together in a conjugal act in itself apt for the generation of offspring' (italics mine). However, canonists are now debating whether this canon means that intercourse with a condom or vaginal sheath does not consummate a marriage.

2. Since I wrote this book in 1982 I have become increasingly unhappy with the expression 'dissent'. I have explained my unease on this point more fully in my book, *New Directions in Moral Theology* (Geoffrey Chapman, 1992), pp. 148–152. Dissent carries negative overtones similar to deny, oppose and contradict. That is certainly how dissent was presented in the 1990 CDF Instruction, *The Ecclesial Vocation of the Theologian*, and in the Pope's 1993 encyclical letter, *Veritatis Splendor*. Both documents use the term 'dissent' to denote an attitude grounded in 'general opposition to church teaching'. That is not an attitude which I and most other theologians who disagree with some aspects of the Church's official moral teaching would want to subscribe to. Hence, I would prefer to use the much more ordinary word, 'disagree'. That fits better into a context of genuine dialogue which involves respectful listening and honest speaking. I make this point more fully on page 151 of *New Directions in Moral Theology*:

The Instruction's restriction of the meaning of 'dissent' is much to be welcomed. It provides moral theologians with a clear distinction between unacceptable dissent and the kind of disagreement which many moral theologians can recognize in themselves and which they believe comes from a very positive attitude towards teaching authority in the Church. It includes such positive elements as respect for tradition, concern for the truth, love of the Church, shared responsibility for the Church's mission in the world, commitment to Vatican II's call to dialogue in a common search for the truth, respect for the place of human reason in discovering and articulating our deepening understanding of the truth, responsibility towards those who are looking for help in major decisions affecting their personal or professional lives, etc. The term 'dissent' misses all this, as Orsy observes: 'The voice of a theologian proposing an answer different from the one given by those in authority may not be an act of dissent at all; rather, it may be a needed contribution to the development of doctrine, coming from someone who is assenting to every part of revealed truth.'

Consequently, in the republished text of my book I have changed 'dissent' to 'disagree' throughout.

3. On p. 89 of my original Appendix (1) I quote with approval a passage from the directives of the South African bishops on *Humanae Vitae*. If I were writing a commentary on that passage today, I would query their use of the phrase, 'though falling short of the ideal'. 'Ideal' is a term which needs very careful handling in moral theology. I believe it is a term which is most helpfully used in an inspirational sense. For instance, ideals can throw light on and help to bring out the often hidden goodness in the down-to-earth difficult decisions we have to make in situations which are often far from perfect. Too frequently we use the term 'ideal' to cast a shadow over such difficult decisions, by implicitly suggesting that they are only second-best and even morally suspect.

4. I ended my original Introduction with an apology to my many women friends for my reluctant decision to settle for the more common traditional usage and use 'he' in an indefinite sense. I now believe that is not good enough and have altered the text in an attempt to use inclusive language throughout.

Some reiterations of emphasis

I would also like to highlight certain passages either because they open out a major topic for discussion or because the point they make has great pastoral importance.

1. As mentioned already, the key section of the book at the level of theological exploration is found on pp. 16–24 where I offer an interpretation of indissolubility which might perhaps be more in line with the Vatican II covenant-relationship paradigm of marriage. It should be noted that on p. 23 I try to refute the objection that this interpretation does not imply that a marriage can only be said to have achieved indissolubility when one of the partners dies. Moreover, on p. 24 I show how the Roman Catholic tradition actually has built into it a two-tier understanding of indissolubility.

2. On pp. 30–31 I argue that the fact that new grounds for nullity can come to be recognized in matrimonial jurisprudence should remind us that the decisions of matrimonial tribunals are fallible and have never claimed to be otherwise. One implication of this is the possibility that people might perhaps have an intuitive sense of the nullity of their own marriage, even though the grounds for it might not yet be accepted in matrimonial jurisprudence. At least, their judgement about their own marriage, though not impartial, might still be worthy of more credence than is often admitted.

3. The grace-filled character of at least some second marriages makes us face the question as to whether there is any sense in which a second marriage after divorce can be viewed as 'sacramental'. I discuss this on pp. 39–41.

4. Although I am not too happy with the expression, 'the law of gradualness', which was used by the bishops in the Synod and which I elaborate on in pp. 51–52, I believe that the basic line of thought presented in those pages is important for the field of pastoral theology. The kind of analysis found in Josef Fuchs' latest volume, *Moral Demands and Personal Obligations* (Georgetown University Press, 1993), would seem to offer a more satisfactory way of exploring this area of morality. Fuchs' approach in that book reassures me in my practical conclusion on p. 52, though, for the sake of accuracy, I think 'many Catholics' should be altered to 'some Catholics'.

Bearing all this in mind I would have no hesitation in saying that entering a second marriage or (even more so) remaining faithful to an already existing second marriage can certainly be envisaged as a *rightly made* decision for many Catholics. And if it is rightly made, I think it can also be described as the right decision for them (i.e. in their present state and at this particular moment in time within this specific situation). And if it is in this sense the right decision for them, it is accurate to describe it as morally good.

5. Archbishop Worlock's impassioned plea at the 1980 Synod on Marriage and the Family for a more open approach by the Church to the divorced-remarried still has a powerful impact on me when I read it. I am not sure that the Church has really heard what he is saying there. The text of his intervention is given on pp. 71–72 of my book.

6. Since first writing pp. 81–82 I have become even more convinced that good pastoral practice needs to develop from the grass roots. For the Church to encourage among pastoral practitioners an attitude which is unwilling to accept personal pastoral responsibility but which only acts in response to an edict on high, to my mind, destroys good pastoral practice. Since I get the impression that, in many ways, the Church is moving backwards rather than forwards in this respect, I wish to highlight one particular passage from those two pages:

> As a normal rule, it is good that changes in pastoral practice should in the first instance occur naturally as a kind of instinctive reaction to a new way of understanding things. This is a much healthier process than that of having practical changes imposed by edict from on high. If they develop naturally, they have more chance of being able to find their own right level as people learn to discern what is appropriate in particular situations. The adoption of these changes as official policy should occur at a later stage in the process. By then what is pastorally helpful would have been sifted by experience from what is harmful or unnecessary. For a change in pastoral practice to occur informally, therefore, should not be regarded as something harmful to the Church. Nor should it be considered to be occurring by accident, if by that is meant occurring without deep theological reflection and serious pastoral concern. In fact, for change to be able to occur in this informal way can be a very healthy sign that the whole Church is beginning to play a more active part in theological reflection and pastoral discernment (p. 82).

INTRODUCTION

Facing the challenge

Marriage breakdown and second marriage challenges all of us in the Church in a number of different ways.

It challenges us to put far more emphasis on proper preparation for marriage and on providing adequate support for married couples, especially during the critical phases of their marriage. It challenges us to be better equipped as a Church so that, wherever possible, we can help couples who are drifting apart to achieve a deep and lasting reconciliation. It challenges us, too, to offer deep understanding and support for men and women who have suffered the painful tragedy of their marriage breaking down completely, without any hope of reconciliation. Such people need support at a whole variety of levels to enable them to regain their balance and self-respect after such a devastating experience; and where there are children involved there are all the difficulties of one-parent families, with the additional problems of tension and rivalry between the separated parents and the consequent confusion and insecurity for the children. If such people choose to remain single as a sign of their commitment to life-long fidelity, the Church should feel challenged to give them every support possible.

These are all challenges which flow naturally from our belief in life-long marriage. However, vitally important though all these challenges are, they are not the ones which are faced in this book. Thank God, they are already being tackled more and more in the Church today and they have been very well highlighted by the Pastoral Congress. This book would like to face a different set of challenges presented to us by second marriages after divorce. These are challenges which we find far more difficult to handle, since they do not fit in so easily with our belief in life-long marriage.

There is the challenge which increasingly many priests are experiencing, of the couple in such a second marriage who are among the best parishioners in the community. Their home is a truly Christian home, their family is exemplary, they are fully participating members of the Eucharistic community and there is evident prayer and goodness in their lives. Priests are challenged by the obvious presence and activity of God's Spirit in the lives of these couples. Unless we are to separate off faith from life, and Vatican II considers this as one of the major errors of our day, there is no denying the Christian goodness of many second marriages of people who have been divorced. That is a challenge to us. How do we fit such marriages into our theology of marriage and our belief in the indissolubility of marriage? And how do we deal with such couples at the level of sacramental life?

Another challenge is one which faces almost all of us but which is felt most deeply by many parents. Someone close to us, perhaps a son or daughter, has gone through the tragedy of marriage breakdown and things have gone beyond the stage where reconciliation can realistically be hoped for. Has such a person no alternative but to remain single for the rest of life? Very often our concern for that person's deep happiness leads us to hope that he or she will find a new partner and will discover in a second marriage the happiness that eluded them in their first marriage. If our concern for that person's deep happiness is genuine, might it not be saying something to us about God's will? Can we be so certain that the life-giving Good News of Christ has no message except one of refusing healing when this is to be found in the love of a second marriage? That is a second challenge which we have to look at.

A further challenge is that of the millions of Catholic men and women now living in a second marriage after divorce. In the parish they may not be among the leading lights referred to above. There might not be anything particularly exemplary about their marriage and family life. But they are brothers and sisters to whom we believe the Gospel is addressed as Good News just as much as it is to the rest of us. The challenge we are faced with in their regard is this. Do we really believe that the Good News of Christ is calling them to break off and surrender the goodness of whatever married love now exists in their lives?

A personal note

This book is an attempt to face these last three challenges honestly. I have not found it an easy book to write, since by temperament I am cautious and very law-abiding, and at first sight this book might seem very brash and dismissive of authority. However, I have been impelled to write it by my conviction that these challenges come to us from the Lord himself. In them I feel he is beckoning us beyond our present certainties and securities. To refuse to face these challenges might be to refuse to listen to the Lord.

Although this book expresses my own personal and sincerely held views, it is the fruit of extensive reading and wide-ranging discussion over many years. My concern for the divorced-remarried was already aroused during the ten years in which I taught moral theology in the major seminary at Upholland. It was greatly consolidated by the very fruitful experience of sharing the problems of so many priests and lay-people while I was involved in Clergy In-Service Training and Adult Christian Education during my five years as Director of the Upholland Northern Institute. During that time I also served on the Working Party set up by the bishops of England and Wales to look at the pastoral issues of the Sacrament to the Divorced-Remarried. And my brief experience in Skelmersdale New Town as leader of the Team Ministry there has only served to confirm me in my convictions. Consequently, if it does not sound too presumptuous, I feel a certain peace and confidence in the position I am putting forward. I know that for the most part it is shared by the vast majority of my colleagues in the field of moral theology and that it is supported by the intuitive Christian sense of so many good priests and lay-people. But most of all I feel supported by the fact that what I have written seems to me to be in tune with what the Spirit is actually working out in the lives of so many people who are divorced and remarried, and in the courageous and welcoming ministry they are receiving from so many priests.

The argument of the book

I would summarize the main argument of this book as follows: At Vatican II the Catholic Church reminded herself that she must accommodate her understanding of the Gospel to the richest insights and knowledge of every age and culture. This does not mean watering down the truth. Nor is it just a matter of mere translation into different and more appropriate language. It is a real challenge to the Church to listen to the wisdom of her age. By so listening she will be able to penetrate more deeply the truth she believes and so arrive at a fuller understanding of it (cf. *The Church in the Modern World*, nn. 44 & 58).

Despite the fact that there are many aberrations abroad today about sexuality and marriage, it cannot be denied that there is also a richer understanding of human sexuality and its relation to growth in married love and parenthood. This deeper insight has been gratefully received and acknowledged by Vatican II and by Paul VI and John Paul II and has resulted in the development of a much more satisfactory theology of marriage as human reality and Sacrament.

There has been a dramatic change of gear in moving from looking at marriage as a contract, to putting the main emphasis on its being an inter-personal relationship of life-giving love. These are not mutually exclusive positions, but one's whole approach to marriage can alter radically depending on which is made the main emphasis.

This change of gear fits in with the thesis proposed by Thomas S. Kuhn in his famous work, *The Strucure of Scientific Revolutions* (University of Chicago Press, 1962). According to Kuhn a particular science comes into being when some fertile imagination discerns an overall pattern which brings together and makes sense of what previously seemed to be a lot of unconnected phenomena; and the science becomes established when others working in the same field accept this overall pattern and conduct all their research in accordance with it. The consequent development of the science occurs through the process of demonstrating how all sorts of other phenomena also begin to make sense within that pattern. Kuhn calls such an overall pattern a 'paradigm'. Phenomena which do not fit into the pattern are often discounted as being outside the field of this particular science, though there are usually some enterprising spirits who refuse to give up the challenge presented by these rogue phenomena. Kuhn maintains that a scientific revolution occurs when the adequacy of the accepted pattern is stretched to breaking point by the phenomena which cannot be accommodated within it, and the moment of breakthrough comes when another fertile imagination conceives a new pattern and suddenly things are seen to make sense in a new and different way. This initiates a new upsurge of scientific research as people explore all the exciting implications of viewing reality within this new pattern.

It seems to me that Kuhn's analysis can help us to understand what has occurred in the field of the theology of marriage. We are currently involved in the process of the change-over from one pattern to another. Society, with theology and the Church in its train, has moved from the 'contract' pattern of marriage to the 'relationship' pattern. Consequently, the present phase involves the exciting work of fitting all the pieces together again within this new pattern. For the Church this has wide implications for different levels of its life – law, pastoral policy, celebration of the sacraments, education etc. It is not surprising that many in the Church today complain of confusion during this phase. But it is not a confusion which is due to the Church having lost her way; it is merely a temporary, transitional confusion such as is necessarily involved in the process of changing position in order to get a better view of things. It is rather like the blurring of vision which occurs while one is trying to get things into clearer focus. In fact, it is a confusion which should eventually give way to a much clearer vision.

In this book I am trying to explore the implications of the 'relationship of life-giving love' pattern of marriage for a belief in the indissolubility of marriage. In no way do I wish to deny the indissolubility of marriage or to weaken it in any way. I want to see whether this new pattern of marriage allows us to see indissolubility in a new and richer light. If it does, I want to see what are the challenges this presents to us and whether it helps us to understand and interpret what is happening in our society, with its tragedy of such widespread breakdown of marriage. This is the main thrust of Chapters 1 and 2. I think it is only fair to state that the re-interpretation of indissolubility offered in these chapters does not carry the same wide consensus among moral theologians as the position and practice I put forward in Chapters 3 and 4. This is not because many theologians have discussed it and rejected it. It is simply that it has not received wide discussion in theological journals; though I have a feeling that it should tie in with the general approach adopted by many of my colleagues. I look forward to their reactions, since I feel sure their comments should help to refine and tighten up the position I am proposing.

I also feel it is important to point out that Chapters 3 and 4 retain their validity independently of whether my re-interpretation of indissolubility is acceptable or not.

A listening Church

I am convinced that as a Church we need to be far more humble in our whole approach to marriage. We need to have the humility to listen to the experience of married people. This was a major strength of the National Pastoral Congress. It found such richness in the contribution of the married delegates that it recommended that the Church 'should listen to the experience of married people and appreciate their unique insights into what is contained within a permanent sexual relationship' (Sector C Report, n. 2). This recommendation was clearly listened to by the bishops (cf. Easter People, n. 102) and Cardinal Hume made it his own in his first address to the 1980 Rome Synod on Marriage and the Family.

As a Church we also need the humility to listen to other cultures. In the 1980 Synod many Third World bishops expressed concern that a false conflict had been created between Gospel values and the values of their own particular cultures. They wanted the Church to be more attentive to the values of marriage and family as embodied in different cultures, since human and Christian values never exist in a non-cultural form. 'It could be left to the local Churches to embody this ideal in their different settings. It seems to be impossible to speak of a single model type of family valid for all people, cultures, and epochs. Each and every model is shaped by social and cultural circumstances' (Bishop Datubara of Indonesia). There is no pure state of marriage. Marriage is an institution which takes on different forms in different cultures.

Marriage in a cultural context

I am very much aware that I am writing this book in the specific cultural context of Western Christianity. Although human sexuality and its link with love and life transcends all cultures, it only exists in reality in particular cultural settings. That is why it is no disrespect to the fine teaching on marriage contained in the Vatican II Pastoral Constitution, *The Church in the Modern World* (nn. 47–52), to suggest that as a picture of the reality of marriage today it is probably a more accurate reflection of Western culture than of other cultures. This should be borne in mind later when I use such expressions as 'the Church's current understanding of the reality of marriage'. I can appreciate that some of the points I will be arguing in this book might lose much of their force in another cultural setting. This is particularly the case when we are looking at marriage as a relationship and trying to understand what happens when a marriage breaks down. I do not think that this invalidates my case. It simply means that to understand the indissolubility of marriage and its practical problems in parts of Africa or Asia, for instance, a different cultural view-point is needed. I respect the statement made to the Synod by Cardinal Rugambwa of Tanzania: 'The local Churches in Africa feel that they have the duty and the right to ensure that marriage and family life within their region are authentically Christian and authentically African. It is up to the local Churches to find solutions on the pastoral level to problems arising from Christianity and African cultures meeting each other.'

Origins of this book

These pages are by no means offered as a final solution. But neither are they merely a preliminary sketch. I have tried to blend together as well as I can the fruits of many people's reflection and practice in various parts of the Church, and I have added in some personal reflections of my own.

These pages were originally prepared as part of a joint work with Dr Jack Dominian. Circumstances beyond the control of both of us led to the abandonment of that venture. I am sure my debt to Dr Dominian still remains evident in what I have written and I have his written assurance that 'You have developed your theme of the internal relationship along lines that I would totally accept.' One sadness I have is that a book devoted entirely to looking at Divorce and Second Marriage might leave its author branded as one who betrays the Church's stand on life-long fidelity and the indissolubility of marriage. I hope I am as much committed to marriage for life as anyone. Although this book is not written jointly with Dr Dominian, I would be delighted if readers would see it as a kind of appendix to Dr Dominian's *Marriage, Faith and Love* (DLT, 1981). That would guarantee that it was read in the context of an overall concern for married love in all its levels and in all its phases of development.

Kevin T. Kelly

1

A FRESH LOOK AT MARRIAGE AND INDISSOLUBILITY

Coming to terms with marriage breakdown

Irreconcilable marriage breakdown is a human reality which the Catholic Church has to come to terms with in some way or other. Although many marriages with better preparation or support or with more adequate remedial care during the crisis periods might not have reached the state of irreconcilable breakdown, regrettably these helps were often not at hand when needed or at least were not made use of. Consequently, very many contemporary marriages which have broken down must be classified as 'irretrievable breakdowns'. In other words, whatever might be said about the future with its prospects of better educational, supportive and remedial care, for the present the Church has on her hands a crisis of marriage breakdown which cannot be solved by the mass reconciliation of divorced partners. The extent of this crisis is evident from the statistics for marriage breakdown in this country.

Apart from a small minority who see marriage as a purely temporary arrangement to be terminated at will, the majority of couples who marry do so in the hope that they will be able to share the rest of their lives together. That is what they think marriage and married love is all about. This means that none of them enter marriage with the intention of causing it to break down at a later date. Many will realize that such a breakdown is theoretically possible, though, like death, they will probably see it as something which happens to others. They do not really believe it could happen to *their* marriage. Therefore, if both of them genuinely intend to marry for life, something quite different to what they intend must happen between them if the situation becomes changed so drastically that they reach the stage of irreconcilable breakdown.

In *Marriage, Faith and Love*, Dr Dominian has described the typical stages of growth or crisis through which most marriages have to pass. The passage through these stages does not happen automatically. All these stages can be painful and in some cases couples may not have the inner resources necessary to make the transition. Sometimes too the external pressures might be too great for them. This might be expressed slightly differently by saying that many couples may not understand what is happening to them when they reach the troubled waters of these stages and they may be thrown badly off course without realizing what is going on. Furthermore, until recently society in general had little appreciation of the different stages involved in the process of development within marriage. And so, much of the external help which was offered to the couple might have been quite unsuitable to their needs.

Consequently, it would seem fair to say that frequently the cooling off of fidelity in marriage is not a positive choice made by one partner or the other. The couple suddenly find it is happening; but why it is happening is a mystery to them. Like any other symptom, its only real cure lies in tackling its root cause but this root cause is not understood by those immediately affected. So the symptom itself is treated since it is thought to be the actual cause. This only leads to disaster in one form or another. The inner love of the marriage continues to disintegrate and the marriage dies. The couple separate or else they settle down to living what is no more than an empty shell of a marriage.

Is the sin of one or both partners the real cause of marriage breakdown? In most cases probably not, I would suggest, since, as already noted, couples normally enter marriage with every intention of staying together and the death of their marriage is the very last thing they want. That might be true, one could object, but their good intentions can easily evaporate when they meet some of the difficulties involved in married life and it is this hardly perceptible transition from good to bad will, which causes their marriage to come asunder.

But does this really correspond to people's experience? Many couples who have been through this traumatic experience would claim that their marriage broke down despite their genuine efforts to save it. It is true that they eventually chose to separate but probably at that stage everyone agreed that such a decision was the only reasonable choice open to them. So it could hardly be described as a sinful decision.

But what about during the actual process of breakdown? Was there not clear evidence of bad will in all the hurt they inflicted on each other or in the way they withdrew their love in various ways? In many instances, these injuries to each other could probably be described as 'sins of passion'. In other words, they did not come out of an evil heart but resulted from an inability to cope with an emotional reaction to a situation which seemed beyond their control and outside their normal experience. 'What on earth is happening to us?' are not just words spoken on the stage; they belong very much to the real-life drama of marriage breakdown.

Is this interpretation fatalistic? Is it suggesting that couples can do nothing to stop their marriage breaking down and that they bear no responsibility for the breakdown? Not at all. This view would in fact be saying that they and they alone are the only ones who are able to make their marriage and that therefore only they can prevent its breakdown. Thank God, more succeed in this than fail. That is why marriage breakdown is still the exception rather than the rule. Surely to say that is a far cry from fatalism! But this view is also suggesting that, although only the couple themselves can make their marriage, nevertheless the reason why so many fail in this need not be their own bad will, but may often be their lack of understanding of what is going on and their consequent inability to cope. However, I am not denying that it can sometimes happen that a marriage can be destroyed through the serious and persistent fault of one of the partners. Nevertheless, I would hazard the generalization that in Western society today the basic attitude of ordinary men and women towards marriage is fundamentally good. More specifically, Vatican II's vision of the human reality of marriage as a covenant of inter-personal love which is faithful and life-giving would seem to correspond to the deepest desires and convictions of most men and women, inside and outside the Church.

If this is an accurate picture, why is there such a vast increase in marriage breakdown? Dr Dominian suggests that this is because of the heightened expectations which men and women bring to marriage. Obviously, these flow from the contemporary view of sexuality and marriage. A few of these expectations (e.g. judging sexual adequacy by false standards of maximum performance) might be quite unreal and artificially cultivated by advertising and the media. Nevertheless, generally speaking most of the expectations can be accepted as good and appropriate, arising as they do from a positive attitude to sexuality and marriage. This means, therefore, that in entering marriage today a couple are making a greater investment in their personal relationship than was ever done in the past. This is very healthy because the human reality of marriage at the present day is such that unless the personal relationship is firmly based there is little hope that the marriage will survive, at least in a form that would be regarded as desirable. It is not realistic to say that contemporary expectations of marriage are too high and that if couples would only lower their sights they would have no problem with their marriage. These expectations do not concern some incidental benefits which they hope to draw from their marriage. They touch the very heart of what the couple believe their marriage to be. Consequently, if these expectations are not fulfilled, their marriage is experienced by them as something which does not make sense, as something which is self-contradicting and a lie. That is why they feel it would destroy them as persons if they were to continue with it. Men and women cannot continue to invest their persons in something which they experience as person-destroying.

The fact that so many marriages today end in breakdown forces us to look again at our belief in the indissolubility of marriage. An outside observer looking at society today would see plenty of empirical evidence for believing that marriage is not indissoluble. Tragically, marriage seems to be far too dissoluble. So can we as Christians still maintain a realistic belief in the indissolubility of marriage? I believe we can and we must. But this belief must be in tune with the reality of marriage as it is experienced and lived today.

The reality of marriage today

The human reality of marriage in Western culture today differs in some important respects from marriage in previous ages and even in some contemporary cultures. Some of these differences touch the very heart of what marriage is understood to mean. For instance, while it is possible to recognize that St Augustine and the Fathers of Vatican II are speaking about the same basic reality when they discuss marriage, it is also true to say that in at least one essential aspect they understand it differently. St Augustine could never have written section 49 of Vatican II's *The Church in the Modern World*, which goes to the heart of how the Church interprets the goodness of married love today. For him it would have been unthinkable to have suggested that sexual intercourse between a married couple could be the vehicle by which their love 'merging the human with the divine . . . is uniquely expressed and perfected'. While St Augustine in some parts of his writings allows for the possibility of a real friendship between husband and wife (even though some of his other remarks are hard to reconcile with this), nowhere does he come near to suggesting that this friendship could be mediated through sexual intercourse.

Today great emphasis is put on the personal relationship which constitutes a marriage and the sexual dimension of this relationship is better appreciated. This is very much in evidence in the current approach to marriage preparation. It concentrates on helping an engaged couple to look at the quality of their relationship so that they can build on its strengths and rectify or at least be aware of its weaknesses. Likewise, as was clearly acknowledged by the Pastoral Congress (Sector C, Topic 2), any sound pastoral policy of support within marriage will try to help couples to move constructively through the various critical phases of their relationship and it will offer the appropriate help needed at each stage. All this is based on a firm belief that it is the human reality of the couple's relationship which forms the heart of their marriage. To use other terms, the matter of the sacrament of marriage is the human relationship of the couple themselves.

This is not ignoring the social dimension of marriage. Marriage is a fundamental social institution and in all societies it is very wisely enhanced and protected by a whole variety of laws, customs and rituals. It is from this angle that down through the ages the Church has concentrated on marriage as a solemn contract. Understandably, this has been the aspect emphasized in Canon Law. Regrettably, until very recently it has also been the viewpoint of most moral theologians over the past few centuries, often due to an amalgamation of the teaching roles of moral theologian and canon lawyer.

Today the Church denies neither the social dimension of marriage nor its character as a contract; but it does insist that the heart of marriage lies in its being an inter-personal sexual relationship of life-giving love, and one which is therefore permanent and exclusive. It is this relationship which is given the legal status of a contract and institutionalized in various other ways; but it is neither the contractual character nor the institutional factors which tell us about the reality of marriage.

For that we have to go to the relationship. It is there that we find the most basic and fundamental reality of marriage.

This is the clear teaching of the Fathers of Vatican II in their Pastoral Constitution, *The Church in the Modern World* (nn. 47–52). It was warmly embraced by Paul VI and finds eloquent expression in his encyclical, *Humanae Vitae*, (especially nn. 8–9). In fact, the reason why so many theologians and lay-people found certain sections of that encyclical so unacceptable was not simply because they did not like what he said, but because it seemed in contradiction to this basic understanding of marriage as a relationship of life-giving love. The disputed passage seemed inconsistent with the rich vision of the earlier part of the encyclical and out of tune with the mind of Vatican II.

This same personalist approach to marriage is also the stance of Pope John Paul II and is spelled out at length in his Apostolic Exhortation, *Familiaris Consortio*, in which he tries to share with the rest of the Church the fruits of the 1980 Synod on Marriage and the Family. Here too there are some practical points with which very many theologians and married people would disagree, but at least the debate can be carried on within a mutually acceptable vision of marriage as a personal relationship of life-giving love.

To say that marriage is for life can make it sound like a life-sentence. The Church's current understanding of marriage is really saying that it is for life (i.e. life-long) because married love is all about giving life and that is a life-long process. This brings out the intimate connection between the couple's love for each other and the fruitfulness of that love, usually resulting in giving life to their children. In speaking of marriage as a personal relationship the Church insists that married love must be 'open to life' or 'life-giving'. I prefer to use the latter expression; its full meaning is appreciated only when the intimate unity between both aspects of married love is understood.

In the first place their love is life-giving to each other. Husband and wife through their mutual love and trust enable each other to become alive in ways they never believed possible. They may be able to heal some of the personal handicaps each brings into the marriage from negative experiences in earlier life. They support each other and are able to help each other grow as individuals and in the process they grow as a couple. Since what is being talked about is not just physical life but the developing life of persons, it is not just romantic imagery to describe the couple's love as being in the first instance life-giving for themselves.

Their love is also life-giving in the sense of giving life to new persons, their children. While it is possible to read too much significance into physical processes, most Christians would be prepared to see the hand of God in the fact that the very act by which a couple is said to 'make love' to each other includes within it the power to give life to a new person. Naturally, the moment of conception or birth is not seen as the end of this second way in which their love is life-giving. They are giving life not just to a living human organism but to a *person*. The 1980 Synod put this very simply: 'The end product of procreation is the person and persons are only fully brought alive when they are properly educated' (Proposition 26, no. 2). In other words, the life-giving power of a couple's love is at work all through the process of the upbringing and education of their children. They are bringing their children alive as loving persons. Once again this is not just mere imagery. Psychologists never tire of insisting that one of the most influential factors in the personal develop-ment of a child is the climate of love, acceptance and security found in a home where parents have a genuine love for each other. If a couple's love is not truly life-giving to each other, it will not be able to be fully life-giving to their children either. Without the secure home background of their parents closely united together, it is more difficult for the children to become more fully alive and develop as persons capable of forming loving relationships. Furthermore, it is probably true to say that normally the growth of the parents' love for each other needs the stimulus of their shared love for their children. In other words, there is a very real sense in which children can actually give life to their parents; they can bring them more fully alive. The wheel of life-giving love turns a full circle.

The Church's current understanding of marriage sees all these facets of life-giving love as intimately bound together. Sadly, at the level of official teaching she has still not been able to draw out the full implications of this as regards life-giving love and family planning. In an Appendix to this book I have included my own attempt to spell out these implications.

There is a richness in the contemporary understanding of marriage that is not to be found in earlier ages. This is something at which Christians must rejoice, since they interpret this deeper understanding as a fuller appreciation of God's truth. Nor is this just at the level of ideas. It has obvious implications for the way people can actually live their marriages. Marriage today offers a much richer personal life than was ever thought possible in times past.

There is no doubt that marriage is for life; that is, it is about giving and sharing life with other persons. There is also no doubt that the Church has always taught that marriage is for life in the sense of being permanent, life-long.

In no way do I want to deny or even challenge that teaching. What I want to do is to see whether the Church's contemporary emphasis on marriage as a personal relationship of life-giving love helps to throw any new light on the way we understand the permanence or indissolubility of marriage.

Indissolubility, a task for life

Indissolubility and the personalist approach to marriage

In earlier ages the fact that marriages were able to last for life was partly due to the many external supports and constraints which helped to hold them together. This is not to suggest that in many instances there was not a deep personal love between the couple. When that was there, a marriage would have an inner permanence of a very different nature to that of many other marriages which would be kept in being almost entirely by these external factors.

Furthermore, the permanence or indissolubility of marriage was not clearly seen as flowing from the nature of the couple's love for each other. That is why their interpersonal love was not thought to be essential to their marriage and its indissolubility. The main point of focus was the institutional character of marriage. The emphasis was put on the solemn contract to which the couple gave their consent. The contract spelled out what marriage was all about, with each partner's rights and duties. Marriage was seen more as an institution which they entered, rather than as an interpersonal reality which they themselves brought into existence. Indissolubility was considered to be one of the essential properties of marriage, rather than something flowing from the very nature of the couple's love for each other. While there was a deep appreciation of its importance for the good of the children and the stability of the family and society, its ultimate binding force was traced back to the command of God 'in the beginning', reiterated by Christ himself.

As already stated, the Church today does not deny that marriage is an institution. It is obviously a crucial element in the fabric of society. But it is not the needs of society which determine what marriage should be. In fact, the very reason why marriage is an important institution within society is precisely because of its nature as an interpersonal reality of life-giving love. That is why the roots of the indissolubility of marriage must not be sought in the good of society but in the very nature of the committed life-giving love of a couple for each other. It can be spoken of as being 'commanded' by God only because it is in fact demanded by our being truly human. And it is in the experience of this truly human fidelity that we get some inkling of and feel for (and even involvement in) the fidelity of God himself.

It would seem that the personalist approach to marriage can give us a renewed and richer understanding of indissolubility. Indissolubility is something which has to be brought into being *within the marriage itself.* When they marry, a couple do not suddenly find themselves tied by an indissoluble bond which has an existence independent of them. When they marry, they give their pledge that they will form an indissoluble union of persons through their love for each other. The indissolubility of their marriage is *a task to be undertaken.*

A closer look at indissolubility

This proposition needs closer analysis. It is not saying that it is up to the couple to decide whether they want a soluble or an indissoluble marriage. Obviously, they are free to choose the former if they so wish, but in that case I would say that what they have chosen is not marriage in the true sense. It is not so much that they are rejecting one of the essential properties of marriage. It is more that they are pledging themselves to married love while refusing that commitment of unconditional trust to each other which is the indispensable first step needed to bring married love into existence.

Indissolubility is in no way an optional extra open to the free choice of the couple. It flows from the very nature of the love they are pledging to each other. This is clearly stated by Vatican II: 'As a mutual gift of two persons, this intimate union, as well as the good of the children, imposes total fidelity on the spouses and argues for an unbreakable oneness between them' (*The Church in the Modern World*, n. 48). This text is taken up and reaffirmed by Pope John Paul II in his Apostolic Exhortation, *Familiaris Consortio*, n. 20. It is beyond the scope of this book to attempt to prove that life-long fidelity is an essential quality of married love. I would suggest that, as well as being taught by Vatican II, recent Popes and the Synod, this view is accepted by all Christians and Christian Churches today. It would also seem to be the prevailing view in society at large, at least in Western culture. It is not contradicted by the fact that there is a widespread breakdown of marriage. On the contrary, the fact helps to prove it. Men and women want a marriage based on interpersonal love and they are refusing to be bound by an indissolubility which they feel has no foundation in interpersonal love. Consequently, they believe that when love in marriage has completely died indissolubility has lost its roots.

This indissolubility is not something independent of the couple of themselves. Their children, other people, the Church and society may expect it from them but its reality lies in themselves. That is why I would prefer to speak of the life-long fidelity of married love rather than of the indissolubility of marriage. I recognize that the latter term is firmly enshrined in traditional usage. Nevertheless, it seems more in keeping with the contemporary understanding of marriage to view its permanence or indissolubility as a consequence of the life-long fidelity of married love. In other words, it is the faithfulness of married love which is really fundamental. It is towards this that the Church should be directing its attention.

I am claiming not only that fidelity is an essential quality of married love, but also that it is a quality which can grow and develop only along with the growth and development of married love itself. Therefore, to understand this fidelity the nature of married love itself needs to be looked at.

It takes two to make love – and to make indissolubility

A catch-phrase common in Marriage Encounter circles today is: *love is a decision*. Since fidelity is a quality of married love, it could also be said that fidelity too is a decision. The meaning behind the catch-phrase is that the decision to love is not taken once and for all and then everything else follows automatically. Love is only real as a decision to the extent that it is continually renewed in big and small matters throughout the course of married life.

The important thing to notice is that it takes two to make love. Consequently, it takes two to make the decision to love. When one partner begins to refuse to renew the decision in the events of their life together, the other is forced into the position of trying single-handed to keep their love alive. This would involve a decision to work at healing, reconciliation, forgiveness etc. If these are continually refused, it becomes impossible to make their love last. Obviously, this will all depend on whether the situation can be mended or not. As long as reconciliation is believed to be a real possibility, fidelity as a decision still retains a true meaning in the context of this marriage. There are definite actions which can be undertaken which are a realistic way of giving practical effect to the decision to be faithful in love. They are realistic because they have a genuine connection with the hoped-for reconciliation. The decision not to re-marry is an obvious example.

However, if the situation is so far gone that there is absolutely no possibility of reconciliation, the picture changes completely. In this case, love no longer exists, because the joint decision on which it depends for its very existence has ceased to operate. Of course, one of the partners, the husband for instance, might still feel he is in love with his wife. Since he considers that he has not refused the decision to love, he might decide to remain faithful to his initial decision. At one level this might be admirable; at another level it could be tragic. He feels he is being faithful to his marriage. I would suggest that perhaps it no longer exists for him to be faithful to. This is not to suggest that his 'fidelity' is without value. Human tragedy can at times be a most powerful witness to the ideals which have occasioned it. Pope John Paul II has a special word of praise for men and women who give such a witness (*Familiaris Consortio*, n. 20).

Irreconcilable breakdown – a denial of God's love?

The Bible often portrays God as the faithful husband who is always ready to forgive his erring wife no matter how unfaithful she may have been. Since marriage is a symbol of this faithful love of God, is not the notion of irreconcilable breakdown a denial of this symbolism? Does the admission that reconciliation is impossible deny the power of God's reconciling love?

This is a serious theological objection and deserves careful attention. Perhaps the following remarks could be made with reference to it.

Married love is a symbol of God's love. However, it cannot be completely identified with God's love. Somehow Catholic theology has manoeuvred itself into the position of holding that whatever can be said of God's love applies without further qualification to the love of every married couple. This is not true. By overloading the meaning of symbol in this area, Catholic theology can be doing married couples a disservice. It can change the privilege of being a symbol of God's love into an intolerable burden for some married couples. The *true* symbolism of marriage is encouraging for a couple, since it invites them to let their human love grow more and more into the likeness of God's own love. To totally identify their love with God's love can dehumanize their love and can leave them confused and dis-heartened by the contrast they see between their own human imperfect love, with all its limitations and imperfections, and the perfection of God's love.

Therefore, to accept that human married love can break down irretrievably does not imply that the same is true of God's love. Despite the mysterious words of Jesus about the unforgivable sin, it is part of Christian faith to believe that no one can be so far gone in sin as to be completely beyond the reach of God's forgiving love. In other words, irretrievable breakdown is an unthinkable notion when applied to God's love for his people. Presumably this is because at the very centre of every human person lies some kind of innate desire for God. This cannot be extinguished without a person's very humanity ceasing to exist. So the reason why the total and irretrievable breakdown between God and humankind is inconceivable is not just because of the nature of God's love, it is also because of the corresponding desire for God's love deep within every man and woman.

This is not true of the love of a particular man and woman for each other. Though there is a beautiful saying, 'Marriages are made in heaven', it is no part of Christian faith to believe that married couples are destined for each other by God. Certainly, what draws them together is far more than a rational decision to love. Every marriage carries its own personal story of what attracts the partners to each other. Usually there will be factors working on all the five levels outlined by Dr Dominian – social, sexual, emotional, intellectual and spiritual (*Marriage, Faith and Love*, DLT, 1981 Part III). These factors have a vital part to play in attracting the partners to each other and in helping them to grow closer together and to develop and mature in their two-in-oneness. The general way in which this process works is clearly described by Dr Dominian. From that analysis it is quite obvious that far more needs to be said than that love is a decision. For love to develop and grow there needs to be some kind of awareness of what is going on at these various levels. Commitment (a better word than decision) is not enough. Without this awareness the various factors which have worked to draw the partners together can begin to have the opposite effect and drive them apart again. Or in some instances perhaps some of the factors which should have been working if the couple were to draw really close together, might not have been operative; and then suddenly they might begin to make their presence felt but only with the effect of showing the couple how far apart they are from each other.

Therefore, although there may be some truth in the saying 'Love is a decision', it is at least equally true to say that married love consists in a number of clearly identifiable components. Each of these needs to be operating at least at a minimum level if married love is to grow properly and mature. When some of the more important components are absent or are ignored or even violated, married love will only be present in a seriously defective form and there is a real danger that it will deteriorate and die. A renewed decision to love will not be enough to stop this happening. The precise factors which are causing the trouble will need to be tackled if there is to be any hope of recovery. However, some of these factors might be outside the control of the couple. For example, despite their willingness to give it another chance, a couple's marriage might still break up simply because they are quite incompatible either sexually or personality-wise. It is possible that a marriage might die, not because the couple were not committed to life-long fidelity, but because they did not know how to love each other. They never lost their belief in life-long fidelity, but the source of their fidelity to each other dried up because they were unable to cope with the process of growing in married love.

Married love has its own very specific needs, therefore. That is why, although it may be a symbol of God's love, it is unhelpful and even misleading to suggest that what can be said of God's love can be applied without qualification to married love.

Does interpreting indissolubility in the way I have suggested mean that I am rejecting the whole tradition of the Church in the West? Far from it. There are various elements in the Latin Church's traditional practice which would offer some support for the position I have outlined.

Some lessons from history

The Catholic Church's current teaching and practice with regard to indissolubility has undergone considerable development throughout history. What most interests us here is the way the Church has gradually evolved a position which recognizes different degrees of indissolubility. In other words, while it believes in the indissolubility of marriage, it also accepts that most kinds of marriage can be dissolved. In fact, the only kind of marriage which it holds to be absolutely indissoluble is a valid marriage between baptized persons which has been consummated. The Church accepts the possibility of the dissolution of every other kind of marriage. How did this come about? After all, it seems a strange development in view of the fact that the teaching of Jesus is so clear: marriage breakdown, divorce and remarriage are not God's plan for men and women. Moreover, Jesus is not giving this as teaching which applies only to his own followers. 'It was not so from the beginning.' In other words, marriage breakdown, divorce and remarriage contradict the very nature of marriage itself. In God's design every marriage is called to life-long fidelity.

Paul took the first important step. He found that the marriages of some of his converts still broke down despite the radical teaching of Jesus. In fact, some broke down precisely because one of the partners became a Christian. To ease the situation Paul told them that if they were not able to live at peace with their non-Christian partners they were no longer bound. Paul's pastoral ruling was later developed still further by the Church: such a Christian could remarry another Christian and in such a case it was recognized that the former marriage had ceased to exist. This is known as the 'Pauline Privilege' and still operates in the Church today.

Moreover, in what has been called the 'Petrine Privilege' which in our century went through some dramatic developments under Pius XII, the Church extended even further the implications of Paul's ruling that one should be able to live at peace as a Christian. The Church will dissolve the marriage of two non-Christians if it can be shown that such a dissolution will help a Christian third party to live at peace in marriage. This same broad-minded pastoral approach was adopted by a series of Popes in the handling of the marriage problems of captives and slaves in the sixteenth century and their decisions still have a place in current Church law. Implied in all these practices of the Church would seem to be the assumption that not being able to sustain their marriage relationship in peace is an essential element in the Church's determining that there is no longer any marriage in these instances.

Another important step was the compromise solution adopted by Pope Alexander III in the dispute between Paris and Bologna as to whether it was consent or consummation which made a marriage. He accommodated both views by ruling that it was consent which made the marriage but it was consummation which finally gave it absolute indissolubility. In practice this meant that Alexander was recognizing two degrees of indissolubilty even in marriages between two Catholics. This is relevant for our discussion of indissolubility since it shows that the Church did not look on marriage as absolutely indissoluble simply because it was a sacrament. Over the years the Church's practice became established: a non-consummated sacramental marriage could be dissolved either by a decision of the Pope or by the relationship ceasing to be effective through one partner taking solemn religious vows.

Indissolubility: its strength and its fragility

Since the above paragraphs have looked at the way in which marriages, called to be indissoluble in the design of God, can actually dissolve, it might help to say more precisely what is meant by the indissolubility of marriage. In this chapter I have been arguing that at least in Western society today the indissolubility of marriage depends on the continued growth and development of the couple's love for each other. This is where its great strength lies, even though it is also the source of its fragility. This is really saying that indissolubility is something to be realized in a marriage. A man and a woman getting married bind themselves by a solemn commitment to love each other faithfully for the rest of their lives. Indissolubility is the fruit of this pledged life-long love. The process of building their love together depends on commitment, trust and understanding from within and an appropriate and timely support from without. It is in the very process of building this love that they create the indissolubility of their marriage. One would be missing the point to argue that this really means that a marriage is only indissoluble when it has actually lasted until one partner has died. That is true if 'indissoluble' is being used in a purely descriptive sense. But Christians believe it has a deeper meaning than that, it refers to the deeper levels of personal being. The initial foundation of the indissolubility of marriage lies in the fidelity of these two persons to their committed word and the trust they invest in each other. That is already a deep basis in their being as persons. They have made solemn marriage vows to God and to each other and they have made an act of faith that each will be faithful to those marriage vows. This in itself is a very substantial foundation for the initial indissolubility of their marriage. An unconditional commitment to life-long fidelity is a personal act of the greatest significance. But it is a commitment to undertake and achieve something. It is not the achievement itself. Personal fidelity to one's committed word is a most sacred obligation, but it can be thwarted. However, as they grow together and become 'two in one flesh' in the sense already explained, the indissolubility of their marriage gains an even deeper basis. It is now founded on the oneness they have achieved as a couple. In a sense, they are now a new being, not just 'I' and 'you' but also 'we'. The Church of England report, *Marriage and the Church's Task*, has expressed this beautifully:

> The marriage bond unites two flesh-blood-and-spirit persons. It makes them the persons that they are. It binds them together, not in any casual or peripheral fashion, but at the very centre of their being. They become the persons they are through their relationship to each other. Each might say to the other 'I am I and I am you; together you and I are we'. Since the marriage bond is in this way a bond of personal *being*, it is appropriate to speak of it as having an 'ontological' character (section 96).

I do not think that the position I have been outlining is a denial of indissolubility. It is merely a different way of understanding it. Admittedly, it accepts the possibility that some marriages (far too many at present) will not attain this inner indissolubility and instead will disintegrate and fall apart so that eventually they no longer exist. This is not to deny that these marriages were never indissoluble in any sense. They were; but their indissolubility during that initial stage drew its binding force from the pledged commitment they had made to each other to become two-in-one at a deep personal level. It was not yet based on the achievement of that personal two-in-oneness. Sadly these marriages never reached that level of indissolubility. To understand indissolubility as having two levels of binding force should not seem too outrageous to Roman Catholics brought up on the earlier way of viewing marriage. As has been noted already, it is only possible to make sense of some aspects of the Latin Church's practice by admitting that some marriages are more indissoluble than others.

No to conditional marriage vows?

It might be objected that my understanding of indissolubility would mean that the commitment given in the marriage vows would in reality only be conditional and so it would be more honest to add in some qualifying clause such as 'for as long as our relationship lasts'. That does not follow at all. The couple's commitment is to life-long fidelity and that is precisely why they are morally obliged to do all in their power to achieve that fidelity. By moral obligation here I mean that their personal integrity is at stake; they have committed themselves to this task. To insert a qualifying clause into their commitment would completely alter the nature of the commitment they are making to each other. It would mean that the breakdown of their marriage could not be described as evil since it would be quite in accord with the pledge they had given each other.

The approach I have been describing is quite different. It sees two distinct but not unrelated elements in the commitment the couple make. One is the obligation by which each is bound by virtue of his or her commitment. This is the obligation to fulfil the task to which they have committed themselves. The other element is the task itself to which they are committed. This is to fuse their lives together into an unbreakable personal union. To admit the possibility that some couples might fail (culpably or unculpably) in the task in no way implies that the original commitment should only be conditional. In fact, from the very nature of the task being undertaken the commitment needs to be unconditional.

2

CAN A CHRISTIAN CHOOSE A SECOND MARRIAGE AFTER DIVORCE?

In the Roman Catholic Church the answer to that question has been a qualified 'Yes'.

A second marriage after divorce is acceptable if the first marriage is not considered to have been a true marriage in the proper sense of the word (null or invalid); or if the first marriage is considered to be no longer binding (Pauline Privilege or Papal Dissolution).

This chapter looks more closely at these possibilities and examines whether any new light is thrown upon them by the change of emphasis in the theology of marriage. Does the shift of emphasis from contract to relationship alter their focus at all and, if so, what implications has this for the way we look at second marriages today? But before we undertake this analysis it might be appropriate to remind ourselves that we are not trying to solve some kind of pastoral puzzle; we are thinking about the lives of people who have been deeply wounded through suffering the human tragedy of marriage breakdown.

The human tragedy of marriage breakdown and divorce

Marriage breakdown is a human tragedy. It causes hurt and suffering to human persons. It can crucify a husband and wife and their children, as well as family and friends. In the home and relationship where they are hoping for mutual healing and support and where they are expecting that atmosphere of trust and security needed for them to grow further as human persons, they eventually find the very opposite – mistrust, insecurity and even hatred. We put things the wrong way round if we assert that divorce is evil because it is forbidden by God. That does not face the question: why is divorce against God's will? The answer to that question is found in a statement of St Thomas Aquinas which could be paraphrased as: God is not offended by us except insofar as we harm ourselves and other people. Marriage breakdown and divorce is evil because of the human hurt and suffering caused by it. It offends God because people precious to him are being harmed and are hurting each other. That is why it is a human tragedy.

Marriage breakdown is a form of dying. For most people it entails an experience of deep pain. Especially for the partners in the marriage there is a crushing sense of rejection and personal failure. There is the guilt of feeling that they have failed God, themselves and their family and friends. This can wreak havoc with their sense of self-worth.

Any major dislocation of a person's life puts him or her under severe personal strain. Marriage breakdown is an experience which involves serious disruption of life at many levels. Emotionally a person is affected very deeply. Often a person becomes so drained at this level that the emotions have to be drawn out of the marriage even before the initial separation. The economic disruption can be painful, for both partners. At a legal level a person can be shattered by the frightening and dehumanizing character of the court procedure, especially when the question of custody of the children and access to them comes before the court. On the social level, the normal pattern of relationships is now broken since much of social intercourse is based on the unit of the couple. A divorced person can be a source of embarrassment to his or her friends. Psychologically a husband or wife has to readjust to the challenge of living alone. As regards the children, they have to get used to the change from a two-parent to a one-parent family as well as the confusion and emotional blackmail they can experience when one of the parents uses them as a pawn against the other.

Many people who have been through the experience of marriage breakdown liken it to the experience of bereavement. There can be similar patterns of behaviour to the grief process – disbelief and denial that this is happening; anger at the unfairness of it; bargaining to put something in its place; depression and final acceptance. Men and women who have been through the tragedy of marriage breakdown are wounded people. They need appropriate care. Most certainly this care does not consist in condemnation or rejection by the community. Nor does it involve encouraging them to bounce on the rebound into a hasty second marriage. In fact, such an unwise second marriage can actually be caused by rejection or condemnation on the part of the community. The appropriate care they need is to be brought back to life again so that they can make a new beginning.

The thrust of our pastoral care must always be one of healing. Sometimes that healing will take the form of reconciliation between the couple and they are helped to rebuild their disrupted life. But sometimes that form of healing is no longer possible. Perhaps the true foundations of a lasting marriage were not there in the first place. Maybe the wounds go too deep and are beyond repair. It might be that one partner or other has formed a new and permanent relationship and there is no going back on this.

In such a situation healing has to take another form. If the community is sensitive to the needs of someone who has been through the painful experience of marriage breakdown, that healing might take place in the context of a positive acceptance of not remarrying as long as such a decision did not flow from a fear of risking a new relationship. Sadly, however, it can happen that some communities are not alert to the needs of such people. What then? In some instances the only setting in which effective healing might be found might be in a second marriage. Experience seems to show that this can and does happen. When it does happen, it must surely be God's healing touch which is being experienced since all genuine human healing comes ultimately from him. Someone who was lost has now found theirself. The Christian is called to rejoice at this, rather than resent it after the manner of the elder brother.

It is only in this context of the Church celebrating the healing action of God in our lives that any discussion of the possibility of second marriage after divorce has any chance of getting a proper hearing among Christians. The fact that Catholics are becoming more conscious of this healing at work in the second marriages of their friends and even their relatives is making them more open to look at the underlying question as to whether a second marriage after divorce is a choice which is open to a Christian.

Nullity and the 'relationship' approach to marriage

To say that a marriage is null is to say that it has never been a real marriage right from the beginning. This is a different notion to that of divorce, which involves saying that a real marriage has now ceased to be or at least is no longer legally binding.

The concept of nullity did not fall down from heaven. It is a human creation which attempts to interpret what is the real truth in a particular situation. In fact, it is based on the belief that appearances do not always correspond to reality. Things are not always what they seem, as the old song says. I do not think anyone would deny the wisdom of this insight. Nullity is just one instance of a broader approach to life which all of us would accept.

What nullity meant in the 'contract' approach to marriage was that, although the couple appeared to make a genuine contract of marriage, this was not in fact so. For some reason or other the contract was null. It might be because one or other partner lacked the requisite knowledge or freedom to undertake the contract of marriage. They might have had totally misguided ideas regarding what marriage is all about, or they might have been forced into marriage through the fear that something terrible would happen otherwise (e.g. threat of suicide). Another reason why the contract can be null is if some condition is added in implicitly by one partner which goes against the very substance of what they are committing themselves to. Or in some rare and bizarre cases the person one is marrying might not be the person one believed them to be.

For any of these reasons what appeared on the surface to have been a genuine contract of marriage might not have been so in reality. It is obvious that in this approach it is the partners' state of mind at the moment of entering the marriage which is put under the microscope. How the marriage worked out is far less important.

This approach still has its place in the marriage tribunal. To put the major emphasis on marriage as a 'relationship' is not to deny its character as a contract. It is simply to maintain that 'relationship' is more at the very heart of marriage than 'contract' is.

Does the 'relationship' approach to marriage have any bearing on the issue of nullity and the work of the marriage tribunals? It certainly has, even though I would suggest that it involves a much broader use of the term 'null'. Strictly speaking, nullity is a concept which is restricted to the field of contractual law. Only contracts can be said to be null. Relationships as such can hardly be said to be null. They can be non-existent, or non-viable, or even terminated, but to call them null is really to misuse language.

To be fair to the marriage tribunals, I imagine that they are blending together the two approaches to marriage. They are not applying the term 'null' to the relationship as such. Rather they are saying that if the relationship is a non-starter the substance of the marriage is not there and so the essential matter of the contract is missing. So the contract is obviously null.

This approach can be strongly defended and there is no doubt that very many people are being greatly helped by the work of the marriage tribunals. The marriage tribunal personnel have every right to claim that they are engaged in real pastoral work and their dedication is rewarded by the peace they help to bring to the lives of many people.

To recognize all that need not blind us to the incongruities of the system as it is currently developing. Many people involved in this field, including many tribunal personnel, are coming to the conclusion that a court of tribunal is the wrong form for helping people in the wake of marriage breakdown. Now that the emphasis has shifted to marriage as a relationship, what is far more appropriate is some kind of Marriage Counselling Service. Its task would not be to pass a judgement of nullity. Rather its task would be to help the people involved to arrive at an honest appraisal of their marriage relationship. Was it really viable in the first place? If not, are some of the reasons for this to be found in themselves and how will this affect future relationships? Did their relationship have a minimum viability, but somehow came to grief? Why did this happen and how can they learn from this? Is there any hope of re-establishing it? Is their relationship completely dead? Why has it died? Could they have avoided it and can they draw lessons for the future from this? What about the future? Is there a conversion process to be completed before they can face the future in peace? Have they the inner resources to accept a challenge of life-long celibacy or can they, for their own sakes or for their children, be open to the possibility of a second marriage?

I know that many tribunal personnel try to help people think through these problems. However, I would still query whether the tribunal is the appropriate setting for this kind of approach. The change of emphasis from 'contract' to relationship in marriage would seem to indicate the need for some major structural changes in the field of marriage care.

However, we have to live in the present so we need to be as clear as possible about the current situation regarding nullity of marriage in the Church today.

It is important to distinguish nullity from the juridical act of a declaration of nullity. When a marriage tribunal declares a marriage null it does not in fact make that marriage null. If it is right in its decision, the marriage is null already and has been null right from the beginning. The tribunal's declaration does nothing to change the marriage itself. Its value lies in its being a public and official act recognizing the already existing nullity of the marriage. In a certain sense a tribunal's decision is a very humble and almost diffident decision. It does not say: this marriage is null. It goes no further than saying 'We agree that this marriage is null' (*constat de nullitate*). Even when it gives a negative decision it refrains from declaring a marriage true and genuine. It will only say 'We do not agree that this marriage is null' (*non constat de nullitate*).

This obviously has important consequences for men and women who have suffered the tragedy of marriage breakdown and who with hindsight now believe that their first marriage was not a true marriage at all. The marriage tribunal offers them a service. Since they themselves are interested parties, it could be called a service in objective impartiality. This group of highly trained and experienced canon lawyers are willing to examine the first marriage and will give their opinion as to whether they think it was null or not. But in the end it is no more than their opinion. It does not change the truth of the situation. It is simply a professional but fallible attempt to discover the truth. If the ruling of the tribunal is that they are not convinced that the marriage was null, the couple have every right to stand by their own conviction that it was null as long as they are doing this in good conscience, really trying to discern what is the truth in the eyes of God.

It might be objected that, unless a person was a qualified canon lawyer or theologian, it would be very presumptuous for them to follow their own opinion in preference to that of the tribunal. After all, they would just be working on their own native wit, intuition and feelings – 'I just don't think that this is what marriage is meant to be.' I would suggest that the sound native wit and intuition of a good honest person deserves a lot of credence. Marriage tribunals are highly fallible institutions and I mean no disrespect by that. Increasingly they are becoming highly professional bodies, but quite naturally they are totally limited by the current situation in law and theology. This means that they have to keep to very strict rules regarding admissibility of evidence etc., and it also means that their criterion for finding the nullity of a marriage is determined by theological and psychological positions in current acceptance. All this is admirable and I do not mention it to criticize it. It is simply the natural limitation of a good human institution.

But it is a healthy reminder to us of the fallibility of this institution. For instance the very praiseworthy developments which are currently occurring in tribunal theory and practice mean that today very many marriages are being declared null which would not have been judged so ten or fifteen years ago. In effect, this means either that the tribunals are making thousands of wrong judgements today, or else that fifteen or so years ago very many marriages were null which had no chance of being declared so by a tribunal. Assuming that the latter is the case, this in turn means that it is possible that ten or fifteen years ago the intuition of the people involved in those marriages might have been a better guide to the truth than the professional judgement of the tribunals.

If that was true fifteen years ago, could it not still be true to some extent today, especially at a time when we claim to be learning so much about marriage from the actual insight and experience of married couples? It was Cardinal Hume himself who stated at the 1980 Synod that 'this experience and this understanding (of married people) constitute an authentic *fons theologiae* from which we, the pastors, and indeed the whole Church can draw' (*Briefing*, vol. 10, no. 32, p. 6). I am sure that no canon lawyer would claim that we have reached the end of the road in matrimonial jurisprudence, and that there will not be further developments in refining the causes for nullity in marriage.

It does not seem unreasonable, therefore, to believe that there are many marriages today which are in fact null and are thought to be 'not real marriages' by the partners involved, but which at present for a variety of reasons will not be able to be declared null by any marriage tribunal. It is encouraging to see this possibility recognized by the bishops of England and Wales: 'There are, however, other situations in which there may be moral certainty that the previous marriage was not valid even though this cannot be adequately established in the matrimonial courts' (*Easter People*, n. 111). If this is so, it would seem grossly unfair to dismiss as presumptuous a person who stood by their own intuition rather than by the judgement of the tribunal. In good conscience, such a person can genuinely believe that they are free before God to enter a second marriage. That is a belief which deserves respect from the rest of us. Such a person should certainly feel free to enter a second marriage and there should be no question of being refused the sacraments. At present Church law does not allow for any official public Church celebration of such a second marriage, but even among those who stand firm in the pre-Vatican II approach to moral theology it would seem acceptable practice for a priest to conduct a more private celebration of such a second marriage and to keep a record of it in a confidential register.

Pauline Privilege, Papal Dissolution and the 'relationship' approach to marriage

The Pauline Privilege and the exercise of the power of Papal Dissolution have in common the fact that what was considered to be a true marriage is considered to be no longer binding. I am including under Papal Dissolution the accepted law in the Church that solemn religious profession automatically dissolves a marriage as long as it has not been consummated. Most canon lawyers would interpret this as a general exercise of the power of Papal Dissolution. The Code of Canon Law (canon 1119) links with this the Papal power to dissolve the non-consummated marriage of baptized persons at their joint request, or even at the request of one partner in the face of the other's unwillingness. These instances of Papal Dissolution are very interesting, since they demonstrate that it is not the actual sacramental status of a marriage which makes it absolutely indissoluble in the eyes of the Church.

Expert canon lawyers dealing with this area of dissolution of the marriage bond make the point that it is justified on the grounds that 'The law of indissolubility is neglected in favour of a greater good, which is ordinarily the "salvation of souls"' (Abate, *The Dissolution of the Matrimonial Bond*, 1962). They quote Pius XII in their support: 'In every case, the supreme norm according to which the Roman Pontiff uses his vicarious power of dissolving marriage is . . . the "salus animarum", in the attainment of which not only the common good of religious society, and of human society in general, but also the welfare of individual souls will receive due and proportionate consideration' (*AAS*, XXXIII, 1941, p. 426).

All this would seem to be a filling out of Paul's original comment in 1 Corinthians 7:15: 'in these circumstances the brother or sister is not tied: God has called you to a life of peace'.

Paul is saying something of deep significance there, and it is something which the Church has taken to heart in its limited practice of the dissolution of marriage. He is saying that the Lord's plan for marriage is one of love and peace. He has not called us to live at enmity with each other. If a marriage has no further future except at the level of constant bickering and fighting, and a kind of cold war neutrality, it can hardly be called a window on God's love which has called us to a life of peace.

The grounds for accepting that a particular marriage has dissolved seem clear enough, therefore. If they are to have a genuine Christian basis, it must lie in the moral impossibility for this couple to live together in peace. The 'relationship' approach to marriage finds no difficulty with this. As long as 'living in peace' is not interpreted superficially, ignoring all the ups and downs, trials and crises of any growing relationship, then it is fully in line with the 'relationship' approach.

As currently interpreted by the Church there is a great difference between the Pauline Privilege and the various instances of the power of Papal Dissolution. With the Pauline Privilege no act of jurisdictional power is considered necessary. The person simply is not bound by the first marriage and this 'being loosed' becomes reality, as it were, by the entry into the second marriage. This fits in perfectly with the 'relationship' approach. Provided the relationship is clearly dead (i.e. no possibility of living in peace), the first marriage no longer binds.

Papal Dissolution, however, brings in an additional element. As understood down through the ages, it requires an act of jurisdiction on the part of the Pope exercising the special vicarious power given him in his supreme office in the Church. In other words, when the Pope dissolves, God dissolves; and so his action does not contradict the words of the Lord 'What God has joined together, let no man put asunder' (Matt. 19:6).

It is at this point that the 'relationship' approach to marriage presents a major challenge. If the heart of any marriage is the personal relationship of life-giving love (which it is agreed is exclusive and permanent), then this is something which cannot be dissolved by any act of jurisdiction whatsoever. Sadly, as we well know, the relationship can dissolve and this can be due to both internal and external factors, but it certainly cannot be dissolved by any act of jurisdiction. Even God cannot give the Pope power to do that.

When the emphasis is put on marriage as a 'contract', there is no apparent difficulty. An act of jurisdiction can release people from a lawfully binding contract. In that context the notion of Papal Dissolution can make sense even though there may be other objections to it. But once it is admitted that the heart of a marriage lies in the couple's relationship, then the institution of Papal Dissolution loses its basic foundation.

If it is to continue to be exercised, it needs to be interpreted differently. It needs to be understood in the same kind of way as a declaration of nullity. In other words, all that the Pope can do is to recognize that the relationship has ceased to exist and so 'declare' that there is no longer any marriage. Consequently, at a public level he releases the two partners from the contractual legal effects involved in their marriage, though the natural rights of the children will obviously have to be safeguarded. If this is a correct interpretation of what actually happens when the Pope 'dissolves' a marriage, there would seem to be no reason why this 'declaratory' function should be reserved to the Pope. Since part of its role should be to make sure that a couple are not giving up too easily, it would seem more helpful if it took place at local level. It could be part of the pastoral function of the local bishop, who would probably be wise to delegate it to some kind of diocesan marriage counselling service, as mentioned earlier in this chapter. Such a service would obviously involve married people trained in counselling and with a sound understanding of the stages of growth in marriage.

'Two in one flesh' – a personalist approach to consummation

Although the Church stands firmly by the truth that indissolubility is an essential property of every marriage, it has no difficulty in accepting that the marriages of non-Christians can dissolve and can cease to exist and be binding. This is an implicit admission that the human personal relationship of life-giving love (which the Church now acknowledges to be at the heart of marriage) can die. To admit this presents a major challenge to the way we have understood the indissolubility of marriage.

I think we have tended to evade the challenge by saying that the fact that the marriage of two Christians is a sacrament gives it a totally new depth of indissolubility and that renders it absolutely indissoluble.

Without wanting to deny what that statement is getting at, I think it is very unsatisfactory as it stands. For one thing, it ignores the fact that the Church has for many centuries claimed the power to dissolve sacramental marriages provided they were not consummated. This means that it is not the sacramental status as such which, in the Church's understanding, makes a marriage of two Christians absolutely indissoluble. According to the Church's practice it must be said that it identifies consummation as the key factor in making a sacramental marriage absolutely indissoluble. However, for most of its history in line with its belief that nature had designed intercourse principally for procreation, the Church regarded a marriage as being consummated provided that intercourse was performed correctly as a natural physical act open to procreation. It was not essential that the act consummating a marriage should be an act of love. In fact, it did not even have to be a fully conscious act. Amazingly, as recently as 1958 a Roman decision stated that a marriage was truly consummated even if one of the partners had to be drugged into unconsciousness to enable intercourse to take place. It stated that 'Consummation can be had independently of consciousness and free consent of the will' (*Canon Law Digest*, vol. 5, on canon 1119).

Along with many other theologians and canonists I cannot accept such an approach to consummation. I do not deny the basic insight that consummation has a bearing on indissolubility and I acknowledge that this intuition goes back to what Paul in Ephesians says about the marriage of two Christians and how their being 'two in one flesh' is a great mystery. However, I reject an excessively physical interpretation of being 'two in one flesh', even though I would not want to deny importance to the act of intercourse. It is a very significant element in the language of love between a couple. But being 'two in one flesh' is more than an interpenetration of two bodies; it is about two persons becoming one in a very real sense. According to this interpretation a marriage is consummated when the husband and wife really experience themselves as a 'couple'. In other words, in their life-giving love for each other each has given and received so much that the words 'I cannot live without you' are no longer just an expression of the promise they have made, but an accurate summing up of what they now know from experience. When this experience is genuinely shared by both of them, their marriage can truly be said to be consummated.

When we are in the presence of a marriage which has been consummated in that sense, we are in the presence of something very precious and sacred. We are in the presence of the sacrament of marriage in the fullest sense of the word. The love of the Lord really is made visible in our midst in and through the love of such a couple. I hope I am saying this without romanticizing it. There will still be pain and suffering, misunderstanding and hurt in their life together. That is not surprising since these were present even in the intimate love between Jesus and his Mother. But there will be an indissolubility in such a marriage, which really is a sacred image of the indissoluble love of Jesus for his Church. I am not claiming that the indissolubility of such a marriage could not possibly be broken, but I would say that to break it would be a sacrilege and must surely involve serious sin on the part of one or other partner. And I wonder whether such a marriage could ever really be dead and beyond all hope of reconciliation. And if the second union of one of the partners was the cause of this, I would find it hard to see how such a union could in any sense be something to be celebrated by the Church. If this sounds unduly hard, maybe it is because I believe that the Lord's love is so intensely present in a marriage which has achieved this degree of indissolubility that I scarcely believe it could be thwarted. Maybe that is how, within the 'personalist' approach to marriage, I rejoin the age-old belief of the Church that a sacramental marriage which is consummated is absolutely indissoluble.

However, not every sacramental marriage is consummated in this way and not everyone might be willing to accept this revised interpretation of consummation, even though a good number of canon lawyers and theologians seem to be saying something similar to this.

Even prescinding from this interpretation of consummation, is there anything else that can be said with reference to the statement that the fact that the marriage of two Christians is a sacrament gives it a totally new depth of indissolubility, and that renders it absolutely indissoluble?

Over ten years ago a very wise priest friend said something very thought-provoking. 'If the bread corrupts or the wine becomes totally diluted in the Eucharist, the real presence of the Lord is no longer there, since the sacramental species has ceased to be. If the heart of marriage (and so the matter of the sacrament of marriage) consists in the personal relationship of life-giving love, what happens to the sacrament of marriage if this relation-ship has become totally corrupted and has ceased to exist?' I can see no answer to that question other than that the sacrament of marriage has ceased to exist.

Such an assertion can sound very bland. 'A marriage was in existence; now it is gone. So what? Life must go on.' If that is all that is being said, a massive untruth is being perpetrated. No one would deny that the untimely death of a human being is a human tragedy deeply affecting many people. Although it may not be due to anyone's fault or sin, and although it is possible for good to come from it, it is certainly an evil.

Something very similar has to be said about the untimely death of any marriage; and it has an added dimension of evil and tragedy when it is the breakdown of the marriage of two Christians. Despite its re-interpretation of the meaning of in-dissolubility, the 'relationship' approach to marriage does not play down the evil of marriage breakdown. If anything, it enables us to appreciate that evil even more starkly. Lady Helen Oppenheimer expresses this very forcefully when she writes:

> Surely there is a real sin in putting asunder what God has joined, a sin which cannot be properly recognized by those who have to say that a broken marriage has not been put asunder at all, because either it is still in being or else it never was . . . The present suggestion is that a broken marriage is a broken marriage; something that stands out as an unnatural smashing of what was built to last, a blasphemy against the unity of Christ and his Church, an amputation inflicted upon a living body . . . The bond of marriage is indeed a real bond, affecting those who are joined in it for evermore. It can never be neatly untied, only harshly severed. When this injury has happened the practical question is how the wound can best be healed, and the temptation is always either to cover it soothingly up at grave risk of it festering, or to keep it open for ever as a warning for others ('Is the Marriage Bond an Indissoluble "Vinculum"?' in *Theology*, LXXVIII, 1975, p. 242).

If according to this approach the first marriage has ceased to exist, can a Christian choose to enter a second marriage? If he or she really accepts the 'relationship' approach to marriage, then one thing at least can be said in answer to this question. If as Christians they decide that they should not enter a second marriage, it cannot be because they believe their first marriage has some kind of extra-terrestrial existence totally distinct from the marriage relationship itself and that, thus existing, it still binds them.

Second marriage – adultery?

This question leads us straight back again to the two different ways of understanding marriage which we looked at earlier. Within the first pattern of marriage the Roman Catholic Church has clearly stated what is to be regarded as adultery. Moreover, by the various procedures already mentioned (nullity, Pauline and Petrine Privilege, dissolution of non-consummated sacramental marriage etc.), it has been able to classify as non-adulterous certain marriages which to an outsider might seem to be adultery, since they are second marriages while the former partner is still living.

However, we have already noted that, even for many who hold this first approach to marriage, these categories do not do full justice to their experience of the kind of second marriages under discussion in this chapter. They have encountered such marriages in which the couples are most certainly deeply loving spouses and parents with a deep Christian faith. This experience forces them to recognize that such marriages are truly vehicles of God's gracious love and it seems almost blasphemous to condemn them as adulterous. Of its very nature the term 'adultery' carries a negative moral evaluation. To call a marriage 'adultery' is not just to give a factual description of it; it is to pass a condemnatory moral judgement on it. That is why, in the various cases of permissible second marriage referred to above (i.e. Pauline and Petrine Privilege, nullity etc.,) the Church would never consider referring to them as acceptable or justified adultery. Instead it maintains that the first marriage was either non-existent or at least is no longer in existence.

A similar kind of approach is suggested by those who work from the second pattern of marriage; the relationship or covenant view. In the types of marriage breakdown under discussion they would claim that the first marriage never reached the state of achieved indissolubility; it was never consummated in a fully personal sense. It never really 'got off the ground' and it deteriorated to such an extent that it no longer exists. If the partners enter a second marriage therefore, they cannot be regarded as being unfaithful to the first marriage since it has ceased to exist. Consequently, their second marriage is not classified as adultery. Obviously, how they stand as regards the law is a separate issue. That will be discussed later.

Second marriage – sacrament?

Some writers today see the answer to this question as bound up with the debate as to whether for baptized Christians there can be a legitimate separation made between a natural marriage and a sacramental marriage. The context in which this debate has arisen is different from the issue under consideration in this book. It is the context in which a Church celebration of marriage is being asked for by two baptized Catholics who have now given up their faith and yet who still desire the solemnity of a Church wedding. The renewed appreciation of the necessity of personal faith for true sacramental practice poses a problem for such an arrangement. It makes it difficult to accept that a marriage can be viewed as a Christian sacrament when it involves two baptized Christians who no longer have any living faith in Christ, and for whom marriage has no Christian significance whatsoever. The 1980 Synod called for an investigation of this issue. The current practice of the Church is proving intolerable to many conscientious parochial priests. They feel themselves in an impossible dilemma. Either they take part in the seeming blasphemy of celebrating an apparently 'faith-less' sacramental marriage; or they refuse to marry the couple, knowing at the same time that the Church teaches that the couple cannot be married validly except before a priest and two witnesses. This pastoral problem has raised again the theological issue as to whether baptized Christians can contract a natural marriage without its being regarded as a sacramental marriage. In some areas such a distinction seems to be implicit in the pastoral policies being followed in an attempt to wrestle with this difficulty. These policies have the approval of the local bishops. For instance, in some parts of France and Switzerland the priest supports the couple through a civil marriage to which he might add some kind of blessing or moment of prayer; at the same time he begins to explore with them the Christian significance of their marriage in the hope that they might eventually be able to accept and celebrate it as a sacrament. It is suggested by some writers that this distinction between a sacramental and a natural marriage offers a solution to the problem of how the Church should regard second marriage after divorce. They would be true, natural marriages. It could be appropriate to bless them with a prayer since they belong to God's creation. But there would be no question of regarding them as sacramental and celebrating them accordingly.

I agree with those who reject this attempt to establish a two-tier system of marriage. Somehow it seems to miss the point of what is meant when marriage is said to be a symbol of God's love. While I share the concern of clergy who are profoundly worried about some of the marriages at which they officiate, I feel that at least in certain cases their worry is misplaced if it is focused on the possible sacrilegious nature of what they are doing. If marriage really is a symbol of God's love, it can never be sacrilegious to celebrate a true human marriage in church. In fact, the Japanese hierarchy are reported to have drawn up a rite of service for marriages of non-Christians, since they have received so many requests from such people asking the Church to help them celebrate their marriages as a sacred occasion. It is probably true to say that in some cases what priests are really worried about is not the couple's lack of faith, but their careless and immature approach to their forthcoming marriage. In such cases the word 'sacrilegious' is hardly misplaced. To bless such a union in church is to attribute the sacredness of marriage to something which really has no claim to be called a marriage. But providing that a couple are really intent on a true marriage, priests should be only too happy to help them celebrate such a sacred occasion in their lives. Admittedly, their lack of faith in the person of Christ might demand some changes in the normal form of service, but that should not prevent the priest from helping them to appreciate as far as possible the sacredness of what they are doing. It is not the theology of marriage which opens a window on to God; it is the actual experience of marriage itself. Even if the priest does no more than help them to deepen their respect for the mysterious experience of life-giving love in which they are involving themselves together, he will be implicitly heightening their awareness of the experience of God in their married love.

In the end, as noted earlier, it is the human reality of marriage itself which is the substance of what the Roman Catholic Church calls the 'sacrament of marriage'. That is why I feel that the Church is so right in its teaching that the sacrament cannot be separated from the human reality. Consequently, if a marriage after divorce is to be accepted as a real marriage, it must be admitted that there is a sense in which it can also be said to be 'sacramental'. Sacraments are not only signs, but signs which bring about what they signify or symbolize: and they do not do that automatically. They can be effective signs in varying degrees. Presumably that is why Pius XI was willing to allow only a very restricted value as a Christian sign to a marriage not involving two Christians. In the case of a second marriage after divorce, it would be fair to say that its power to symbolize what a Christian marriage can be is to some extent impaired. Shared fidelity, which lies at the heart of marriage, can only be the joint creation of two persons. Therefore, in a second marriage after divorce one of the partners is bringing into the second marriage his or her personal history of failure in fidelity. This means that, viewed as a public sign or even as an experienced reality between the couple, there is a negative element present which makes the sign or the experience imperfect. The Eastern Church has catered for this by building into the celebration of the second marriage some kind of penitential element, though it seems that this is not always adhered to in practice. Something similar has been suggested for the Church of England, though many are opposed to it. Whether such a penitential note is present in the celebration or not, it is important to recognize that to accept the second marriage as sacramental does not imply that it should be put fully on a par with the first marriage from a sacramental point of view.

The radical, life-giving teaching of Jesus

Is this position an outright rejection of the clear words of Jesus in the New Testament? I do not think so. I would not for a moment claim that the original words of Jesus were anything but totally uncompromising. Any 'except' clauses appear to have been added by the Gospel writers to cope with pastoral problems in the early Church. Jesus refused to be drawn into the casuistic Rabbinical debate regarding when divorce might or might not be allowed because of the sinful situation created by the hardness of our hearts. His teaching was radical. It went right back to the roots or foundation of God's plan for marriage. He refuses to accept that divorce is part of that plan.

This teaching is not an intolerable burden laid on us. It is Gospel, good news. And it is good news that we urgently need today. There are people today who are claiming that to expect a man and a woman to pledge themselves to each other for life is to demand the impossible. Such a life-long commitment would be inhuman, they say. This is a message which is gaining credence and yet it is not a message which seems to bring deep happiness and it is certainly not a message that most people entering marriage want to hear. They embark on their marriage with the hope that they are going to share their whole lives together. For them the words of Jesus are good news. Your hope is really possible, he promises them. Life-long fidelity is a gift that is truly on offer to you. It is a grace, and God's grace is freely given. But the Church in her wisdom reminds us that grace must build on nature. Life-long fidelity is a gift freely available to us – but it is also a task to which we must apply ourselves. If we want really to live, we must accept the pattern of dying and rising.

Jesus proclaimed his radical, life-giving teaching on marriage in the terms imposed by the thought-categories of his own age and culture. These must have been his own thought-categories. Dr Dominian's elaborate analysis of the phases of growth in marriage would have been quite foreign to him, as would any talk about nullity or Papal Dissolution. It is surely not irreverent to say that today we know far more about marriage and growth in marriage than Jesus knew. For him divorce could only be thought of within the category of human sin and so any remarriage after divorce had to be condemned as adultery.

Fidelity to the teaching of Jesus does not oblige the Church to remain locked within the thought-categories of his time and culture. In fact, the Church today can only be truly faithful to his teaching by presenting it enriched by the best insights of our own age and culture. This does not imply any dilution of his teaching. Today the radical teaching of Jesus must become incarnate within our new way of understanding marriage.

For Jesus divorce was a positive action by which one partner (usually the man) sent away the other. Divorce was an action which repudiated the contract of marriage and which treated the other partner unjustly. As such it could only be thought of within the category of human sin and so any remarriage after divorce had to be condemned as adultery. All the complexities of growth in marriage, with the subtle role of sexuality within that growth, would have been a foreign language to Jesus. Despite his great compassion towards all who were wounded and in need of healing, he would not have been able to see marriage breakdown as a terrible human tragedy which left people desperately wounded and in great need of healing. This would not have been blindness on his part. It would have been because marriage breakdown in his day and in his culture would have been a different human reality to what it is today in our Western culture. Despite his welcome for people who were categorized as sinners and made outcasts by the community, he would not have seen anyone who gave his marriage partner a bill of divorce in that light. Jesus would see such a person as acting out the hardness of his heart. He would probably be angry with him as he was with the scribes and Pharisees. But for us today many who suffer the tragedy of marriage breakdown are often victims of sin rather than perpetrators of sin.

Jesus could not see that way in his own day because things were different then. But he does see that way now – in and through us, and in and through his Church. Our task is, as it were, to let his heart shine through our eyes. We must not sell our age short by minimizing the radical challenge and invitation in the teaching of Jesus. But neither must we deny our age the compassion of Jesus by closing our eyes to those whom we can now recognize as deeply wounded and in great need of healing and bringing back to life again.

There must be a two-way process going on, therefore. There must be an interpenetration of the radical teaching of Jesus and the best insights on marriage available in our own day. We do not preserve the treasure of the faith by burying it as the man in the Gospel buried his one talent. That is wasting it and letting it die and stultify. To use a phrase of the Pope when still Archbishop Wojtyla, to defend and preserve the deposit of the faith 'entails its growing understanding, in tune with the demands of every age and responding to them according to the progress of theology and human science' (quoted in *Theological Studies*, 1979, p. 96). Therefore, simply to accept the new under-standing of marriage on its own is not enough. Somehow it must be enriched by being infused with the radical teaching of Jesus. Unless this happens, the Church is merely repeating the teaching of secular experts on marriage. While what they say may be extremely valuable and must be listened to and received respect-fully by the Church, it is still not the Gospel. A further question has to be asked, therefore: what does the radical teaching of Jesus imply with regard to indissolubility as it is made incarnate in the new way of understanding marriage? The radical demand of Jesus does not add some new ingredient to marriage. It is not creating a new reality called 'Christian marriage'. Rather, it is reminding men and women of the deeper significance of marriage. This natural human reality of marriage involves the mysterious process by which distinct persons become one in a very real sense even though they retain their distinctness and individuality. This 'oneness in communion' language is familiar to the Christian. It occurs in the one-in-threeness of the Trinity, in the person Christ being truly man and God, in the one Church being a communion of churches, in the one body of Christ being made up of many members, in the one vine having many branches etc. Oneness in communion is seen to be at the very heart of God himself and the whole of reality seems shot through with this hallmark of God.

It is seen most clearly in the sphere of personal relationships, among which marriage has a very special and unique place. In rejecting divorce on the grounds that 'it was not so from the beginning', Jesus is propounding teaching which is truly radical. That is, he is going back to the real roots of the indissolubility of marriage. The oneness in communion in marriage is a symbol of the oneness in communion of God himself. In other words, through this human experience a couple gain a glimpse of what God is like and actually share in his love. And in reverse, since the oneness in communion of marriage is itself a reflection of God's oneness in communion, a new light is thrown on marriage itself. This oneness in communion, if it is to be true to its roots, cannot be merely transitory. It is only fully authentic if it achieves a permanence which reflects the faithfulness of God himself. This applies to all marriages, not just to the marriages of Christians.

Jesus is recalling *all* married couples to their origins. What is really new, however, what is 'revelation', is Jesus himself who in his person is the oneness in communion of God with man. In his person he is the sacrament of oneness in communion between God and man; and his body, the Church, is called to continue this sacramental presence and mission throughout history. That is why, if marriage today is to be true to its roots, it must reflect the fidelity of oneness in communion revealed in Christ and his Church. This does not demand a new kind of fidelity from marriage, but it does open our eyes to a new dimension of fidelity in marriage. The couple's faithful love is not only a deep and very privileged aspect of their being an 'image of God' and a sharing in his love. It is also a 'real presence' of the faithful love of Christ himself. This makes us even more aware of just how precious is the human reality of faithful love in marriage. This realization by itself does not cause married love to be any more faithful. That can only come from the growth and development of the human reality of married love itself. That is why the only way to make the radical teaching of Jesus really effective within today's understanding of marriage is by giving top priority to fostering the growth and development of this human reality of life-giving, faithful married love. It can hardly be said to be a top priority unless the following challenges are accepted and faced up to:

1. An initial challenge to the Church (and to society in general) to demonstrate its faith that married couples really are capable of such God-like oneness in communion, by providing the helps needed to enable their marriages to reach the state of inner indissolubility. In other words, the first challenge is to the community, rather than to individuals.

2. A challenge to all couples to prepare properly for their marriage and to really work at it once they are married, making full use of all available resources, internal and external. This is not a lack of faith in each other or in their marriage. Grace builds on nature. Normally speaking, they can only hope to enjoy the faithful love they are invited to share if they are prepared to take all the human steps necessary to safeguard and develop it.

3. A challenge to those who are enjoying the fruit of achieved indissolubility (i.e. their marriages are sacramental in the full sense of the word) to accept their mission in the Church to share this gift with other married couples by helping them in their turn to reach and become confirmed in a similar personal indissolubility.

4. A challenge to the Church to recognize that it is marriage breakdown itself which goes counter to the oneness in communion in which we reflect and share in the life of God himself. It is not the legal divorce nor even the second marriage. These both come afterwards. What is really against oneness in communion in marriage is the slow corrosive process by which the relationship gradually deteriorates and finally dies altogether. To the extent that the Church recognizes this, it will be able to concentrate its efforts on the educational, supportive and remedial work needed to sustain fidelity in marriage; and it will not feel the same need to penalize those who have been unfortunate enough to have lost this pearl of great price, whether through their own fault or through force of circumstances beyond their full control.

5. A challenge to couples to recognize that growth in fidelity will only normally occur through phases of crisis and that in a very special way in their marriage each will have to live the Gospel invitation of losing self in order to find the true self. This inner conviction of faith that the cross which leads to new life will be experienced within marriage should provide the inner strength and conviction to keep going in times of darkness.

This final point is important and deserves further elaboration. It is frequently said that any change in the Church's policy in the direction of admitting the divorced-remarried to the sacraments would deprive married people of an essential support in their moments of crisis. They need a strong external law to sustain their fidelity in the difficult times of inner weakness. Without it many couples would easily give up the struggle and they would miss the opportunity of allowing a crisis-point to develop into a growth-point in their marriage. This may well have been true formerly. It would seem to be less true today. This may be because nowadays more people are experiencing marriage, at least implicitly, according to the pattern of the new understanding of marriage. If this is true, the crisis situation which formerly was so well catered for by the strong law has to be catered for in some equally effective way within the new approach to marriage. As suggested above, this will be provided for at two levels: first, by the local Church (and particularly by loving married couples within the local community) being alert to the needs of married couples in these crisis times, and being actually organized to provide any external help needed; and second, by the couples, through adequate preparation, being more aware of the nature of these crises and thus being helped to cope with them and experience them in faith as transition phases to a new level of relationship.

Conclusion

By comparing today's experience and understanding of marriage with that which was widely accepted until very recently, this chapter has come to the conclusion that these two views result in two different interpretations of indissolubility. It is difficult to see how these two positions can possibly be reconciled. This is not to suggest that the former position cannot be updated to some extent so as to incorporate at least some appreciation of marriage as growth in relationship. Neither is it to suggest that the position I am proposing does not appreciate the important role of law in safeguarding the good of marriage. However, when it comes to the critical issue of marriage breakdown and the possibility of remarriage, it is there that the two views go their separate ways. Nevertheless, it would be unfair for either position to accuse the other of not really believing in the indissolubility of marriage, even though each might be tempted to think that the other is failing to concentrate on the central core of the issue.

If they cannot be completely reconciled, are they available as two alternative positions within the Church, or at least for the Church? Although at first sight that might seem an attractive way out of the impasse, I feel it is not a solution open to the Church. The Church is committed to interpreting the Gospel in the light of the best insights available to it in any age, even though in the process it must always keep one eye on the way earlier Christians have undertaken this same task. It would seem that the current best insights on the human reality of marriage leave the Church no choice but to accept the new position. In fact, it could be argued that the official acceptance of the change-over to this position is implied in the approach to marriage adopted by Vatican II in *The Church in the Modern World*.

I firmly believe in the indissolubility of marriage and I also believe that the Church must never fail to uphold this, even though, as stated earlier, I prefer the more personalist term of 'life-long fidelity' to indissolubility. If I became convinced that the position outlined in this chapter denied that truth, I would not hesitate to renounce it. To reinterpret indissolubility in the light of the Church's richer understanding of the human reality of marriage should not be construed as a denial of indissolubility. In fact, it is trying to unearth the full riches of this precious gift of faithful married love in order that it can be better appreciated and lived out in today's world.

3

SACRAMENTS FOR THE DIVORCED-REMARRIED – THE THEOLOGICAL ARGUMENTS

The rest of this book is concerned with the possibility of Holy Communion for Catholics who are involved in a second marriage after divorce, either because their own first marriage has broken down or because they have married one of the partners of a broken marriage. Though this and the following chapter come naturally after our discussion of indissolubility, it is worth noting that the position I am about to develop does not depend completely for its validity on the interpretation of indissolubility I have suggested in the previous chapter. As already mentioned, in the world of theological writing there seems to be a fair measure of agreement with the main lines of the position expressed in this chapter, whereas there has been far less discussion of how the modern approach to marriage affects our understanding of indissolubility.

I would also like to stress that this chapter is focusing on just *one* of the needs of those in a second marriage. It is the need felt by many in this situation to share more fully in the sacramental life of the Church. In the actual everyday life of the Church and of the local Christian community this need cannot be viewed in isolation from the many other important human needs of such people (e.g. their need for acceptance, practical support, legal and financial aid, help with the children, involvement in the community, etc.). If these needs are ignored, there is a danger that the sacraments will be experienced merely as religious actions with no relevance for, nor roots in, the ordinary life of the community. Nevertheless, the sacramental question can and needs to be examined in its own right. The Church has a growing concern for the pastoral care of the divorced-remarried as regards all their other needs. But when it comes to their sacramental needs, there it draws the line.

Many people find this hard to understand. It gives the impression of an unsympathetic and unforgiving Church which does not really understand what these people have been through and which cannot in its heart of hearts bring itself to fully accept them. In this sense, the sacramental question becomes for many a test of the Church's credibility. If the Church cannot cope with marriage breakdown today, it cannot cope with life; and so it becomes hard to believe that it is the sign of God's love for all men and women in the world of today.

Therefore, this chapter will deal with the theological question: can the Catholic Church allow to the sacraments those who are involved in a second marriage after divorce?

It is a basic principle of Catholic pastoral theology that no one should be refused the sacraments unless he or she is manifestly unworthy or would give grave scandal or is barred from the sacraments by the Church. This chapter will examine whether those in a second marriage after divorce are manifestly unworthy or whether grave scandal would be caused by their receiving the sacraments. The next chapter will consider whether they are forbidden the sacraments by any law or teaching of the Church; and, if so, what is its current binding force and should it be changed?

Are they 'living in sin'?

Until recently most Catholics would have said that couples in a second marriage after divorce are 'living in sin'. Many of the couples themselves would have accepted that, at least in theory. What was meant by this expression was that the couple were living in 'a state of mortal sin'. In other words, the sin in question was personal sin. They were alienated from God.

Personal sin?

Though there are still many Catholics who would view such couples in this way, it is not the position which is adopted in most of the more recent official statements in the Church. And it is rarely found even in those contemporary theologians who are still unable to accept their admission to the sacraments. Their writings frequently imply that God's grace may be alive and active in the lives of these people and they nearly always encourage such couples to develop their prayer life and to share in the Church's mission and worship, short of receiving the sacraments. This is very beautifully expressed in the authoritative Chapter 11 of the 1980 French pastoral directives. It speaks of them 'building an authentic spiritual life, inspired by the Spirit and rooted in hope in God who never abandons those who trust in him.'

The recent utterances of Pope John Paul II are more ambiguous. He too insists that the divorced-remarried 'do not consider themselves as separated from the Church, for as baptized persons they can, and indeed must, share in her life' (*Familiaris Consortio*, n. 84). He calls on the whole Church to encourage them to be actively involved in all aspects of the Church's life. Yet at the same time he insists that they need sacramental reconciliation and that this must be refused to them unless they radically change their way of life. This sounds very harsh and condemnatory teaching but is softened somewhat by the Pope's describing their situation as '*objectively* contradicting that union of love between Christ and the Church which is signified and effected by the Eucharist'. In this he seems to pull back from passing any judgement on their inner personal stance in love before the Lord. Certainly the advice to be actively involved in the prayer and missionary life of the Church is hardly consistent with the judgement that the couple are at enmity with God and living in a personal stance of mortal sin.

A living contradiction

This is probably why there has developed another way of presenting the 'living in sin' argument. This is not directly concerned with the personal state of the couple, how they stand before God. It is using the word 'sin' almost in the sense of 'contradiction'. Marriage is about faithful love, whereas a second marriage after divorce contradicts faithful love. So such a second marriage is really a living contradiction.

At first sight, the new way of presenting the 'living in sin' argument might seem to be simply another way of saying that their second marriage is wrong but they are in good faith about it. However, I think it is saying more than this. It is talking about couples who are fully aware of the Church's current teaching that their second marriage is wrong. Yet they are deciding that in their particular situation it is right for them to remain in this marriage. To maintain that they are 'in good faith' is not a satisfactory explanation since it implies that they do not know that what they are doing is wrong. They do know that the Church teaches it is wrong; yet they are also convinced that it is right for them. This might sound like double-think. But it is a fair description of the state of mind engendered among many Catholics by the Church's approach to morality in recent centuries.

Making a right decision: the law of gradualness

In fact, it was precisely this state of mind (though in the context of the contraception debate) that the bishops in the Synod were addressing themselves to when they found great help in what they called 'the law of gradualness'. The law of gradualness refers to the kind of dilemma situation in which two different points of focus have to be kept in view even though for the present they cannot be fully aligned with each other. The first focus (it could be called the 'universal' focus) is the universal value or law which is concerned with the good of human persons in general and which challenges the individual regardless of their particular situation. The second focus (the 'particular' focus) involves both the individual's capacity at this stage in the history of their personal development and also any features in their particular situation which may have special human significance. The law of gradualness is directed towards a growing alignment of the particular with the universal focus. However, it accepts that the 'particular' focus will be the determining one when the individual comes to make his or her personal decision at this point in time in this specific situation. Nevertheless, there will always be something unsatisfactory about any decision in which the 'particular' and the 'universal' focus cannot be properly aligned together. The law of gradualness recognizes that this process of alignment takes time; it is a gradual process. In the case of certain individuals or in some particular circumstances, perhaps it will never be open to more than a partial achievement. Certain values may never be able to be achieved, however gradually, by some persons unless there first occurs some change in the situation in which they have to live their lives and this might be beyond their control and might never occur in their lifetime. Incidentally, the discrepancy between the two points of focus would be roughly the equivalent to what contemporary moral theologians would refer to as 'non-moral evil'. That is their way of recognizing that there is something unsatisfactory as long as both foci are not aligned. However, they would insist that the law of gradualness must not be restricted to the subjective field of inner personal development. The personal sphere cannot be divorced from its social context. Pope John Paul rightly warns against an abuse of the 'law of gradualness' which would take all creative tension out of a humanly unsatisfactory situation (one which is not properly focused) by saying that each situation is virtually independent and has its own law. This would be tantamount to extreme 'situation ethics' and would receive no support from contemporary Catholic moral theologians.

What might seem a highly theoretical discussion is in fact very relevant for the issue of people living in a second marriage. The law of gradualness is a way of saying that people can only start from where they are. That is where their decisions have to be made. And where they are includes their present stage of development on all levels: emotional, psychological, intellectual, moral and spiritual. What is demanded of them is not some super-human decision totally beyond their present capabilities. What is asked of them is a decision which according to their own capacity is rightly made, i.e. gives due importance to the most important values insofar as they see them. Moreover, as already noted, part of starting from where they are involves starting from their present interpersonal and social situations.

Bearing all this in mind I would have no hesitation in saying that entering a second marriage or (even more so) remaining faithful to an already existing second marriage can certainly be envisaged as a *rightly made* decision for many Catholics. And if it is rightly made, I think it can also be described as the right decision for them (i.e. in their present state and at this particular moment in time within this specific situation). And if it is in this sense the right decision for them, it is accurate to describe it as morally good. (See New Preface, pp. xxii–xxiii, n. 4).

If that is the case with regard to the second-marriage decisions of many Catholics, it is not appropriate to use the term 'sin' in any sense to refer to their marriages. That is not to deny that there is evil involved in their second-marriage situation. But this is not moral evil. It is what many theologians today would refer to as 'non-moral evil'. The evil in question is the regrettable fact that their second marriage is not and cannot be fully aligned to the important focal point of life-long marital fidelity. The term Pope John Paul uses to describe this evil is 'objective contradiction'.

Living in contradiction to the Eucharist

This leads us on to the changed emphasis in the 'living in sin' argument. It has now developed into a 'living in contradiction to the Eucharist' argument. In the Eucharist we celebrate the indissoluble love of Christ for his Church. And the marriage of two Christians is called to be a symbol and living presence of that love. That is why earlier in this book I embraced Helen Oppenheimer's description of the evil of marriage breakdown: 'a blasphemy against the unity of Christ and his Church'. This being so, a strong case can be made out for describing a second marriage after divorce as a living contradiction to the Eucharist. Certainly it is living witness that the faithful love of the first marriage is no longer in operation.

In one of their propositions to the Pope, the Synod bishops state: 'They cannot be admitted to eucharistic communion since their status and way of life *objectively* contradicts the indissolubility of that covenant of love between Christ and the Church which is signified and actualised by the Eucharist' (Proposition 14, n. 3). The Pope obviously took their words to heart since in his recent Apostolic Exhortation, *Familiaris Consortio*, he has written: 'They are unable to be admitted thereto (i.e. to Eucharistic Communion) from the fact that their state and condition of life objectively contradicts that union of love between Christ and the Church which is signified and effected by the Eucharist' (n. 84).

The argument that the divorced-remarried must be refused Holy Communion because they are living in objective contradiction to the Eucharist was put forward by the International Theological Commission in its 1978 statement. It is echoed in the statements of the Italian and French bishops. As far as I can ascertain it is only in recent years that the argument for necessary exclusion from the Eucharist has been articulated in this way. It is an argument which I used myself in *The Clergy Review*, 1970, pp. 123–141. As will be clear in what follows, honesty now forces me to say that I am no longer convinced by it as an argument *necessitating* exclusion from the Eucharist.

An unconvincing argument for exclusion

The question to be faced is: what is the force of this 'living in contradiction to the Eucharist' argument? I do not think that the contradiction can be really denied, but does it entail exclusion from Holy Communion as a necessary consequence? By way of parenthesis it might be noted that since this 'living in contradiction to the Eucharist' form of the argument does not presume sin in any personal sense (although it does not deny its possibility), the sacrament of reconciliation would not seem to present an insuperable obstacle at the level of pastoral practice.

Roman Catholic theology of the Eucharist has developed considerably in recent years. Many of the liturgical changes introduced by Vatican II are the fruits of this development. For instance, today far more emphasis is laid on the fact that we celebrate the Eucharist as a community. It is seen as a celebration in which the whole Christian community has its part to play. And the Christian community itself is seen less as a gathering of the saints and more as a coming together *en route* of the pilgrim church in which all are at the same time saints and sinners. This is one of the points highlighted by the bishops in their post-Congress document, *The Easter People*, n. 22. Every Eucharist significantly begins with a short service of confession of sinfulness and grateful acceptance of forgiveness; the communicant's final words before receiving are 'Lord, I am not worthy...' Moreover, 'full, conscious and active participation' is seen by Vatican II to be demanded by the very nature of the liturgy and is to be regarded as 'the aim to be considered before all else' (*Liturgy Constitution*, n. 14). Furthermore, the Council also speaks of the Eucharist as having a twofold meaning and purpose: it should be both a sign of unity and a means to unity (cf. *Decree on Ecumenism*, n. 8).

It is the development in Eucharistic theology that has enabled the Church to open the way to allowing non-Catholic Christians to receive the Eucharist in certain situations. As long as we look at the Eucharist exclusively from the angle of its being a sign of unity achieved, it is difficult for us to understand how non-Catholic Christians can be admitted to the Eucharist since their objective status contradicts that unity. But once we open our eyes to the Eucharist as a means to achieving unity the impossibility vanishes and we even become more humble in acknowledging our own contribution to disunity in the Church.

In the light of this current understanding of the Eucharist, an absolute prohibition of Communion to the divorced-remarried can hardly be claimed to be a necessary theological conclusion and the pastoral wisdom of maintaining such a prohibition needs to be seriously questioned. For one thing it lays too much emphasis on the Eucharist as a sign of already existing community and it ignores the power of the Eucharist in helping us to achieve a greater unity. It also turns a blind eye to the many ways (small and great) in which the lives of other members of the community might be out of focus; in fact, a conclusion of the view I am criticizing could well be that the main body of the Church in the so-called 'developed' West should not be admitted to Communion because it is involved in structural (i.e. objective) injustice vis-à-vis the Third World! The Justice Sector of the Pastoral Congress had the humility to confess this on behalf of the Church in this country but the bishops in *The Easter People* did not draw the conclusion that we should all be put under an interdict!

Furthermore, to recommend the divorced-remarried to attend the Eucharist without communicating seems contrary to the participation demanded by the very nature of the Eucharist. Likewise, the pastoral advice sometimes given that they might receive the sacraments in a church where they are not known seems to conflict with our understanding of the Eucharist as the celebration of *this* (usually local) community.

All this would seem to point to the conclusion that it is a theological exaggeration to state that the couple's admission to Communion would totally contradict the meaning of the Eucharist and so is impossible. On the contrary, the understanding of the Eucharist in contemporary theology could produce equally strong arguments in favour of their admission.

Would their receiving the sacraments cause scandal?

Maybe this Eucharistic argument which I have been criticizing is merely a theological superstructure erected as a defence of a very practical and understandable concern of the Church. This would be the Church's concern to uphold the indissolubility of marriage because it believes this is necessary if the institution of marriage is to be preserved and the happiness of married people safeguarded. For instance, the section of Proposition 14 of the Synod referred to above continues: 'Furthermore, there is a special pastoral reason [i.e. why they should not be admitted to Communion], namely, because this would cause the faithful to be misled and confused about the Church's teaching on the indissolubility of marriage.'

Once again the Pope makes these words his own in *Familiaris Consortio*, n. 84. Perhaps, then, the basic reasons for the absolute prohibition run along lines such as the following: so that people will not be misled into thinking that the Church is no longer committed to indissolubility; so that those struggling with crises in their marriage will not give up but will be supported in their struggle by the Church's unambiguous witness; so that those entering marriage will really accept that they are pledging themselves to a life-long commitment etc. If these are really the fundamental concerns underlying the theological argument, then that argument is the same as the 'scandal' argument. Let us now examine that argument in more detail.

Scandal – arguing from consequences

This maintains that the strength of the Church's witness for indissolubility will be weakened by allowing these couples to the sacraments. As a consequence of this, more marriages will end up in the tragedy of breakdown. In this sense, by such a practice the Church would be implicitly helping to spread the evil of marriage breakdown. That would be a scandal in the true meaning of the word. It would be leading others into evil and perhaps even into personal sin. That is an argument based on consequences. How can it be proved true or false? Short of actually implementing the suggested policy for a period of time on an experimental basis (and even that would hardly provide convincing proof), the only ways of testing the validity of the scandal argument would seem to be:

a) Investigate situations where this policy has been in operation already, e.g. some local communities in the Roman Catholic Church; other Christian Churches who have followed a similar policy.

b) Investigate whether there are any experimental findings drawn from parallel situations which might be helpful.

c) Look more closely at the scandal argument itself in order to evaluate its internal strength as an argument.

To the extent that the first two investigations are feasible, it is important that they should be undertaken. Ultimately, there is no real substitute for sound experimental data in considering an argument from consequences. However, since I do not have access to such experimental data and since such investigations would be beyond my field of competence, I have no option but to restrict myself to the third choice. I hope that others might be able to carry out the investigations mentioned. If they do, I look forward to learning from their findings.

A question of priorities

The scandal argument states that, if it were to admit such divorced-remarried people to the sacraments, the Church would be contributing to the increase in marriage breakdown. The basic premise of this argument seems to be: the Church must not do anything which would contribute to the increase in marriage breakdown. This sounds very convincing and it might seem to be a statement which no Christian could question. Nevertheless, it does need to be looked at more closely. Should it be accepted as an absolute rule? Or should it be interpreted merely as emphasizing a value which ought to be given a high priority? If the former, then the Church can never allow anything to overrule it. Yet in fact the Church does weigh it in the balance with other values. For instance, the group whose marriages are most at risk are those who marry under the age of twenty-one, especially when there is a pre-marital pregnancy. The Church could make a law prohibiting such marriages. However, it refuses to do this because of the respect it has for another basic human value, that of human freedom. It is therefore willing to contribute to the breakdown of marriage through its act of omission (i.e. not forbidding such marriages by law) because it fears that such legislation would violate this other basic human value of personal freedom.

Therefore, to say that the Church must never do anything which would contribute to the increase in marriage breakdown does not seem to be completely accurate as a statement of the Church's position as revealed in its practice. A more accurate statement might be: because the Church is very conscious of the great evil involved in marriage breakdown, it will do all in its power to lessen this evil and it will try to do nothing to contribute towards it insofar as this can be reconciled with its concern for other basic human Christian values.

To look at how convincing the scandal argument is, therefore, we need to look at two questions related to it. The first is: is refusal of the sacraments the most effective way to bear witness to the Church's belief in the indissolubility of marriage and thus help to prevent more marriages from breaking down? The second is: is there another important value at stake which might justify the Church in adopting a pastoral policy which might in the eyes of the world weaken its stand on indissolubility?

Witnessing to a belief in the indissolubility of marriage

Before it takes a stand against anything, the Church must always stand for something. In other words, it must be committed to some positive human and Christian value which it sees to be threatened by this negative phenomenon. In the instance we are examining, the Church stands for life-giving and life-long faithful love in marriage. The Church cares deeply about this value because it cares about people and this value is intimately bound up with the deepest good of people. People's true happiness is at stake here. Love is God's greatest gift to humanity and the Church is concerned that love be genuine and true to itself. In fact, through this precious human reality a window is opened, allowing men and women to get a glimpse and an experience of what God himself is like.

It is this concern for true life-giving and faithful love in marriage which makes the Church so strong in its determination to safeguard people from the pain and suffering of marriage breakdown. That is why it refuses to weaken in its belief in the indissolubility of marriage.

However, it is fair to ask whether refusing Communion to the divorced-remarried is an effective way of giving this witness. Paradoxically, the people who are most convinced about the evil of marriage breakdown and who have the deepest belief that life-long faithful love is one of God's most precious gifts, are those who themselves have been through the painful agony of marriage breakdown. They have experienced in their own persons its dehumanizing effects. They have seen at first hand the shattering impact it has on their children. If the Church really wants to mobilize a body of people who see how precious is the gift of faithful love in marriage, she could make a good start by enlisting all those who have been through the tragedy of marriage breakdown. The fact that some of them have remarried could hardly be used as an argument against their belief in the goodness of life-long faithful love. In fact, this belief has probably been part of their motivation in remarrying. They want to find that precious gift which eluded them in their first marriage.

In terms of public witness, therefore, refusal of Communion comes over to people more as a form of punishment and victimization. I honestly believe that the Church would be more effective in combating marriage breakdown if it made the divorced-remarried feel completely at home at the table of the

Lord and from there drew them into active involvement in the apostolate of preparation and support for marriage.

In the end, the only effective way the Church will overcome the evil of marriage breakdown will be by making the marriage apostolate a top priority in its pastoral policy. In fact, until recently it could be argued that a major scandal was the fact that the Church gave such a low priority to the kind of work needed to enable marriages to become truly indissoluble. Through its sins of omission in this field it could even be argued that the Church has actually contributed greatly to the breakdown of marriage. However, it is probably unhelpful to labour this point since, after all, the Church can only do its best within the limits of its understanding of marriage at any point of time. The law of gradualness even applies to the Church itself, though I am tempted to complain that it has been far too gradual in giving proper recognition and realistic support to a major prophet in this field, Dr Jack Dominian.

Nevertheless, what can hardly be denied is that if the Church today is to be a credible witness standing for the indissolubility of marriage, it must give a real (and not just notional) priority to the kind of pastoral care which will be needed if marriages are to become indissoluble in fact rather than just in theory. As Paul VI wrote in *Evangelization in the Modern World*: 'Modern man listens more willingly to witnesses than to teachers, and if he does listen to teachers it is because they are witnesses' (n. 41).

Thank goodness, things have been changing in recent years. With a richer appreciation of marriage as a process of growth in relationships, there has been a move to introduce into the Church's pastoral policy an emphasis on training and support during the initial phases of growth and development. The Catholic Marriage Advisory Council has led the field in this area with their educational, pre-marriage and remedial work. In the past few years a particularly important contribution has been made by the Marriage Encounter movement and this shows every sign of being a major influence for good in the years ahead.

Perhaps this change of emphasis in pastoral policy could be linked with two approaches to marriage and indissolubility discussed in the previous chapter. The change could be described as a shift from an external to an internal emphasis. The external approach would say: we believe in the indissolubility of marriage and we show this by our absolute stand against divorce and remarriage and by our refusing the sacraments to the divorced-remarried. The internal approach would say: we believe in the indissolubility of marriage and we show this by the high pastoral priority we put on doing everything possible to help marriages become really indissoluble.

The value of healing and forgiveness

There is another aspect of scandal which needs to be considered. In many instances, it would be truer to describe those whose marriages have broken down as victims of sin rather than as perpetrators of sin. Certainly, many will emerge from the traumatic process of marriage breakdown as wounded people. They are men and women needing help and healing, not judgement and condemnation. It should be a scandal if the Church were to turn its back on them in their time of need since it is committed to doing all in its power to bring healing to hurt and wounded people. Many people whose marriages have broken down come into that category. They have been through a form of dying and they need help if they are to be brought back to life again and if they are to find real healing. Obviously, the question arises: can this new life and healing come through entering into a second marriage? I have no doubt at all that this can and does happen in a fair number of cases. Clearly such a statement would carry far more weight if it had the backing of some good research into the healing potentiality of second marriages. Careful research into this field might make it possible to draw up some kind of picture of the healing process after marriage breakdown. This could be helpful in discerning whether a prospective second marriage might offer genuine healing or whether it might simply be leading into a repetition of what went wrong in the first marriage. It might also help towards a deeper appreciation of the special needs of those for whom healing will have to be found in living singly or as single parents.

If a second marriage brings true healing, and especially if for some men and women it is the only way of finding true healing, I feel that the Church has no choice but to accept it as good. 'Is it against the law on the sabbath to do good, or to do evil; to save life, or to destroy it?' (Luke 6:9). To deny healing in the name of God's law comes perilously close to the position of the Pharisees which Jesus opposed so strongly.

The need for repentance

The thrust of the Church's pastoral care is always in the direction of healing and forgiveness. Obviously, therefore, the need for inner repentance and forgiveness must be given a high priority. If a marriage reaches the stage of irreconcilable breakdown, although that means that resumption of married life is now impossible, it does not mean that there is no need for some form of reconciliation ard forgiveness. Both partners should be ready to accept responsibility for any ways in which they contributed to the breakdown of the marriage, and to the extent that this was due to their deliberate fault they should be sincerely sorry for it. In their hearts they must also want to forgive the other for his or her share in the breakdown process with all its attendant sufferings to both of them and to the children.

Although the English law has dropped the distinction between the 'innocent' and 'guilty' party in a marriage breakdown and although it is probably true that both partners share responsibility to some extent in every breakdown process, nevertheless at the level of personal responsibility before God perhaps it would be unrealistic to ignore these categories altogether. Especially when we are dealing with marriages which seem to have been real marriages and which no one is claiming to have been null, the breakdown process may have begun in some instances through factors within the control of one or other of the partners. Consequently one or other might carry a greater responsibility for the breakdown of the marriage. In that case it might be fair to think of that person as the 'guilty' partner and the other might be more sinned against than sinning. If this is true, it has implications both at the level of scandal caused in the community and at the level of the quality of repentance and forgiveness needed.

This distinction needs to be kept in mind in any consideration of pastoral practice. In instances where it would seem appropriate to speak of a 'guilty' and an 'innocent' party, some kind of differentiation of practice would seem to be indicated. This is obviously in the thoughts of Pope John Paul II reflecting the mind of the Synod:

> Pastors must know that, for the sake of truth, they are obliged to exercise careful discernment of situations. There is in fact a difference between those who have sincerely tried to save their first marriage and have been unjustly abandoned, and those who through their own grave fault have destroyed a canonically valid marriage (*Familiaris Consortio*, n. 84).

In the case of a 'guilty' partner, for a pastoral practice to respect the needs of healing and forgiveness, some additional requirements such as the following might seem to be indicated:

a) a sincere desire for the innocent partner's forgiveness and willingness to change as far as possible whatever in the present situation is hurtful to the innocent partner.

b) an appreciation of the scandal he or she has caused in the local community and a determination not to do anything that might increase that scandal still further. This might mean that even though sincerely repentant, they might judge that receiving the sacraments would further disturb and disrupt the community rather than express and increase communion. And so at least for a time they might voluntarily but regretfully refrain from receiving the sacraments. When the public celebration of the sacrament of reconciliation becomes more confidently re-established in the life of the Church, perhaps that might provide the context for celebrating the reconciliation of one who had caused such public scandal in the local community.

The individual and the public good

I am not denying that on occasion individuals have to suffer to avoid much greater harm being done to people in general. Nor am I denying that willingness to give one's life for others is a hallmark of the disciple of Jesus. But it does not follow that those who have suffered the human tragedy of marriage breakdown should be forced (or should be willing) to carry their cross to the end by accepting the loneliness of a life of non-chosen celibacy. That would only follow if it could be proved that their not re-marrying would certainly help others to avoid the tragic suffering they themselves have been through. Unless that were proved, it would be unjust to put moral or legal pressure on such people to sacrifice their personal well-being for a cause which might be completely unfounded. It is true that restrictive laws can be made to avert probable dangers to the common good, and this is precisely why it is reasonable to have civil and ecclesiastical legislation governing the area of marriage breakdown and second marriage. Nevertheless, such laws must not restrict individual liberty beyond the needs of the common good. Increasingly, civil legislation is judging that some level of acceptance of second marriage is on balance beneficial rather than harmful to the common good. If this judgement is well-founded, the Church cannot but take note of it if it is going to employ the same criterion of concern for the common good.

Conclusion

The position outlined in this chapter is totally different from what is called a 'divorce mentality'. That is a vision of marriage which would see no particular value in life-long fidelity. In fact, some versions of it would even claim that the pledge of life-long fidelity is a denial of human freedom and turns marriage into a life-sentence rather than an occasion of personal enrichment for both partners.

The 'divorce mentality' would, therefore, see nothing harmful or evil in marriage breakdown. It would see it merely as a perfectly normal phase in the transition from one close friendship to another.

According to the way of understanding marriage which I have been proposing, irretrievable marriage breakdown is definitely seen as an evil. It is not in accord with God's plan for human living and loving. And to the extent that its causes can be laid at the doorstep of human responsibility, it can truly be regarded as the fruit of sin. To what extent any particular breakdown can be attributed to the personal sin of the couple themselves is quite a different question. Yet even when it would seem to be principally due to their sin and they themselves are willing to accept this humbly and in a spirit of repentance, it is not regarded as an unforgivable sin. Consequently, if, as is being assumed here, their repentance cannot take the form of the resumption of married life together, and if they subsequently find healing through entering a second marriage, there are no convincing grounds for saying that they cannot be admitted to the sacraments. Neither the 'living in sin' argument nor the 'scandal' argument prove the case against admission to the sacraments.

4

SACRAMENTS FOR THE DIVORCED-REMARRIED – WHAT CAN WE DO IN PRACTICE?

The previous chapter considered the theological question: can the Catholic Church allow those in a second marriage after divorce to receive the sacraments? The answer was 'Yes'. This final chapter will move to the level of practice. In other words, the question now becomes: *may* those in a second marriage after divorce receive sacraments in the Catholic Church? This in turn will need to be broken down into three separate questions:

a) Does the Catholic Church forbid them the sacraments?

b) If so, how strictly should this prohibition be interpreted by such couples themselves and by those who administer the sacraments?

c) Would a divergent practice lead to pastoral chaos?

It should be noticed that in what follows I am constantly referring to the 'divorced-remarried'. Obviously, for most practical purposes my remarks apply equally to those who are not themselves divorced and remarried but who have married a divorced person.

Does the Catholic Church forbid the sacraments to the divorced-remarried?

The impression has been given throughout the second part of this book that the Catholic Church does forbid the sacraments to the divorced-remarried. However, what this means needs much closer examination. At a popular level virtually all Catholics believe that the divorced-remarried are forbidden to receive the sacraments. Is this belief correct? Does the Catholic Church forbid the sacraments to the divorced-remarried? Within the Catholic Church a prohibition can arise from two different sources. It can come from the Church's law or it can flow as a direct consequence of the Church's doctrinal or moral teaching. This division is not meant to suggest that the Church's laws have no grounding in its doctrinal or moral teaching. It is merely recognizing that not everything which is regarded as forbidden in the Church needs to have a special Church law made against it.

Not excommunicated

Many Catholics think that the divorced-remarried are excommunicated. Even more tragically, some of the divorced-remarried themselves believe this to be true and this has caused them to drift away from the Church. In fact, whatever other reasons might be offered for their not receiving the sacraments, all experts in Church law would agree that there is absolutely no question of the divorced-remarried being excommunicated in the proper sense of that word.

Not forbidden by Church law

Although not all experts in Church law would agree with it, a strong case can be argued for saying that the category of divorced-remarried men and women under consideration here are not forbidden by any Church law to receive the sacraments. This involves a highly technical legal argument which is based on detailed analysis of the Church's laws dealing with non-admission to the sacraments. It would be out of place here to try to spell out all the points of the argument and the objections of those who reject it. For the purpose of this book it is enough to note that this interpretation is sufficiently well-founded to bring into play the accepted principle that 'a doubtful law does not bind'. In other words, because there is sufficient doubt whether any prohibition exists in law against such people receiving the sacraments, for purposes of practical decision-making no obligation should be presumed to exist. Consequently, if it is held that the Catholic Church forbids the sacraments to the divorced-remarried, the source of this prohibition must be sought in her doctrinal and moral teaching since it is not enshrined in her laws.

This is an important distinction. It means that if any such prohibition exists, it should be interpreted according to the principles of moral theology and not of Church law.

Not forbidden by theology

In the previous chapter it has already been shown that such a prohibition is not a necessary consequence of our contemporary theological understanding on marriage and the Eucharist. In fact, current developments in theology in both these areas would tend to point in the opposite direction. They would seem to indicate that in the kind of divorce-remarriage situation under consideration it would be more appropriate to admit them to the sacraments rather than refuse them.

Official statements of authoritative teaching

However, it cannot be denied that at the level of official Church teaching it is quite clearly taught that such couples should not be admitted to the sacraments. Pope Paul VI spoke in this vein and the same position is expressed by the International Theological Commission (1978) both in its own statement and in a paper by G. Martelet to which it gave general approval. The Congregation for the Doctrine of the Faith has adopted the same position in its dealings with some bishops' conferences, particularly in its letter from Cardinal Seper sent to the bishops in 1973. Pope John Paul II's closing address to the 1980 Synod reiterates this position, as does his Apostolic Exhortation, *Familiaris Consortio* (1981). (For post-1982 official statements, see New Appendix)

Public proclamation and pastoral practice

Although all these statements seem to present a total and absolute prohibition, it is worth noting that some commentators who have studied the Vatican's style of dealing with such matters would argue that this is far from being the case. Such statements need to be interpreted in the light of the Roman approach to moral theology which makes a distinction between moral principle and pastoral practice. According to this view, if a principle is to have any real effectiveness, it must be stated clearly, unequivocally and without any qualification. Provided this is done, there is then room for some flexibility in pastoral practice. It is claimed that this approach has been drawn from the standard writers in moral theology in recent centuries. Consequently, even the apparently uncompromising letter of the

Congregation for the Doctrine of the Faith could be understood as giving a hint of a much more liberal approach in its cryptic footnote, 'Consult the approved authors'. This could also explain why the Congregation for the Doctrine of the Faith has given what seem to be unnecessarily ambiguous answers to very clear questions put to them on this matter.

Put very crudely, this approach means that authority says a very clear 'No' to the possibility of the divorced-remarried receiving the sacraments but this unambiguous 'No' is intended only for the purposes of public proclamation. It is meant as a clear public witness of the Church's commitment to indissolubility. But it is not intended as a guide for pastoral practice. Pastoral practice operates on a different level altogether and is the concern of pastoral theology. This is the level at which guidance has to be offered for the difficult process of decision-making in a situation where other values besides indissolubility have also to be considered and where all the particularities of an individual's stage of personal growth and his or her unique situation have to be taken account of. An instance of this two-tier approach was quoted in *The Clergy Review* a few years ago. In 1975 the Sacred Congregation for the Doctrine of the Faith issued a document entitled *Declaration on Certain Questions concerning Sexual Ethics*. In its treatment of homosexuality it shows a good grasp of the issues at stake and tries to tackle the pastoral problem with compassion and sensitivity. However, it insists that 'According to the objective moral order, homosexual relations are acts which lack an essential and indispensable finality' and it states that 'homosexual acts are intrinsically disordered and can in no case be approved of' (n. 8). It is common knowledge that one of the co-authors of this declaration was Fr Visser C.Ss.R., professor of moral theology at Propaganda Fide. One of Fr Visser's colleagues makes the following comment about his approach to homosexuality:

As a moral theologian he has no doubt in categorically stating that homosexuality is intrinsically immoral. A homosexual relationship just does not make sense in terms of principles, and therefore it is always intrinsically wrong. But when he comes to deal with the person who is homosexual, Fr Visser's one concern is to help the person to live as stable a Christian life as possible in his situation. In an interiew in the magazine *L'Europa*, on 30 January, 1976 (after the publication of the Declaration) Fr Visser said 'when one is dealing with people who are so deeply homosexual that they will be in serious personal and perhaps social trouble unless they attain a steady partnership within their homosexual lives, one can recommend them to seek such a partnership, and one accepts this relationship as the best they can do in their present situation'. Fr Visser justifies this on the grounds that the lesser of two evils is often the best thing for people in a particular situation and that one can pastorally and positively recommend the lesser evil as the best thing here and now. He would see no incompatibility between such a pastoral attitude and the adherence to the general, abstract principle that homosexual acts are always intrinsically evil (Sean O'Riordan, 'The "Declaration on Certain Questions concerning Sexual Ethics"' in *The Clergy Review*, 1976, p. 233).

Naturally, the Anglo-Saxon mind finds this approach quite foreign and difficult to understand. It smacks of double-standard morality and can easily lead to a loss of credibility of the Church's moral teaching. Despite our dissatisfaction with this approach, we have to bear it in mind when we are trying to interpret to what extent the authors of these official statements intended them to be understood at the level of practical decision-making.

Divergent voices among the bishops

The 1979 statement of the Italian Episcopal Conference probably belongs to the same type of expression as these official Roman statements. This is not the case with the very delicately worded pastoral letter issued in 1979 by the bishops of the French-speaking cantons of Switzerland or with the equally sensitive pastoral directives of Bishop LeBourgeois of Autun some years previously. From these and from various first-hand and second-hand reports of initiatives being taken in some dioceses or regions I have gained the impression that the practice of admitting some groups of the divorced-remarried to the sacraments is growing in various parts of the Church, and that it is receiving some level of informal approval from a number of bishops either individually or even in groups. Unfortunately, I have found it impossible to gather any official documentation on this point.

The 1980 Roman Synod on Marriage and the Family

However, the views voiced by various bishops in the 1980 Synod are a good indication that there is a desire in some countries that a way should be found to permit the divorced-remarried in some circumstances to receive the sacraments. In fact, one of the forty-three Synod propositions handed over to the Pope includes a request that the practice of the Eastern Church in this matter should be closely studied. The Eastern Church's notion of 'economy' tries to accommodate the demands of the Gospel within the reduced possibilities of the imperfect situation following marriage breakdown. Remarriage is usually allowed but it is not put on a par with a first marriage. This is an ancient practice in the Eastern Church and must be accepted as part of the Christian heritage we share in our diversity. This was acknowledged at the Council of Trent. Canon 7 of Session XXIV, which appears at first sight to be a hard-line approach on indissolubility allowing no possibility of remarriage, was in fact very carefully worded so as not to offend Christians of the Eastern Rite. Very deliberately it refused to state that their divergent practice did not have equal claims to be founded on the Gospel and tradition. Furthermore, a recent study has suggested that this practice of the Eastern Church had a certain counterpart in the West for many centuries: those in a second marriage were allowed to continue living together as man and wife once they had done the penance required by the Church.

It is obviously the hope of the Synod that we in the Roman Catholic Church might be able to learn something from this ancient practice in the Eastern Church.

Another part of the Synod proposition already referred to recognizes a great difference between those whose marriage has broken down despite their real efforts to make it work and those who by their sinful conduct have actually destroyed their marriage. 'Out of love of the truth pastors are obliged to discern between such situations.'

Pope John Paul II

This is a theme which is taken up and expanded by the Pope in *Familiaris Consortio*, n. 84:

> Pastors must know that, for the sake of truth, they are obliged to exercise careful discernment of situations. There is in fact a difference between those who have sincerely tried to save their first marriage and have been unjustly abandoned, and those who through their own grave fault have destroyed a canonically valid marriage. Finally, there are those who have entered a second union for the sake of the children's upbringing, and who are sometimes subjectively certain in conscience that their previous and irreparably destroyed marriage had never been valid.

The Pope does not say what this discernment means in practice. Perhaps it is a veiled reference to the kind of pastoral guidance offered by pastoral theology and so stoutly defended by Fr Visser. If it is, it would explain the rather puzzling statement at the end of the Pope's treatment of divorced persons who have remarried, where he says that the position he has adopted shows the Church's 'motherly concern for these children of hers, especially those who, through no fault of their own, have been abandoned by their legitimate partner.'

I do not share the views of those who believe that the remarks of Pope John Paul II in his closing address to the Synod have put paid to any developments in this direction. A careful analysis of what he actually said is most revealing. In the first place, he received all forty-three propositions 'as a singularly precious fruit of the works of the Synod' and he even called them a 'rich treasury'. There are no grounds for thinking that he excluded the Synod's concern for the divorced-remarried from these words of praise. Moreoever, when he moved on to speak specifically about the question of the divorced-remarried and the sacraments, his remarks were phrased in such a way as to give the impression that he was not adding anything new of his own but was merely articulating for the Synod Fathers what seemed to be their own mind on this matter. He summed this up in three points:

1. The Synod reaffirmed the Church's practice of not admitting to Communion the divorced-remarried.

2. Those who come into this category should be given special pastoral care by 'Pastors and the whole Christian community'.

3. It must not be denied that they can receive the sacraments if they show sincere repentance by living as brother and sister and if there is no scandal.

Respect for the Synod and consultation

It could easily be interpreted as the Pope's final decision that there must be no change in this matter. I feel that is too pessimistic an interpretation. Pope John Paul II knew well enough the alternative solutions which were being proposed in the Church. As he sat through the Synod debates he had heard some of the bishops arguing that these alternative solutions should be given serious consideration.

One of the strongest of these pleas came from Archbishop Worlock. He was not speaking purely as an individual. He spoke out of the experience of listening to groups of committed Catholics at parish level all over England and Wales discussing this issue. The consensus from such discussion comes over clearly in the summary of the Diocesan Reports prior to the National Pastoral Congress:

> Almost every report makes an urgent plea for a re-examination of present policy on this matter (admission to the sacraments for divorced and remarried people). A new pastoral strategy should come from the bishops, with special consideration of the spiritual needs of divorcees.
>
> People cannot understand the rigidity of the Church in this regard: 'Jesus would not refuse to come to them. The Church forgives anything, even murder, but not remarriage': this feeling is echoed in many reports.
>
> Reports ask for . . . a blessing on the second marriage (*Liverpool 1980*, p. 68).

This same conviction was repeated in the Congress itself:

> They (the bishops) should look at ways of showing compassion to those whose marriages have broken irreconcilably, whose second marriage is a living witness to Christ and who seek to re-establish unity with the Church through the Eucharist (*Liverpool 1980*, p. 173).

In *The Easter People* (n. 109) the bishops showed themselves not unsympathetic to these pleas but it was Archbishop Worlock who gave them most eloquent expression in his powerful intervention in the presence of the Pope during the opening week of the Synod:

> Yet despite our best efforts, some marriages fail and family unity is destroyed. To these victims of misfortune, not necessarily of personal sin, or of sin which has not been forgiven, the Church, both universal and local, must have a healing ministry of consolation.
>
> Moreover, many pastors nowadays are faced with Catholics whose first marriages have perished and who have now a second and more stable (if legally only civil) union in which they seek to bring up a new family. Often such persons, especially in their desire to help their children, long for the restoration of full eucharistic communion with the Church and its Lord. Is this spirit of repentance and desire for sacramental strength to be for ever frustrated? Can they be told only that they must reject their new responsibilities as a necessary condition of forgiveness and restoration to sacramental life?
>
> Some pastors argue that the Church's teaching on marital fidelity

and contractual indissolubility are here at risk. They fear lest other Catholics would be scandalised and the bond of marriage weakened. Our pre-synodal consultation would question this assertion. Those who vigorously uphold the Church's teaching on indissolubility, also ask for mercy and compassion for the repentant who have suffered irrevocable marital breakdown. There is no easy answer. But our Synod must listen seriously to this voice of experienced priests and laity pleading for consideration of this problem of their less happy brethren. They ask that the Church should provide for the spiritually destitute to the same degree as it strives today to meet the material needs of those physically starving (*Briefing*, vol. 10, no. 32, p. 8).

By calling the Synod the Pope was trying to implement the process of consultation and shared responsibility in the Church. It is worth noting that with regard to the National Pastoral Congress he congratulated the Church in England and Wales 'for the initiative you are taking in shared responsibility' (*Liverpool 1980*, p. 108).

It would be contrary to the spirit of the Synod and a denial of the Pope's commitment to it to suggest that in his closing speech or in *Familiaris Consortio* he was simply putting a stop to an ongoing process of reflection, consultation and shared responsibility. It seems to me that he was merely stating what was a fact, namely, that the Synod could not bring itself to take the step of reversing the Church's current official position. That is entirely different to uttering a definitive statement declaring the matter closed for now and for ever. I prefer to look on the Pope's statement as a holding operation. The current debate will continue. Pressing pastoral problems will still have to be faced and solved at local level. But for the moment the *official* position in the Church still holds, even though, as mentioned earlier, there are grounds for believing that at the level of practice the official position might be far more flexible than might appear at first sight.

Living as brother and sister

Perhaps a word should be said about the so-called 'brother and sister arrangement' which the Pope states is a required sign of repentance for a couple who for serious reasons are unable to separate. It might be thought that this is insisting on a requirement found in the traditional manuals of moral theology. This is not quite true. Although it is mentioned as a possibility in most of the pre-Vatican II moral theology text books, it is usually accompanied by the caution that it should rarely, if ever, be recommended to a couple. In fact, in the very rare instances where the authors would see it as being a possibility, they add in conditions which belong to another age and which would be impossible for most people, with the current housing situation.

Furthermore, more serious objections can be raised against the 'brother and sister arrangement'. This arrangement demands, in the words of the Pope, that the couple 'take on themselves the duty to live in complete continence, that is, by abstinence from the acts proper to married couples'. If it is the relationship itself which lies at the heart of a marriage, this is a strange require-ment. It insists on the non-practice of one aspect of marriage but allows what constitutes the heart of marriage to remain. It allows a couple to continue loving each other faithfully but it forbids them to express that love in the language of sexual intercourse. Moreover, it is totally ineffective as a measure to obviate what is considered to be a public scandal and a counter-witness to indissolubility. In the public eye such a couple will be remaining as they were, continuing to live together as man and wife. I know of no moral theologian, however pre-Vatican II, who would insist that a couple in this situation should make a public decla-ration that they are only living together as brother and sister. And if they made such a declaration I would suspect that it might well cause even greater scandal!

The Synod and concern for human persons

One important point comes out strong and clear from the Synod. In their approach to marriage the bishops were primarily concerned about the good of persons and so they were deeply committed to fostering and supporting loving relationships in marriage. It was this same concern for persons which was the guiding spirit in their discussion of the divorced-remarried and it is this attitude that the bishops want to share with the Church at large. The Synod offered no support for those who would argue that persons are made for the sabbath and not the sabbath for persons; laws are to service the good of persons, not to be a burden crushing them. If we are going to err in any direction, it seems to me that it is more in line with the climate of the Synod to err in the direction of pastoral openness towards persons seeking healing for the wounds of marriage breakdown. I draw support from the fact that, if the approach I have adopted in this book is erroneous, at least it errs in the direction in which the spirit of the Synod is pointing. The Pope's closing words on the subject of the divorced-remarried clearly show the direction he would like the Church to take during this holding operation: 'Meanwhile the Church, praying for them and strengthening them in faith and hope, must show herself a merciful mother towards them.'

In the light of all this we need to face the following question: as long as the official position of the Church remains as it is at present, how strictly should the prohibition of the sacraments to the divorced-remarried be interpreted?

How strictly is this prohibition to be interpreted?

Widespread rejection of theological and pastoral grounds for refusing Communion

Since this prohibition is not enshrined in any Church law, but is upheld by Church authorities as a *necessary* consequence of the Church's understanding of marriage and the Eucharist, it would seem that the degree of its obligation depends to some extent on whether this 'necessary consequence' view is correct or not. We have seen already that weighty reasons against it can be drawn from the Church's current understanding of marriage and the Eucharist. I am not alone in thinking this. One only needs to look through the theological and canonical journals of the last decade to realize that the majority of theologians and canonists writing on this subject reject the view that the Church has no choice but to maintain such a prohibition. Two years ago I sent a question-naire round all those teaching moral theology to seminarians in England, Ireland and Scotland. Out of the 26 replies received, 21 favoured a more open practice (involving the sacraments under the kind of conditions I mention in the following pages); they said that such a practice was in accord with sound theology and that even now they would be prepared to follow it themselves in appropriate circumstances. Three took the opposite view and two felt unable to give a definite answer. Nor are these the views of isolated individuals. The French Association of Teachers of Moral Theology have agreed that a milder practice is both theo-logically possible and pastorally desirable. A similar conclusion was reached by a sub-committee of the Catholic Theological Society of America and by a working party set up by the Canon

Law Society of America. An Austrian commission chaired by Cardinal Koenig also favoured a more open pastoral policy, even though there was no final consensus on the moral and theological reasoning in favour of it. Furthermore, in the course of various meetings with different groups of lay-people over recent years I have found that what theologians are saying at a professional level corresponds to what many good married Catholics feel should be happening. It is not that they reject the Church's teaching as too demanding. In a sense, they see it as not demanding enough: it is too unbending at the level of negative prohibition but too undemanding at the more positive level of personal investment in the process of preparing for and developing the growth of relationship in marriage. The desire voiced by the National Pastoral Congress for a more open pastoral policy towards the divorced-remarried seems to have been a faithful expression of the voice of many Catholic men and women.

Therefore, if it is true to say that the degree of the obligation of the current official prohibition is linked to the validity of its theological basis, it seems to me that the widespread questioning of this theological basis implies that its obligation is *qualified* rather than absolute.

The decision of responsible disagreement (cf. New Preface, pp. xx–xxi, n. 2)

In recent years all Catholics have been forced to accept the fact that at least for others, even if not for themselves, a situation can arise when one has to resolve a dilemma in decision-making due to a conflict between what remains the fallible teaching of the Church and what one believes oneself. It is accepted teaching that within certain limits disagreement can be a fully responsible Christian decision and should be recognized as such by fellow-Catholics. Such people should in no way be branded as disloyal Catholics for taking this stand. It is being assumed in this teaching that such people are basing their disagreement on serious reasons, usually shared by others in the Church; and it is also being assumed that they remain sufficiently open to admit that, since in any such situation of disagreement it is unlikely that an adequate expression of the truth has yet been reached, it might be necessary for them to revise their position at a later date.

This is not just a question of intellectual disagreement which has no bearing on life. It means disagreement which justifies a person's acting in apparent contradiction to the official teaching. Obviously, the relevance of this teaching which has a long pedigree in Catholic theology, came very much to the fore after the publication of *Humanae Vitae*. Shortly before *Humanae Vitae* was issued, this teaching was given a thorough airing in a magisterial document issued by the German Hierarchy. Since *Humanae Vitae* it has been reinforced by many other hierarchies in their pastoral guidelines to help married couples with decision-making in the wake of the encyclical. A good example is found in the statement of the Scandinavian bishops:

> Should someone, for grave and carefully considered reasons, not feel able to subscribe to the arguments of the encyclical, he is entitled, as has been constantly acknowledged, to entertain other views than those put forward in a non-infallible declaration of the Church. No one should, therefore, on account of such diverging opinions alone, be regarded as an inferior Catholic. Whoever, after conscientious reflection, believes he is justified in not accepting the teaching and not applying it in practice, must be answerable to God for his attitude and his acts (Horgan edit., *Humanae Vitae and the Bishops*, p. 238).

A much fuller version of this same teaching is found in the statement of the Canadian bishops and is quoted in Appendix 1 of this book.

This position can sound very much like an extreme form of 'follow your own conscience' and might appear to be completely individualistic and totally opposed to the common good of the community. Far from it, however. It presumes that the individual believes in the community and is concerned about the truths and values to which the community is committed. Moreoever, it presumes a person who, as a Christian, believes that the Lord's Spirit is active in the community, helping us to discern the truth in action. It was this kind of presumption which enabled the Pope (then Cardinal Wojtyla and writing as a phenomenologist philosopher) to describe this stance of disagreement as 'essentially an attitude of solidarity'. In the section of his book *The Acting Person* (Reidel, London, 1979) which deals with what is needed for any human community to be healthy, he stresses that opposition is vital to any community's growth and well-being. 'The one who voices his opposition to the general or particular rules or regulations of the community does not thereby reject his membership' (p. 286). In fact, it is an obligation on the community to recognize the constructive role of loyal opposition and to structure itself to enable this to be effective:

In order for opposition to be constructive, the structure, and beyond it the system of communities of a given society, must be such as to allow opposition that emerges from the soil of solidarity not only to *express* itself within the framework of the given community but also to *operate* for its benefit. The structure of a human community is correct only if it admits not just the presence of a justified opposition but also that practical effectiveness of opposition required by the common good and the right of participation (pp. 286–7).

For many of us brought up to believe in a doctrine of absolute obedience to all human authority and particularly to Church authority, the notion of responsible disagreement might seem hard to swallow and a denial of all that we have held dear in our tradition. In fact, it has a very solid basis in tradition, especially in the thought of St Thomas Aquinas. It also has a good pedigree in our native culture in England and Wales. To deny responsible disagreement in theory or in practice is to take the path that leads to totalitarianism. No doubt that is why Cardinal Wojtyla, writing in the context of Poland, was able to see the need for it so clearly.

In practice

Applied to the situation under discussion, the notion of responsible disagreement would mean that a Catholic who is involved in a second marriage after divorce could in certain circumstances be making a fully responsible Christian decision in presenting oneself for absolution or Holy Communion. The kind of conditions which most writers would regard as essential if such a decision is to be genuinely responsible are the following:

1. The first marriage is irretrievably broken down and there is no possibility of its being restored again.

2. All obligations in justice towards the other partner and the children of the first marriage are being fulfilled as far as is humanly possible.

3. The second marriage is being lived in good faith. In other words, it is being experienced as 'What God wants us to do'. This might seem a very vague statement and hardly the equivalent of the 'serious reasons' mentioned above. However, the theologian, Karl Rahner, has argued convincingly that in an area of human experience such as marriage and in a climate

of open theological discussion, such a way of putting it could be a genuine expression of the same truth that others are expressing in more theological language.

4. The desire for the sacraments must be motivated by genuine faith. One would hope that this could normally be presumed to be the case.

Nevertheless, the presence of these conditions is not the end of the matter. The reception of the sacraments needs a minister. It is one thing for an individual to disagree with the official teaching of the Church and to follow his or her own conscience. But that does not give them the right to violate the conscience of the minister from whom they are requesting the sacraments. Anyone administering the sacraments does so in the name of the Church whose minister he or she is. Does not that imply a special obligation of fidelity to the official teaching of the Church?

It does in the sense that if such a person is exercising a teaching function in the Church they have a duty at least to present the official teaching as well as they can, even though this does not release them from their duty in honesty to express any important reservations they may have about this teaching, if they deem this appropriate. However, that is a completely different matter from refusing the sacraments to someone with the kind of disagreeing conscience referred to above. They should not consider themselves duty-bound to refuse such a person the sacraments. This is implicit in the teaching of a number of episcopal conferences in their pastoral commentaries on *Humanae Vitae*. As already mentioned, in this they are not propounding new teaching; they are simply repeating and applying the traditional teaching of the 'approved authors'.

Does responsible disagreement open the flood-gates and lead to pastoral chaos?

Eliminating genuine scandal

What about the situation when a person whose matrimonial situation is truly scandalous and is causing serious disedification in the local community asks for the sacraments on the grounds that they are in good faith and are merely following their conscience? In such a situation most priests would try gently but firmly to change their alleged 'good faith' into 'bad faith'. This would merely be exercising that aspect of their pastoral ministry which is called 'judgement' by the Old Testament prophets and which today might be better described by the phrase 'healing diagnosis'. This might take time, of course, but in the meantime few priests would have any qualms about firmly but kindly refusing such a person the sacraments. If a person is manifestly causing public scandal, both truth and compassion demand that they be challenged to face this, so that they can be helped to repentance and true healing. This would be an example of the 'discernment' that the Synod bishops were referring to. In an extreme case, the local bishop might have to be called upon to intervene, rather in the way that a doctor would call in a second opinion.

Opening the flood-gates

It might be objected that once the right to disagree is acknowledged in this area, the flood-gates would be open and all the divorced-remarried would be queuing up for the sacraments. I do not think for one moment that that would happen but, for the sake of argument, let us suppose that it did. Would this be a major disaster? I must confess that I would not be at all dismayed if all the divorced-remarried who fulfilled the conditions outlined earlier returned to the sacraments. And even if there were some who did not fulfil all the conditions, their hunger for the sacraments would be a healthy starting point for helping them to see what still needs to be done. I feel it is closer to the spirit of the Gospel to rejoice at such a happening than to lament at it. The latter attitude would be reminiscent of that of the elder brother in the parable of the prodigal son.

Responsible disagreement and celebrating a second marriage

In Chapter 2 I argued that in some instances a second marriage after divorce can be acknowledged as good and even, in a restricted sense, as sacramental. Does this mean that there is no problem about celebrating such a marriage in church?

This brings us back again to the question of Church law and public pastoral policy. The official celebration of marriage is an official act within the Church. As such it is governed by Church law which is drawn up by the legitimate authorities with the common good and public order in mind. Clearly it is beyond the competence of any individual minister to change the public law of the Church. While it is true that a conscience in disagreement can on occasion be sufficient justification for the non-observance of law, such a conscience cannot confer the jurisdiction required by law for certain official acts. In this area of second marriage, therefore, a priest could not claim legitimate jurisdiction for his action if he officiated publicly at a second marriage after divorce while the first marriage is still recognized by the Church as valid. However, the couple in such a situation might with reason feel justified in not observing the Church's law by getting married in a registry office.

In the preceding remarks I feel that I have introduced a note of caution which seems inconsistent with the rest of my line of argument. Perhaps it would be more consistent to acknowledge that in a very exceptional case a priest might be acting responsibly in agreeing to celebrate in church a second marriage after divorce. Maybe a distinction needs to be made between the liturgical significance of such a celebration and its juridical validity. The fact that no official validity could be claimed for it would not automatically empty it of all liturgical significance. Maybe my unwillingness to entertain the possibility of a church celebration is simply a sign of my own lack of courage and my natural cautiousness. There is little doubt that to act in this way would sometimes put a priest in dispute with his bishop and perhaps also with many Catholics in his parish. Although that would not prove that his action was not justified, yet these are factors which cannot be dismissed as irrelevant. While it is true that Christian witness will often provoke opposition, it is also true that peace in the community is a matter of Christian concern, even though it should not be interpreted as peace at any price. Certainly I would have no hesitation in saying that if a priest believes that a person is making a genuine decision of responsible disagreement in entering a second marriage, he should feel no qualms about expressing his support and encouragement by helping the couple to celebrate the religious significance of their marriage by sharing some form of prayer or blessing with them. But he would be wise to make it clear to all concerned that this is not an official Church celebration of their marriage.

What about the clear statement of the Pope in *Familiaris Consortio*?

The respect due to the sacrament of Matrimony, to the couples themselves and their families, and also to the community of the faithful, forbids any pastor, for whatever reason or pretext even of a pastoral nature, to perform ceremonies of any kind for divorced people who remarry. Such ceremonies would give the impression of the celebration of a new sacramentally valid marriage, and would thus lead people into error concerning the indissolubility of a validly contracted marriage (n. 84).

Does the advice I have given above square with what the Pope is saying? My answer would be 'Yes' and 'No'. 'Yes' in that it squares with the basic concerns that the Pope is trying to safeguard and promote, i.e. respect for marriage, for the couple and their families, for the community and for the Church's belief in the indissolubility of marriage. 'No' in that, unlike the Pope, I do not believe that any kind of ceremony whatsoever would offend against this respect. I suppose the basis for my disagreement is in fact the whole approach to marriage, indissolubility and second marriage which I have outlined in this book. If this is interpreted as opposition, at least I think it satisfies the Pope's two criteria by being constructive and in solidarity.

At the level of more general pastoral policy I believe that, in the kind of instance under discussion, the Roman Catholic Church should devise some kind of programme of more positive support for a couple who have made a conscientious decision to enter a second marriage.

The process of change in pastoral practice

It would hardly be a good thing to reverse virtually by accident a pastoral discipline which has held almost uninterrupted possession, at least in the Western Church. But would that be an accurate description of what I am suggesting should happen with regard to the sacraments and those in a second marriage? In other words, would such a change be happening *by accident*? To answer this question we need to consider the relationship between pastoral change and theological development.

Theology, authority and life

It is only to be expected that any major change in theological understanding will automatically result in some kind of change of emphasis in Christian living. This does not need to wait to be mediated through some legal process, as though Christians were expected to sit back and wait for alternative instructions for Christian living to be issued. As a normal rule, it is good that changes in pastoral practice should in the first instance occur naturally as a kind of instinctive reaction to a new way of understanding things. This is a much healthier process than that of having practical changes imposed by edict from on high. If they develop naturally, they have more chance of being able to find their own right level as people learn to discern what is appropriate in particular situations. The adoption of these changes as official policy should occur at a later stage in the process. By then what is pastorally helpful would have been sifted by experience from what is harmful or unnecessary. For a change in pastoral practice to occur informally, therefore, should not be regarded as something harmful to the Church. Nor should it be considered to be occurring by accident, if by that is meant occurring without deep theological reflection and serious pastoral concern. In fact, for change to be able to occur in this informal way can be a very healthy sign that the whole Church is beginning to play a more active part in theological reflection and pastoral discernment.

Obviously, what is very important is the quality of theological reflection which precedes and accompanies such change in pastoral policy. In such an area as the living out of marriage for Christians, there is no doubt that theological reflection cannot be considered adequate if Christian married couples are not given the opportunity to make their full contribution to the discussion. Yet clearly they are not the only ones with something to say in this area. Many others can contribute to the Church's understanding of marriage by their practical experience or their research. Even moral theologians have a role to play, though probably a very modest one, in this discussion!

The fruit of such open discussion in the Church should be teaching which is rich in its content and easily understandable in its presentation. It should also be teaching which makes sense of people's experience, interpreting and challenging it in the light of the Gospel. A number of bishops in the 1980 Synod made a strong plea for teaching of this calibre.

The best and most authoritative teaching document on marriage to come from the Roman Catholic Church in recent years is undoubtedly the Vatican II Pastoral Constitution, *The Church in the Modern World*, nn. 47–52. It was welcomed by all concerned as an extremely good, though necessarily incomplete, expression of what they as Christians really believe about marriage. In a sense, this 'reception' confirms and even increases its authority. The same cannot be said of some more recent statements dealing with specific issues of marriage and sexuality, e.g. *Humanae Vitae*, and the *Declaration on Certain Questions of Sexual Ethics*. These have not been 'received' in the same way. Incidentally, one of the main reasons given, especially by theologians, for their critical reception has been the fact that in some respects these documents seem to retreat from rather than develop the teaching of Vatican II. This critical reception lessens the authority of these statements and is an indication of their inadequacy as expressions of what Catholics really believe in this area. This is not reducing Catholic teaching to a head-count or a majority vote; but it is recognizing the essential, though admittedly partial, role played by the Christian common sense of the ordinary faithful. Difficult though this notion is to apply in practice, it is not completely devoid of practical significance. At least one of its immediate implications would seem to be the need to have confidence in the process of open discussion in the Church.

It seems to me that the position put forward in this book, including its practical consequences as outlined in this final chapter, is trying to draw out the implications of the Christian vision of marriage as taught authoritatively by the Second Vatican Council in its Pastoral Constitution, *The Church in the Modern World*. This probably explains why, as far as I can judge, this position is in tune with the deeply-felt convictions of many Christian married couples. The opposite seems to be the case with the position which would refuse the sacraments to the divorced-remarried unless they separate or live as brother and sister. It is not so easy to present that position as flowing from Vatican II's theology of marriage and it seems to go contrary to the pastoral sense of many married Christians.

I would suggest, therefore, that serious theological reflection has prepared the way for such a pastoral development in the Church and this reflection has not been undertaken independently of the teaching authority of the Church. In fact, its starting point has been given authoritative standing in the Church in the teaching of Vatican II. I am not denying that currently there is disagreement about pastoral practice in this question among those who in their different ways exercise teaching authority in the Church. However, what is ironic is that those whose role is to give official articulation to the Church's position sometimes seem committed to positions which are not fully in line with the fundamental teaching of Vatican II; whereas those whose teaching authority is more associated with a combination of experience and theological reflection (i.e. married couples and theologians) favour a view which seems more committed to the teaching of Vatican II. Regardless of how this divergence of view is finally resolved, it is hardly accurate to say that the kind of pastoral development discussed in this chapter would be occurring by accident or without deep theological reflection and concern for the authoritative teaching of the Church.

Change seen in context

In considering whether a change in an ancient practice might not be occurring by accident and so be something to be deplored, the other factor to be borne in mind is that the impact of a particular change can only be assessed by looking at its wider context.

If the new way of understanding marriage is accepted as the basis for developing pastoral care in the field of marriage, what will be experienced initially by people will be a major re-deployment of attention and resources into the area of marriage education, preparation and support. In an age in which divorce can too easily be taken for granted, this should be seen as a radical alternative to a permissive attitude to marriage breakdown. The Church is refusing to go along with any kind of 'divorce mentality'. For her the promotion of the stability of marriage is a prime pastoral priority. Because it will be concentrating so much of its resources into this work, far from overturning its traditional belief, the Church will be giving it a power and an effectiveness which it has never had before. The overall context will be one of a strengthening and a healthy development of its traditional concern for the indissolubility of marriage. In such a context where very positive steps are taken to enable couples to develop at a very personal level in their marriages that indissolubility to which they have pledged themselves, there will be less danger that a milder sacramental policy towards the divorced-remarried will be interpreted as a denial of indissolubility by the Church. It has more chance of being seen for what it really is: the Church trying to care for these people with that Gospel-inspired attitude which Pope John Paul described so beautifully in his closing address to the 1980 Synod: 'The Church . . . must show herself a merciful mother towards them.'

APPENDIX 1
(APPENDIX TO THE ORIGINAL EDITION)

Life-giving love and family planning*

According to the teaching of Vatican II, the answer which a couple should give to the question 'Why do you not want to have a child at present, or even for the foreseeable future?' should always be: 'Because we want to respect the life-giving character of our married love.' For some this might be why they decide not to have a child in the first few years of their marriage; they want to give themselves sufficient time to grow more alive as a loving couple. However, they would need to realize the great contribution that a child of their own can bring to the growth of their love for each other; and they would also need to face honestly where they are putting their priorities. Their own rich love for each other is far more important for their future family than a well-furnished house and the million other amenities of our consumer society. In their desire to get everything just right before having their first child the couple will need to face honestly the possibility that the growth of their own love for each other might need the shared stimulus of a child of their own long before they are able to set up the model household materially.

For other couples 'Because we want to respect the life-giving character of our married love' might be the reason why they decide not to have any further children. They feel that their responsibilities to each other and to their existing children make it prudent for them not to have any further children. Once again this is a decision made for life-giving reasons. The decision is theirs to make but at times they might be wise to get advice from others. For instance, a couple who are absolutely ideal parents might be helped to realize what a great gift God has given them as a couple. This might lead them to decide to have a larger family than is commonly the practice today. Their love might be so rich in life-giving potential that it might be ungenerous not to make a fuller gift of it.

*See above, pp. 13–14.

What needs to be made clear, therefore, is that the *intention* not to have a child for the present or for the foreseeable future can be (though not necessarily is) a life-giving decision and so one which is a fully responsible Christian decision. A calm discussion about methods of birth control is impossible unless this teaching of Vatican II which is repeated in *Humanae Vitae* is clearly understood.

When the question of methods of birth control is discussed, it might be helpful to begin by looking at the various methods with the following question in mind: 'How does this method fit in with the life-giving character of a couple's married love, understanding life-giving in the full sense outlined above?' In order to undertake such an evaluation a person would need to have accurate factual knowledge of the various methods and would also need to know about reliability, health hazards etc. To answer the above question one would need to break it down further and ask:

a) 'How does this way of acting affect their love as life-giving to each other?' In other words, does it interfere with the natural flow of their making love together, does it put all the responsibility on either husband or wife, does it subject one partner to great discomfort or even a health hazard or a bodily mutilation, is it a method in which they carry a shared responsibility, is it permanent or can they change their decision later etc?

b) 'How does this way of acting affect their love as life-giving in the sense of giving life to children?' In other words, they would need to see whether a particular method works by way of an abortifacient.

In looking at the various methods from both these angles, the question of a method's reliability must also be looked at. The importance to the couple of the reliability factor will depend on how important it is to them not to have a child at present. For a few it might even be a matter of life or death; or a wife might have such a dread of another pregnancy that an unreliable method would turn sexual intercourse from a language of love into a virtual nightmare for her.

The method of evaluation outlined above flows as a consequence from the understanding of married love put forward by Vatican II. In that sense it is 'determined by objective standards' as is demanded by the Pastoral Constitution, *The Church in the*

Modern World, n. 51. The criteria flowing from the different aspects of life-giving love provide these objective standards. As Paragraph 51 goes on to say: 'based on the nature of the human person and his acts, they preserve the full sense of mutual self-giving and human procreation in the context of true love'. Decision-making according to these criteria involves trying to respect life-giving love to the fullest extent that one's personal and social situation allows.

This personalist approach to marriage and married love is also presented very beautifully by Pope Paul in section 9 of *Humanae Vitae*. However, the Pope goes even further and insists in section 11 that 'any use whatever of marriage must retain its natural potential to procreate human life' and in section 14 he spells out what this means in practice. His basic argument in favour of this teaching is that the human person is not the master of the sources of life but rather the minister of the design established by the Creator (n. 13) and part of this design is the 'inseparable connection . . . between the unitive significance and the pro-creative significance which are both inherent to the marriage act' (n. 12).

Many Catholics have welcomed this teaching of Pope Paul but many others have found it either unacceptable or not providing a practical solution to their personal problems. To help them in their dilemma many national hierarchies or conferences have issued pastoral guidelines. Basically the guidance given by many of these hierarchies can be summarized as follows:

a) Those who for genuine reasons of conscience cannot accept the Pope's teaching on this precise point should not regard themselves as guilty of sin nor should they be branded by others as disloyal or inferior Catholics.

b) Those who for motives of life-giving love see no practical alternatives but to use some method of birth-control forbidden by the Pope should not regard their decision as sinful provided they are also sensitive to the demands of their life-giving love both in the choice and in the implementation of the method chosen.

The theological competence of these episcopal statements, their integrity, their loyalty to the teaching of the Church and to the Holy Father, cannot be impugned or called into question. All have emphasized their own acceptance of the Encyclical and the obligations on all Catholics to try to do the same.

It might be helpful to give an example of the kind of advice offered with respect to both dilemmas mentioned above.

a) 'It is a fact that a certain number of Catholics, although admittedly subject to the teaching of the encyclical, find it either extremely difficult or even impossible to make their own all elements of this doctrine. In particular, the argumentation and rational foundation of the encyclical which are only briefly indicated, have failed in some cases to win the assent of scientists, or indeed of some in the area of culture and education who share in the contemporary empirical and scientific mode of thought. We must appreciate the difficulty experienced by our contemporaries in understanding and appropriating some of the points of this encyclical and we must make every effort to learn from the insights of Catholic scientists and intellectuals, who are of undoubted loyalty to Christian truth, to the Church and to the authority of the Holy See. Since they are not denying any point of divine and Catholic faith nor rejecting the teaching authority of the Church, these Catholics should not be considered, or consider themselves, shut off from the body of the faithful. But they should remember that their good faith will be dependent on a sincere self-examination to determine the true motives and grounds for such suspension of assent and on continued effort to understand and deepen their knowledge of the teaching of the Church' (Canadian Bishops, 27 September 1968, full text in Horgan, *Humanae Vitae and the Bishops*, pp. 76–83).

b) 'Situations will, no doubt arise in which another pregnancy is unacceptable for reasons such as health or difficult domestic conditions, and where a regime of continence would threaten family peace, marital fidelity or the future of the marriage itself. Here, in common with many other hierarchies, we would say that it is best for the parents to decide what in their given circumstances is the best or only practical way of serving the welfare of the whole family. In this conflict of duties their responsible decision, though falling short of the ideal, will be subjectively defensible since the aim is not the selfish exclusion of pregnancy but the promotion of the common good of the family' (South African Bishops, 4–8 February 1974; full text in *The Tablet*, 23 March 1974). (See also New Preface, p. xxi, n. 3).

APPENDIX 2
(NEW APPENDIX)

SECTION A: THE THREE GERMAN BISHOPS OF THE UPPER RHINE PROVINCE AND THE CONGREGATION FOR THE DOCTRINE OF THE FAITH (CDF)

THE BISHOPS' PASTORAL LETTER OF 10 JULY 1993*

Pastoral Ministry: The Divorced and Remarried

Most people seek their personal happiness in marriage and family. Marriage and the family are the basic cell of human society. It is part of the dramatic change of our times, however, that many marriages break down and that divorces have increased enormously.

The difficult human situation of divorced people and of those who have entered into a civil marriage after a divorce is a serious question facing the Church. For the joy and hope, the grief and anguish of the people of today are also the joy and hope, the grief and anguish of the followers of Christ.[1]

Therefore synods, diocesan forums, bishops' conferences and pastoral and priests' councils have repeatedly concerned themselves with this question over the last two decades. As this problem exceeds the area of responsibility of an individual bishop, the three bishops of the ecclesiastical province of the Upper Rhine have decided to direct a joint pastoral letter to their faithful and to give common pastoral guidelines for those responsible for pastoral care.

---

*Permission to use copyright translations of texts from *Origins* in articles 1, 2, 4 and 5 of this section is gratefully acknowledged.

I. *Situation of divorced and remarried Christians*

First we would like to comment on the present situation. It appears to be of a dual nature. If one asks younger people especially how they envision their future happiness, most will wish for a marital partnership based on mutual love that will last a lifetime. These expectations stand in clear contrast to the fact that in our society very many marriages break down. Christian and ecclesiastically solemnized marriages are here no exception. Many divorced people find a new partner and join in a civil marriage or else they live together without benefit of marriage. There are more and more stepfamilies with children from different families. The number of single parents, both mothers and fathers, is also increasing.

The causes that have led to this situation are extremely diverse. To a not inconsiderable degree, they lie with social changes: The separation today between the family and the world of work and the resulting tension between family and profession, new understandings of the roles of men and women, the increased length of a marriage, the dissolution of the traditional extended family and isolation of the nuclear family, and the insufficient support given to marriage and family in this social climate all play a role. Alongside these there are diverse personal reasons: unreasonable expectations of happiness that will necessarily be disappointed, human immaturity and personal failure in daily life, mutual misunderstanding and insufficient dedication to the point of infidelity and culpable destruction of the marital community or even physical abuse in the marriage.

The consequences of a divorce are usually disappointment, sadness, personal injury, self-doubt and feelings of guilt. A divorce affects relationships with society, the family and with friends; not infrequently, it leads to isolation. Added to that are fear and uncertainty about the future. Those who bear the principal burden are the children. They are torn between the parents; they lose their home and their emotional shelter.

Divorced people and those who have divorced and remarried feel that the Church and society lack understanding and that they are left alone with their problems. Many feel discriminated against, cast out, even condemned. They can accept the Church's rules and regulations only with great difficulty or not at all; they find them incomprehensibly hard and merciless.

This situation is a serious question for the Church. We must ask ourselves how we can be credible witnesses to the closeness of God to the divorced and to the divorced and remarried in their difficult human situation. How can we stand by them and help them, how can we give them new perspectives, courage for life and reconciliation? For many people today the Church's credibility rests on the answer to this question.

II. The gospel standard

In its pastoral care of the divorced and of divorced-and-remarried people the Church is not simply free. It cannot proceed based on the approval of individuals or even of majority opinions. The standard for the Church is the word, will and example of Jesus. The practice of the Church must be measured against them.

The word of Jesus is clear. As the question of the divorce practice of his time was laid before him, he made it clear that, once entered, a marriage was no longer subject to human desires and powers: 'But from the beginning of creation, "God made them male and female. For this reason a man shall leave his father and mother [and be joined to his wife], and the two shall become one flesh." Therefore what God has joined together, no human being must separate.' (Mk. 10:6–9)

Thus by his response Jesus refers to the original order of creation. According to which God made man and woman completely equally in his image (Gn. 1:27). At the same time he made them for each other and gave them to each other. They were to become one flesh, i.e., a concrete community (ibid., 2:24); and they should also be fruitful in their children (ibid., 1:28). Such mutual love demands lasting fidelity. Only fidelity opens up the space in which a man and woman can realize their marital partnership and responsibly bring children into the world.

Through sin, a person refuses love, shutting himself up in himself. That makes him – as Jesus said – hardhearted. Thus the original order of God and the original happiness in marriage are disturbed. Already in the Old Testament law detailed regulations for divorce were necessary.

Jesus did not permit himself to become entangled in the dispute at this level. He answered neither by increasing the severity of the law nor by adding exceptions to it. He placed his answer concerning marriage and divorce within the framework of his message regarding the coming of the kingdom of God. This last will overcome the inimical power of hate, of selfishness and of force. Jesus' word is therefore no crushing law, but rather an offer, an invitation, an exhortation and a gift, which is to realize the original sense of marriage in lifelong fidelity. For where God gives himself completely, there too can man and woman fully and finally give themselves and unite themselves in love and fidelity.

Therefore, Christian marriage, entered into according to the norms of the Church, makes God's covenant present to people. That is why the Church calls Christian marriage a sacrament. That means that the love of God embraces, strengthens, heals and sanctifies the love and fidelity of the couple.[2] God's love and fidelity were proven finally in the cross and resurrection of Jesus. The cross and suffering therefore belong to a Christian marriage but so do also an ever new forgiveness and an ever new beginning.

Clearly the Church's experience from earliest times shows that despite the radically new beginning in Jesus Christ the power of sin continued to be effective within its own ranks and that even marriages among Christians could fail. The Church cannot assume the right to disregard the word of Jesus regarding the indissolubility of marriage; but equally it cannot shut its eyes to the failure of many marriages. For wherever people fall short of the reality of redemption, Jesus meets them in mercy with understanding for their situation. Even in failure and guilt he opens to them the path of conversion and new life. Thus it has been necessary for the Church throughout its history to distinguish among the most varied circumstances and to ask itself how it can remain unreservedly true to the word and example of Jesus while still helping concretely those whose marriages have failed. It must ask itself how it can stand by them in solidarity and be a helpful companion along the way.

III. Responsibility of the Christian community

Faithful to the word and example of Jesus, Christians should be in the forefront of the struggle for successful marriages of lifelong fidelity. In a Christian community an atmosphere should reign in which it should not even come to a situation in which divorce appears to be the only way out. We must therefore with united energy work against the trend that would regard divorce and remarriage as something normal. This mission will best be served by proper preparation for marriage, by support for marriage and by counselling where marriages have broken up.

As part of the same attitude, we should greet with respect and sympathy fellow Christians whose marriages have broken up yet who out of inner conviction do not intend to enter into a new relationship but rather to give witness as single people to the indissolubility of their validly contracted marriages. The person who does not undertake a civil marriage following a divorce suffers no restriction with regard to his or her rights or position in the Church. If the Church does not want to betray the message of Jesus, it cannot set up a legal order in which divorce followed by remarriage can be made a normal event or even a right. Precisely by respecting and protecting the indissolubility of marriage, the Church renders an indispensable service to humankind.

However, the Church must offer solidarity to those who have failed in marriage and who have decided upon a second, civil marriage. Despite some mistaken opinions and information, it must be said that all divorced people and divorced-and-remarried people belong to the Church and thus to the parish community in which they live. Even though their membership rights are somewhat reduced, they are neither excommunicated nor excluded from the Church; they are and remain members of the Church. The Church must, in fact, give them special care because of the difficult situation in which they find themselves.

In his apostolic exhortation *Familiaris Consortio* (1981), Pope John Paul II pointed out in direction-giving fashion the enduring membership in the Church of those whose marriages have failed but who have not remarried. 'The ecclesial community must support such people more than ever. It must give them much respect, solidarity, understanding and practical help.' The pope says specifically that there is not 'any obstacle to admission to the sacraments'.[3]

As for the divorced who have remarried civilly, one must, according to the pope, 'exercise careful discernment of situations.' There is a difference whether one has been abandoned unjustly or whether one has destroyed an ecclesiastically valid marriage through one's own grievous fault. One should help divorced-and-remarried people, too, 'with solicitous care to make sure that they do not consider themselves as separated from the Church.' They can – indeed they must as baptized Christians – share in the life of the Church, listen to the word of God, attend Mass, pray regularly and contribute to works of charity and community efforts to promote justice. The Church should pray for them and encourage them. They should be confident that they 'will be able to obtain from God the grace of conversion and salvation.'[4] Divorced-and-remarried people should realize that they remain part and should feel a part of the community and are welcome at all church services and activities. Unfortunately, in our congregations there is much hardness and intransigence side by side with a willingness for healing relationships. Divorced-and-remarried people should feel that they are accepted by the congregation and that the congregation understands their difficult situation. They should experience the Church as a healing and helping community. The congregation should help them to rebuild their lives and their faith, to recognize guilt but also to experience forgiveness. That presupposes discussion and advice, because a new orientation of one's life is only possible when the shadows of the past have been overcome in intensive discussion.

This goal is served by support groups of family members and friends such as already exist in many congregations as well as by church, marital and family counselling services and pastoral discussion with a priest or expert laypersons. In the final analysis, the responsibility of the entire congregation is demanded.

IV. Participation in the sacraments?

Leading divorced-and-remarried people to active participation in the life of the congregation will usually proceed step by step, during which there are many different grades and possible forms of participation depending on the individual's situation in life and in the faith. One must not take an all-or-nothing stance here. In the end, there is of course the question of participation by the individual divorced-and-remarried person in the sacraments of reconciliation and the eucharist.

The more recent ecclesiastical pronouncements declare, in adherence to the instructions of Jesus, that divorced-and-remarried people generally cannot be admitted to the eucharistic feast as they find themselves in life situations that are in objective contradiction to the essence of Christian marriage.[5] Anyone who acts otherwise does so contrary to the order of the Church.

Canon law, however, can 'set up only a valid general order; it cannot regulate all of the often very complex individual cases.'[6] Therefore it ought to be clarified through pastoral dialogue whether that which is generally valid applies also in a given situation. This cannot be generally presumed, especially when those involved have, based on good grounds, satisfied their consciences of the nullity of their first marriage but no legal proofs exist to obtain a declaration of nullity from an ecclesiastical tribunal. In these and similar cases a pastoral dialogue can help those involved to reach a personal and responsible decision according to the judgment of their own consciences that must be respected by the Church and the congregation. To accompany others on their way to such a mature decision of conscience is the service and mission of pastoral care, especially by priests, who are officially commissioned with the service of reconciliation and unification.

In guidelines specifically prepared for those responsible for pastoral care we have formulated some basic tenets for the pastoral accompaniment of people whose marriages have broken up. We must of course be clear that there cannot be a simple, smooth solution to the complex situations of divorced-and-remarried people. The grace of reconciliation is always postulated on personal conversion. We must not make it 'cheap grace.' Neither an exaggerated strictness nor a weak flexibility will help. The model for our speech and action must be only Jesus Christ. It is a matter of continually entering a relationship with him and of giving his Spirit room to work. Such continual conversion is not only the duty of divorced people and those who are divorced and remarried, but of all Christians and the entire Church.

Finally, we would like to thank all who labour in the pastoral care of divorced people and of the divorced and remarried. We intend to expand such efforts in the future and must make clear that God's fidelity and mercy await each person in that situation, each person who is prepared to repent and open his or her heart anew to God. We beg you all, brothers and sisters, for your prayers for all young people who are preparing for marriage, for married people and their families, and for those whose marriages have failed. It is true for all: God is faithful; he will strengthen you (cf. 1 Cor. 1:9, 10:13; 2 Thes. 3:3).

Trusting in the unbreakable fidelity of God we ask for you the blessing of the triune God, Father, Son and Holy Spirit.

(Translation from *Origins*,
10 March 1994, pp. 670–673)

Notes

1 Vatican Council II. Pastoral Constitution on the Church in the Modern World, 1.
2 Ibid., 48–49.
3 Pope John Paul II, *Familiaris Consortio*, 83.
4 Ibid., 84.
5 Ibid.
6 German bishops' conference, Catechism for Adults, 'The Creed of the Church,' p. 395 (German edition).

THE BISHOPS' PRINCIPLES OF PASTORAL CARE

Principles for the pastoral care of those whose marriages have broken up and of the divorced and remarried in the Church province of the Upper Rhine (issued with July 1993 Pastoral Letter).

I. The situation

One of the most valuable elements of a civilization moulded by the gospel is the Christian understanding of marriage as the personal companionship for life of man and woman, a relationship marked by partnership and parenthood as well as by unconditional exclusivity and life-long mutual reliance. This lofty demand has admittedly not been able to be met by many Christians right from the start. Every period of history, every form of society has had its share of trouble. Today this is something the Churches are especially painfully aware of, often to their disappointment. In our society something like a third of marriages end in divorce. In conurbations the figure is even higher. Nevertheless many long for a marital relationship based on mutual affection and providing the assurance of reliability and security through irrevocable fidelity. After the disappointment of a marriage that has broken down many do admittedly remain single, in many cases with children to bring up. Many are no longer willing to commit themselves to marriage as a form of life marked by mutual obligation and prefer a non-marital relationship. But even today many people whose first marriage has broken down are looking for a new life in a second marriage contracted merely according to the norms of civil law. This has its effect on their relationships within society, within their families, and among their friends, as well as on their relationship to Christianity and the Church and on the religious upbringing of their children. Frequently it leads to an overt or covert break with the Church.

1: A variety of distress

Even divorced people who remain single or who are single parents often have difficulty in finding understanding and help for their situation in the Church. How people cope with a broken marriage is something that for the most part remains hidden from public view. The collapse and failure of many marriages is often linked to a number of inter-connected social and individual factors which even the individual frequently is not sufficiently aware of. Often people are aware simply of the statistical changes:

- a considerable increase in divorces;
- a growing number of single parents;
- people living together after a divorce without getting married;
- the re-marriage of divorced people, whether to another divorced person or to someone who is single;
- the greater frequency of step-families with children from different original families.

Often too little consideration is given to the fact that profound emotional processes are reflected in these statistics. One cannot ignore the lowering of self-esteem, the shock to one's whole system, finding expression in grief, isolation, feelings of guilt, fear of loss, depression, and self-doubt. More profound psychological damage cannot be ruled out.

It is particularly the children who are drawn into sharing this suffering. Often the loss of a parent through divorce and separation is something they experience as even more of a burden than the death of their mother or father. Experiences of this kind, especially when they are not faced up to and tackled, often have their effect on such children's own later relationships.

The divorced and the divorced-and-remarried not infrequently find in these situations that even fellow parishioners keep their distance from them. They feel they are no longer understood by the local Christian community and that they are left on their own with their problems. Hence they often believe that the Church is no longer the place for them. In addition, because of their own personal experience, they find it difficult to accept the Church's rules about Christian marriage. Catholics who marry someone who is divorced feel the Church's attitude to be unbelievably harsh. Many are also of the opinion that they are being punished for the collapse of their partner's first marriage.

2: What the Church has been trying to do

The joint synod of the dioceses of the German Federal Republic held between 1971 and 1975, an international working party attached to this, discussion with the competent authorities in Rome and the contributions of many theologians have followed these developments with great concern. There are in addition many statements by bishops and bishops' conferences. Great effort has been taken in all this to discover justifiable 'solutions' that on the one hand do justice to Jesus's radical instruction on the indissolubility of marriage and on the other help those concerned in their difficult situation. Nearly every diocesan synod held since the Second Vatican Council has been faced with this problem.

Thus the Rottenburg-Stuttgart diocesan synod tackled this question in 1985. The same applies to the consultative bodies of other individual dioceses, as for example the archdiocese of Freiburg-im-Breisgau in the years 1991 and 1992. Diocesan councils continually have this question on their agenda, for example in the diocese of Mainz. It is with the aim of evaluating these diocesan initiatives that the bishops of the Church province of the Upper Rhine are publishing a joint pastoral letter and preliminary guidelines for the pastoral care of those whose marriages have broken down and of the divorced and remarried.

The pastoral guidelines that follow are of course drawn up with the aim of remaining within the framework of the communion of the universal Church and of taking fully into account this fundamental solidarity with the Pope as the focus of unity and with the Church as a whole. But at the same time we wish to take into account the need and distress that is evident among many people today in many different places and to make use of whatever initial means are available to help them. These endeavours are intended to support parishes and priests in their concern gradually to lead those whose marriages have broken down and the divorced and remarried back to full participation in the life of the community of the Church, to the extent that this is possible. In this the bishops have been instructed and shown the way particularly by John Paul II's apostolic exhortation *Familiaris Consortio* of 22 November 1981. They have sought to fulfil this task in numerous meetings.

II. Christian marriage as a pattern of life that creates obligations

1: The evidence of scripture

The starting-point, norm and criterion for principles and forms of assistance can only be the biblical and Christian witness with regard to marriage. According to the statements of scripture the linking together of man and woman corresponds to the will of the creator. He created men and women to experience security and love in acceptance by a partner for life of the opposite sex and from this love themselves to pass on the gift of new love. Hence in marriage, as a special form of personal community, man and woman accept each other unconditionally and without qualification. This kind of acceptance in mutual love makes possible and demands constant fidelity. It is only this that completely opens up the domain in which man and woman are able to make their community of marriage a reality and in which children can be gratefully accepted and can thrive.

The high regard the Bible has for marriage is shown by the fact that in both the Old and the New Testament it serves as the image and metaphor for God's continual concern for his creation and for his people. What is said about God's covenant with the human race is re-inforced by Jesus Christ's irrevocable bond with his Church (cf Eph. 5:21–33). Hence according to tradition the marriage bond between man and woman is a sacrament, since it has as its model God's covenant with humanity: an effective sign of God's lasting presence with men and women in the actual situation of marriage.

In an age when the prevailing practice with regard to divorce put women at a particular disadvantage, Jesus Christ underlined the creator's original intention and over against all human arbitrariness emphasized that a marriage once concluded remain exempt from human whim and discretion. 'But from the beginning of creation, God made them male and female. For this reason a man shall leave his father and mother and be joined to his wife, and the two shall become one flesh. So they are no longer two but one. What therefore God has joined together, let not man put asunder' (Mark 10:6–9).

In this way Jesus liberated marriage from its distortions and made God's original intention clear once more. Its deformation Jesus ascribes above all to 'hardness of heart' (cf. Mark 10:5, Matt. 19:8, and cf. also Mark 16:14). This hardness of heart no longer has any feeling for the person once loved, turns away from genuine love, and becomes incapable of discerning someone else's grief and suffering. This pitiless insensitivity is the origin and foundation of all sin. People reject love and become locked up in themselves. They then think they have a 'right' to divorce. 'Regulations' to govern the practice of divorce – whether in civil or canon law – cannot really restore to order this profound injury and the chaos that has arisen but merely prevent an even greater disorder and worse evil. What is involved here is the necessary and difficult attempt to restore order when this is really impossible.

Jesus does not become involved in the dispute then raging over the legal prescriptions. Rather he places what he has to say about marriage and divorce within the context of the proclamation of the reign of God that has broken in on us with his appearance. This overcomes the powers of pitilessness, hardness of heart and violence. With his message Jesus would like to renew the hearts of men and women and effectively to grant them salvation in the situation of marriage, so that through being converted to genuine love man and woman can make marriage a reality according to God's original plan in life-long fidelity. This love includes a continual readiness to forgive, to start love anew and to seek reconciliation (cf. Luke 17:3–4, Matt. 18:21–22). In this life it remains always disputed and challenged: it is vulnerable and under threat. Genuinely to overcome these temptations demands of married couples sacrifice, subordination of one's own interests, patience with each other, and not infrequently also putting up with dissatisfaction with each other. What Jesus says about life-long fidelity in marriage is at one and the same time a gift and a challenge which continually obtains new strength and renewed courage from the cross and resurrection of Jesus Christ.

The New Testament reflects this situation and provides a sophisticated witness. Throughout it emphasizes the prohibition of divorce. The gospels according to Mark (10:2–9) and Luke (16:18) present it without qualification. The exception on the ground of unchastity which is to be found in Matthew (5:32, 19:9) – and which is so difficult to interpret – and the Pauline 'directive' (cf. 1 Cor. 7:10–11, 7:15) allows the recognition of the limited possibility of a separation of the partners, and at least the toleration of this. Such an approach to individual borderline cases does not however seem in any way to contradict Jesus's instruction but rather to put it into the context of actual cases and to modify and supplement it in a particular situation. In any case it does not mean abolishing the principle of an absolute prohibition of divorce. A second marriage is understood as adultery. There is no permission for remarriage.

For this reason every interpretation of these sayings must remain cautious. Admittedly it is completely in keeping with the message of Jesus to seek after those who are lost (cf. Luke 15) and to forgive without qualification (cf. John 7:53–8:11), as well as not to exclude sharing the meals and company of 'sinners' (cf. Mark 2:13–17), but it is also questionable to apply these sayings of scripture immediately and comprehensively to the situation of the divorced and remarried. Jesus's unrestricted mercy and compassion is in fact closely linked to a serious readiness to be converted (cf. John 8:11). When people fail Jesus meets them with kindness and compassion by opening up to them the way to conversion and new life.

2: The tradition of the Church up to the present

Jesus's attitude to marriage and divorce stood out sharply and decisively from the surrounding Jewish and Hellenistic world. The Church has remained faithful to this legacy of its Lord and has to the present day been indefatigably concerned to protect the permanent partnership of man and woman in marriage. But despite the fundamentally new beginning in Jesus Christ the power of sin continues to be at work even among Christians. The Church has continually asked itself the question how it can remain faithful to Jesus's word and example and how at the same time it may show God's mercy to those whose marriage has failed.

Throughout the Church's long history the age-old dramas of human history have been played out again and again: one spouse's infidelity; one spouse furtively deserted by the other; marriages and families being split up by main force thanks to war, imprisonment and abduction. The Church was not able to prevent marriages continually being broken up in practice, despite its proclamation of the message of Jesus Christ. Nevertheless it did not allow any remarriage after separation. This is the Church's unequivocal and obedient witness, a witness that cannot be overlooked and that binds us too. Admittedly respected Fathers of the Church in both East and West, for example Augustine and Basil, have come to a more differentiated conclusion in individual cases.

According to the evidence of some Fathers of the Church, in individual cases, and for the sole reason of avoiding greater evil, the Church has adopted an attitude of hesitant toleration with regard to remarriage. But this was linked with doing public penance and for the most part was explicitly acknowledged as contradicting the statements of scripture. Hence the relatively few items of evidence that have been transmitted are painfully aware of this unbridgeable tension and therefore as individual borderline cases were never separated from the one genuine obligation, namely lifelong fidelity.

Clear and impressive evidence for this is provided by Origen in his commentary on Matthew: 'Already some of the Church's leaders have gone against what is written and have allowed a woman to marry while her husband is alive. They have done this against what is written when we read: "A wife is bound to her husband as long as he lives" (1 Cor. 7:39) and: "Accordingly, she will be called an adulteress if she lives with another man while her husband is alive" (Rom. 7:3), but not however completely without reason. It is indeed reasonable to allow this indulgence in order to avoid worse evils against what has been ordained and written from the beginning' (*In Matth.* 14:23, PG 13:1245). There is a continual awareness that this kind of practice contradicts the view of the New Testament, and that it also involved a regrettable lack of equality in the treatment of men and women. On the whole these bits of evidence are not easy to interpret. It is something that scholarship has to wrestle with. The texts bear witness to a more flexible practice which however also shows traces of a laxer attitude and of foreign influences – such as civil legislation, for example – but which cannot simply be excluded despite these clearly recognized and avowed weaknesses (cf. for example also Basil Ep. 199, can. 6; Ep. 188, can. 9; Synod of Arles 314, can. 10–11; cf. also Leo the Great, DS 311–314).

Thanks to a long struggle Augustine knew about the difficulty of the question: about the dark depths of the meaning of scripture, the riddle of the human heart, and also the inadequacy of his own position (cf. *De fide et operibus*, 19; *Retractationes*, II:57, 84).

Recent research has shown that even the Council of Trent knew about this tension recorded in the Church's tradition, even if this is not immediately recognizable in the conciliar documents themselves. What this Council does is to declare the indissolubility of marriage and the prohibition of remarriage to be 'in keeping with the teaching of the gospel and of the apostles' (cf. DS 1807 = NS[11] 741), without wanting thereby to condemn the practice of the Eastern Churches as well as Catholic interpretations of the exception on the grounds of unchastity that take a different line.

The Catholic tradition continues to hold firmly and without abridgement to this doctrine of the Church (cf. *Katholischer Erwachsenenkatechismus. Das Glaubensbekenntnis der Kirche*, published by the German bishops' conference, Bonn 1985, pp. 386–397; *Catechism of the Catholic Church*, London 1994, §§1601–1666, pp. 358–372).

III. Basic directions for pastoral care

1: The basis for pastoral efforts

This survey of the biblical origins and of the expression of the Christian message in the Church's tradition provides the foundations for pastoral practice today and in the future whatever transformations may take place in society. Its first and most important task consists of bearing witness, to the men and women who are following Jesus, to the glad tidings of God's loving concern for the world and on this basis of accompanying with God's blessing the human paths of love between man and woman in marriage and the family. Even today this is a quite basic service of the Church for people. Hence the preparation for Christian marriage at all levels of instruction in the faith and the support of marriage constitute a priority.

In this service the Church remains perpetually bound to Jesus Christ's instruction on marriage and thus to the prohibition of divorce. Fundamentally it can want nothing else than always to proclaim this decisive goal and to help it to be realized. This conviction must not remain something that is solemnly paid merely lip-service to but must be lived out in actuality by the Church, in other words by its members. In its tradition the Catholic Church has sought to keep strictly to this unequivocally attested will of its Lord in its teaching and preaching, in its pastoral practice and canon law. This may strike many as a 'naïve' clinging to the letter of the gospel; but in reality it is an actual and practical, credible sign of determined fidelity to God as the Lord of creation and the founder of the New Covenant.

Pastoral guidelines and assistance for people whose marriages have broken down and for the divorced and remarried are only possible within the framework of this message of mutual love in lifelong fidelity. Those who do not continually make the Christian understanding of marriage visible and credible as the foundation, as a positive pattern of life that serves the genuine well-being of humanity, also lack real concern for people whose marriages have broken down and are not acting in the sense of the gospel and of the Church. There cannot be any pastoral treatment of the divorced all on its own isolated from the core of the gospel.

2: Reasons for the crisis in many marital relationships

The number of marriages that are breaking up is incomparably greater than formerly. The reasons for this are well known: marriages are to a much greater extent than formerly linked to the almost exclusive relationship of the partners to each other; hardly at all, if ever, are they supported by the wider family, by the network of relatives and friends. For those who get married today their span of life is often twice as long as it used to be. A constituent element of marriage is a partnership of equals. In a period when the social understanding of the roles of husband and wife is no longer closely established conflicts can arise which must be jointly overcome within the marriage. This also increases the demands on the couples' capability of establishing and maintaining their partnership. The pressure of the views on sexuality, love and fidelity circulating in society has a lasting effect even within the realm of the Church and has a stronger effect even in the case of committed Christians. The insights of modern psychology and sociology, if used sensibly, cannot simply be passed over: awareness of the profound problems of establishing one's identity experienced by people today, of the dependence of the capacity to love on one's successful development as a person, of the need to test and purify erotic love so that this does not remain stuck at the level of mere infatuation and projection or even becomes led astray to a less than human level. If such psychological deficiencies are lurking beneath the surface difficulties in and pressures on the marriage quickly bring them to light. Hence the question rightly arises in many cases whether the psychological disposition for a valid marriage actually exists. Without a doubt there are grey areas here. Often it is only with the benefit of hindsight that one can see how fragile somebody's acceptance of another as his or her partner was.

3: The question of the validity of the marriage

When people whose marriages have broken down are looking for new possibilities it is in this context today that the question of the validity of the first marriage is brought up. The pastor will honestly and openly indicate the possibilities of the Church's marriage tribunals to those concerned. Experience shows that many people with a first marriage that has turned out unhappily can be helped. It is not the only way, but it should not be neglected. Great sensitivity, delicacy and tact are needed here. The diocesan marriage tribunals can provide both advice and practical help if the local pastors find that too great demands are being made on their time or competence.

4: The divorced between exclusion and acceptance

The starting point of all our efforts is the firm conviction that people whose marriages have broken down retain their right of domicile in the Church. It is of elementary importance to bring home to these people, who often continue to suffer from profound psychological wounds, the fact that they are at home in the Church, and to do so in a way that they can experience.

This should not remain merely a theoretical statement. People who have experienced collapse and failure in their marriage must find a place of understanding and acceptance in the parish community. Hence their fellow-parishioners should treat them with courtesy and without prejudice. This applies especially to the children of people whose marriages have broken down. They often go on mourning the breakdown of their parents' marriage for a long time and bear the scars of painful wounds.

There is much to be made up in this field, for in our parishes there is still much harshness and irreconcilability alongside a fundamental readiness to treat people in a way that brings healing. Not infrequently people are judged and condemned thoughtlessly and on the basis of hearsay, without, for example, consideration being given to strains and pressures arising from people's personal history and to unfortunate entanglements. If the Church is really a place of acceptance of those in need of hospitality and reconciliation, then the parish community must practise turning in a special way towards all who have been deeply wounded by separation. Visible and welcoming symbols are needed for this.

The pastor and the various pastoral and charitable services inside and outside the parish must do everything to show in good time to the partners in a marriage under threat the way to counselling and to a fresh start together inspired by the spirit of the gospel. The parish must also turn particularly towards those who are separated and divorced without having married again, especially if they are the innocent party. 'The ecclesial community must support such people more than ever. It must give them much respect, solidarity, understanding and practical help, so that they can preserve their fidelity even in their difficult situation; and it must help them to cultivate the need to forgive which is inherent in Christian love, and to be ready perhaps to return to their former married life' (*Familiaris Consortio* §83). There are not a few divorced people who maintain the troth they once plighted and live it out. 'In such cases their example of fidelity and Christian consistency takes on particular value as a witness before the world and the Church. Here it is even more necessary for the Church to offer continual love and assistance, without there being any obstacle to admission to the sacraments' (ibid.).

In such situations parishes should not demand too much of the divorced. This applies also to single parents. Many still have a hard time coping with the pain of separation and are struggling to keep their heads above water economically. They are absorbed by these cares and often face an uncertain future. Parishes should offer them a friendly place of unprejudiced acceptance where they can stay undisturbed, as well as practical assistance. This can contribute to those concerned not rapidly entering into new relationships rashly and in a panic, often in distress, relationships which not infrequently plunge them once again into misfortune. The Church must be aware that for such people on their path through life it represents a roof and provides a canopy over their heads, but that many after an initial healing will as it were continue along the path of their life with the possibility of their contacts with the Church becoming weaker or even ceasing completely. Here it is a question of genuine *diakonia* which should not seek any benefit for itself (cf. Matt. 6:3).

IV. Special concerns regarding divorced-and-remarried people

All that has previously been said applies in large part also to those who after divorce have entered into a civil marriage.

The Church can do a great deal precisely for this group, even though the second marital partnership is not recognized as ecclesiastically valid and there can be no general admission to the sacraments. It is necessary in this regard to discard widespread misinformation and prejudices. Divorced-and-remarried people are not excluded from the Church nor are they excommunicated, i.e., completely and thoroughly shut out of the community of divine worship and the sacraments.[1] Since these people, however, according to the conviction of the Church, stand in objective contradiction to the word of the Lord, they cannot be admitted indiscriminately to the sacraments, especially to the eucharist. That sounds, and certainly for many is, disappointing. Nevertheless, one thing is clear: Divorced-and-remarried people are at home in the Church and are inside the community of the Church even though they are to some extent restricted with regard to some of the rights of all Church members. They belong to us. Under no circumstances may one simply deny these people the real possibility of salvation.

1: Divorced-and-remarried people in the eyes of church and community

In this area too the apostolic exhortation *Familiaris Consortio* gives some substantial instructions that up to now have been too little regarded: Divorced-and-remarried people must not simply be left to themselves; the Church will always invite them to participate as much as possible in its community. The pope says:

> Together with the synod, I earnestly call upon pastors and the whole community of the faithful to help the divorced and with solicitous care to make sure that they do not consider themselves as separated from the Church, for as baptized persons they can and indeed must share in her life. They should be encouraged to listen to the word of God, to attend the sacrifice of the Mass, to persevere in prayer, to contribute to works of charity and to community efforts in favor of justice, to bring up their children in the Christian faith, to cultivate the spirit and practice of penance and thus implore, day by day, God's grace (No. 84).

We are concerned here in the first place with the active witness of everyday Christian life. This is also required of the divorced and remarried. Anyone who neglects or omits this dimension of active Christian life or remains in fatal isolation insisting only on 'admission to the sacraments' would be on the wrong path.

Divorced-and-remarried people, as members of the Church, can give an important witness when, despite the limitation regarding admission to the sacraments, they continue to work in the community. For example, they can share the experiences of their unsuccessful first and not infrequently more successful second marriages in discussions about marriage and family. Consider, for example, inviting them to collaborate in family circles, in retreats, etc.

Those who are divorced and remarried should find help in coming to terms with their difficulties. The shadows of the past must be overcome in candid discussions. The Church should include precisely these people in its intercessions. It 'should pray for them, encourage them and show herself a merciful mother and thus sustain them in faith and hope' (*Familiaris Consortio*, 84). This should be manifest strongly in public liturgical services.

2: 'Admission' to the sacraments

The more recent official pronouncements explain clearly that divorced-and-remarried people cannot be admitted to the eucharist because 'their state and position in life objectively contradict that union of love between Christ and the Church that is signified and effected by the eucharist' (ibid.). This is a general statement that precludes any general admission of those who are divorced and remarried to the sacraments. Anyone who acts otherwise does so against ecclesiastical regulation.

The Church has long granted admission to the sacraments to those divorced and remarried who form a close partnership of life, but live as brother and sister with regard to their personal relationship to one another, i.e., in complete continence (cf. ibid., and Congregation for Bishops, letter to bishops of April 11, 1973). This is also called the 'tried-and-true practice of the church' (*probata praxis ecclesiae*). Many consider such a position unnatural and unbelievable. Any judgment here calls not only for realism and sobriety, but also for discretion and tact. Not just a few divorced-and-remarried people have indeed chosen this extraordinary, even occasionally heroic path with bravery and self-sacrifice. They deserve respect and recognition. Clearly, in the long run such a way of life cannot be achieved by all people who are divorced and remarried and only seldom by younger couples.

3: Need for a discriminating view of the individual situation

Bishops as well as priests understand the plight of many such divorced-and-remarried people and sympathize with them. It would be of considerable help if, in keeping with the previously shown possibilities, this were more generally known and appreciated. *Familiaris Consortio*, however, leads us one step further. The exhortation states, namely, that the pastors of the churches are duty bound

> to exercise careful discernment of situations. There is in fact a difference between those who have sincerely tried to save their first marriage and have been unjustly abandoned and those who through their own grave fault have destroyed a canonically valid marriage. Finally, there are those who have entered into a second union for the sake of the children's upbringing and who are sometimes subjectively certain in conscience that their previous and irreparably destroyed marriage had never been valid (No. 84).

The apostolic exhortation *Familiaris Consortio* points out these differences in situation, but clearly leaves concrete consequences up to the wise pastoral judgment of the individual spiritual adviser. This must not be considered *carte blanche* for arbitrary caprice. The evaluation of various situations, however, cannot and should not be left merely to individual opinions.

After long effort on many levels (theologians, advisory boards, synods, forums, etc.), more and more common criteria are recognizable today. They are of assistance in that discernment and judgment of the various situations called for also by Pope John Paul II.

Only an honest accounting can lead to a responsible decision of conscience.

An examination of the following criteria is therefore indispensable:

- when there is serious failure involved in the collapse of the first marriage, responsibility for it must be acknowledged and repented;
- it must be convincingly established that a return to the first partner is really impossible and that with the best will the first marriage cannot be restored;
- restitution must be made for wrongs committed and injuries done insofar as this is possible;
- in the first place this restitution includes fulfilment of

obligations to the wife and children of the first marriage (cf. Code of Canon Law, Canon 1071, 1.3);

• whether or not a partner broke his or her first marriage under great public attention and possibly even scandal should be taken into consideration;

• the second marital partnership must have proved itself over a long period of time to represent a decisive and also publicly recognizable will to live permanently together and also according to the demands of marriage as a moral reality;

• whether or not fidelity to the second relationship has become a moral obligation with regard to the spouse and children should be examined;

• it ought to be sufficiently clear – though certainly not to any greater extent than with other Christians – that the partners seek truly to live according to the Christian faith and with true motives, i.e., moved by genuinely religious desires, to participate in the sacramental life of the Church. The same holds true in the children's upbringing.

Divorced-and-remarried people must seek to clarify and evaluate these various situations and circumstances in candid discussion with a wise and experienced priest. Such a discussion is necessary in any case for basic clarification of the facts. For this, criteria have just been stated. The pastors should also point out to those concerned the ways and means given within the Church for a legal resolution of their situation.

4: The possibility of an individual decision of conscience to participate in the eucharist

In conjunction with all this falls the decision regarding participation in the celebration of the sacraments. As already stated, there can be no general, formal, official admission because the Church's position on the indissolubility of marriage would thereby be obscured. Nor can there be any unilateral admission in individual cases, admission, that is, for which an official of the Church alone would be responsible. But through clarifying pastoral dialogue between the partners of a second marriage and a priest, in which the situation is thoroughly, candidly and objectively brought to light, it can happen in individual cases that the marriage partners (or else just one of the partners) see their (or his/her) conscience clear to approach the table of the Lord (cf. Canon 843.1). This is especially the case when the conscience is convinced that the earlier, irreparably destroyed marriage was never valid (*Familiaris Consortio*, 84). The situation would be similar when those concerned already have come a long way in reflection and penance. Moreover, there could also be the presence of an insoluble conflict of duty, where leaving the new family would be the cause of grievous injustice.

Such a decision can only be made by the individual in a personal review of his or her conscience and by no one else. However, he or she will be in need of the clarifying assistance and the unbiased accompaniment of a church officeholder; such assistance will sharpen the conscience and see to it that the basic order of the Church is not violated. Those concerned must therefore submit to advice and accompaniment. Each individual case must be examined: There should be no indiscriminate admission or indiscriminate exclusion. Without such a basic spiritual and pastoral dialogue, which should include elements of repentance and conversion, there can be no participation in the eucharist. The participation of a priest in this clarifying process is necessary because participation in the eucharist is a public and ecclesiastically significant act. Nevertheless, the priest does not pronounce any official admission in a formal sense.

The priest will respect the judgment of the individual's conscience, which that person has reached after examining his own conscience and becoming convinced his approaching the holy eucharist can be justified before God. Certainly this respect has different degrees. The divorced-and-remarried person may be in a certain borderline situation that is extremely complex, where the priest cannot in the end forbid his approach to the Lord's table and must therefore tolerate it. It is also possible that an individual, despite the presence of objective indications of guilt, may not have incurred any grievous guilt subjectively. In this case the priest could, after diligent examination of all circumstances, strongly encourage an examination of conscience.

The priest will defend such a decision of conscience against prejudice and suspicion, but he must also take care that the parish does not thereby take offence. If after an examination of conscience receiving communion is not an option, that still does not mean – as was already explained – that one simply has been excluded from the community of the Church or that his salvation has even been denied. Such people are not excluded from appealing for grace and for faith, hope and charity, and they especially are not excluded from intercession on the part of others (cf. *Familiaris Consortio*, 84). There are still other ways open to them for committed participation in the Church's life.

5: The place of divorced people who have remarried in the whole community

There remains the question whether divorced-and-remarried people are subject to still other aspects of a reduced position as members of the Church. For baptismal and confirmation sponsors, a way of life is required that corresponds to the doctrine of the faith and to the duties to be assumed (cf. Canons 872, 874, 893.1). For work in the pastoral area, good morals are required, for example (cf. Canon 512.3). Divorced-and-remarried people are not automatically excluded thereby. Of course the parish priest must ask himself, together with those concerned, whether the qualification demanded for specific duties can be fulfilled as a general rule. Here again it depends upon the already-presented discernment of individual situations.

Divorced-and-remarried people are not, as a matter of course, excluded from participating in church activities and from membership in advisory councils. Details for the various diocesan committees are explained in the respective diocesan statutes. More appropriate is participation in various volunteer services that have no representative character, although not in public leadership positions. For similar reasons, helping to prepare children and young people for the sacraments is inappropriate.

For the rest, the parish priest is not only responsible for the administration of the sacraments and thus has competency over participation in their celebration, but he must also take into consideration the position of divorced-and-remarried people in the Church as a whole and within the specific context of a particular congregation. The responsibility of divorced-and-remarried people is not limited to their own lives but also includes the common welfare of the Church. This is especially important in the possibility of assuming representative services. The parish priest must consider discomfort and scandal in the congregation. In any case it always comes back to the actual extent divorced-and-remarried people become rooted and are at home in their parish. In particular, external motives such as recognition and improvement of status, for example, or even an increase in prestige should be prevented from playing a decisive role.

Unreasonable demands regarding reception of the sacraments especially must be avoided with respect to the sick and the dying, as has always been the practice of the Church. Refusal of Christian burial can usually be avoided today in most cases, although there still must have been 'some indication before death of repentance' (cf. Canon 1184.1.3).

6: Prayers and church services for divorced-and-remarried people

The Church should pray for divorced-and-remarried people. This is especially true for the pastor. It is, however, strictly forbidden for 'any pastor for whatever reason or pretext even of a pastoral nature to perform ceremonies of any kind for divorced people who remarry' (*Familiaris Consortio*, 84). An official liturgical ceremony would not only lead to serious misunderstandings among many of the faithful regarding the indissolubility of a validly contracted Christian marriage, but would also introduce official liturgical acts that create the impression of a new, sacramentally valid marriage. Communal prayer with the marriage partners concerned fulfils a discerning pastoral care of people from broken marriages. This can take many forms. One could consider, for example, personal prayers or an invitation to the parish worship services and specific intercessions. Ritual and formal prayers that approach an official liturgical act are inappropriate. Misinter-pretations in such situations are almost unavoidable. This is especially true of special Masses celebrated at specific times, namely in conjunction with the civil marriage. In the interests of a specific pastoral care, the pastor can and must avoid public appearances of this kind. Divorced-and-remarried people must not ask this of him. One can express support in other ways such as through visits, discussions, letters and the like.

7: Concrete responsibility for pastoral care

Everyone engaged full time in pastoral care can lead those concerned back closer to the congregation within the given principles. The clarifying dialogue must be led by an experienced priest, who must in any case inform the parish priest of an approach to the eucharist. This is demanded by the parish priest's responsibility for the order of the celebrations and for the reception of the eucharist in the congregation, but also for all forms of reconciliation with the Church (cf. 2 Cor. 5:11–21).

The question whether in the future there ought to be an experienced priest available in each deanery for especially difficult situations can for the time being remain open, but it should at least be brought up here. Certainly the ecclesiastical authorities can be consulted.

These last considerations show in particular how much sensitivity and a sense of responsibility are required on the part of all pastoral workers, especially pastors and other priests. This is also valid regarding the regular proclamation of the word and for instruction in the faith from Sunday homilies to religious instruction. This goal cannot be reached without intensive attention to these basic principles in training and in continuing education.

V. Prospects: Gospel strength and borderline situations

The pastoral care of people from broken marriages and for divorced people who have remarried must not become narrow or isolated. It should be integrated into the overall care for marriage and the family as a whole. It should be aware of the vulnerability of human relationships and of their need for support. It should help in the formation of conscience and know that conscience is irreplaceable. It should be aware of the need for discriminating pastoral dialogue. Only within such an all-embracing approach can the special care of these people be successful. Long and patient processes of theological, spiritual and pastoral education are also needed here.

These principles need corresponding application in other areas such as church employment policies and labour laws. The German bishops' conference is giving attention to such clarification.

Furthermore, judgments regarding those living together before marriage or of those living together in long-standing nonmarital relationships as well as of Christians who contract merely a civil marriage also require discernment. Blanket condemnations or indulgences regarding the question of admission to the sacraments are as inappropriate here as with divorced-and-remarried people.

Many of the problems treated here represent general duties of contemporary pastoral care as well. Strict demands need not be addressed solely to divorced-and-remarried people, for example regarding requirements for reception of communion; discussion of the pastoral care of people from broken marriages also covers deficits in other areas that concern everyone such as the required correct disposition for participation at the Lord's table. One might also recall in this connection the rediscovery and revival of 'spiritual communion.'

With that we are brought back to a basic requirement. Only when the theory and practice of marriage are fundamentally strengthened in the Christian community can the Church intervene on behalf of those from broken marriages and most especially for divorced-and-remarried people without creating misunderstandings. In the end, everything depends on the living witness of Christian married people. This is irreplaceable. The lived strength of the Gospel yields the wisdom to treat border-line cases correctly. This is especially true at a time when these cases are on the increase and even beginning to gain the upper hand. A well-considered basic attitude is therefore all the more necessary and of course requires continual renewal. The great church father St. Gregory of Nazianzus gives this measure: 'Do not oppress by strictness, do not destroy by weak indulgence.'

(Translation of sections I–II by Robert Nowell; sections IV and V from *Origins*, 10 March 1994, pp. 673–676)

Notes

1 Discussion of Canon 915 of the Code of Canon Law has indeed shown that a universal application of these norms to divorced-and-remarried people as a group is not possible and that to this extent Canon 915 does not preclude discussion such as in the present paper of a discriminating 'admission' to the sacraments.

DIVORCE AND REMARRIAGE:
A GERMAN INITIATIVE

Ladislas Örsy

Twice in the past (23 October 1993 and 16 April 1994), *The Tablet* has referred briefly to the pastoral letter issued by the bishops of the Upper Rhine Province in Germany. The letter's subject-matter was the pastoral care of the divorced and remarried. The authors are Bishop Karl Lehmann of Mainz, president of the German bishops' conference, Archbishop Oskar Saier of Freiburg, vice-president of the same, and Bishop Walter Kasper of Rottenburg-Stuttgart. It is a remarkable document, both for its approach and its content: it deserves to be widely known.

In composing it, the bishops acted, undoubtedly, on their own initiative: there is not the slightest evidence of a hidden *nihil obstat* from an office of the Holy See – an approval which increasingly is becoming sought for the pronouncements of episcopal conferences. It appears that the three bishops took to heart the doctrine of Vatican II that they are the vicars of Christ in their own dioceses, and that they have a power conferred on them directly through their sacramental ordination. They balanced their unfailing communion with the universal Church with the quiet assertion of their own authority.

They profess their respect for the Pope's teaching as contained in his apostolic exhortation *Familiaris Consortio* (1982): they uphold the general prohibition against the admission of the divorced and remarried to the sacraments. They stress, however, the need to examine every individual case on its own merits. In this they are on solid ground: Aristotle held that at times even the best of laws may need the tempering force of equity. Aquinas accepted his doctrine and enriched it by giving a role to Christian mercy as well.

This respect for the singular, however, is no permission for arbitrary decisions: the bishops repeatedly stress the importance of a well-informed conscience. They demand that those living in a canonically invalid union and desirous to be admitted to the

Eucharist should always seek counselling by a priest. Once, however, the couple has received all the help they need, they, man and woman, should be able to judge their own position before God. The role of the priest is to respect their conclusion; not to impose one on them. In other terms, the bishops recognize the primacy of conscience. (In this recognition, they are close to the spirit, even to the letter, of *Dignitatis Humanae*, Vatican II's declaration on religious freedom.)

The bishops are certainly moved by a spirit of compassion, yet they are not offering, in their own words, a 'cheap grace'. For them, there cannot be full reconciliation without genuine repentance; and there cannot be repentance without the testimony of prayer and good works sustained for a long time. They enumerate the concrete criteria by which the good will of the couple should be judged.

The bishops are aware of the problem of scandal. They insist, therefore, on the need to educate the communities toward understanding the complex situation where a couple in a legally irregular marriage is incorporated into the eucharistic community. In no way should this weaken the universal Catholic belief in the duty to keep marriages indissoluble; it should rather strengthen our faith in Christ who can provide healing for a wound in the community even when we are unable to do it by ordinary legal means.

We should keep in mind that this pastoral letter is more than a statement signed by three individual bishops: it is the collective teaching of the episcopate of an ecclesiastical province. By the ancient tradition of the Church, when the bishops of a region gather in the Lord's name, he is with them in a special way. Besides (a valid consideration although on a different level) all three bishops are recognized scholars, two of them (Lehmann and Kasper) theologians of international repute.

The document is a model of what today a pastoral letter ought to be. It is brief, its language is courteous and humble, its style is clear and pleasant to read; it has theological depth and yet it is thoroughly down to earth when it speaks of practicalities.

Whether the bishops have intended it or not, their letter in fact complements the teaching of the Pope's encyclical, *Veritatis Splendor*, which puts a strong emphasis on the objective norms of morality. They, on their part, speak of the importance of the well-informed conscience; by its judgment everyone has to abide. Thus, the doctrinal teaching of the successor of Peter blends with the pastoral directions of the successors of the apostles. They together reveal the wealth of a tradition that – as Cardinal Newman has pointed out – no single person can ever fully describe.

The Tablet reported also (16 April 1994) that the 'three bishops were called to Rome to discuss their point of view'. One hopes that the significance of this invitation is that those who by their offices are called to legislate for the universal Church are anxious to be enriched by the experience and the insights of the bishops who have the direct care of the souls.

In this document, we have indeed a fine example of that ancient tradition that today is perhaps more alive in the Eastern than in the Western Church: the faithful observance of the laws, *akribeia*, ought to be coupled with the spirit of mercy, *oikonomia*. This mercy transcends all human reasonings: its source is in the healing power of Christ – never absent from his people and always beyond our comprehension.

(Ladislas Örsy, 'Divorce and remarriage: a German initiative', *The Tablet*, 18 June 1994, p. 787)

CDF LETTER TO THE WORLD'S BISHOPS OF 14 SEPTEMBER 1994 CONCERNING THE DIVORCED-REMARRIED AND HOLY COMMUNION

1. The International Year of the Family is a particularly important occasion to discover anew the many signs of the Church's love and concern for the family[1] and, at the same time, to present once more the priceless riches of Christian marriage, which is the basis of the family.

2. In this context the difficulties and sufferings of those faithful in irregular marriage situations merit special attention.[2] Pastors are called to help them experience the charity of Christ and the maternal closeness of the Church, receiving them with love, exhorting them to trust in God's mercy and suggesting, with prudence and respect, concrete ways of conversion and participation in the life of the community of the Church.[3]

3. Aware however that authentic understanding and genuine mercy are never separated from the truth,[4] pastors have the duty to remind these faithful of the Church's doctrine concerning the celebration of the sacraments, in particular the reception of the holy eucharist. In recent years in various regions different pastoral solutions in this area have been suggested according to which, to be sure, a general admission of the divorced and remarried to eucharistic communion would not be possible, but divorced-and-remarried members of the faithful could approach holy communion in specific cases when they consider themselves authorized according to a judgment of conscience to do so. This would be the case, for example, when they had been abandoned completely unjustly although they sincerely tried to save the previous marriage, or when they are convinced of the nullity of their previous marriage although unable to demonstrate it in the external forum, or when they have gone through a long period of

reflection and penance or also when for morally valid reasons they cannot satisfy the obligation to separate.

In some places it has also been proposed that in order objectively to examine their actual situation, the divorced and remarried would have to consult a prudent and expert priest. This priest, however, would have to respect their eventual decision in conscience to approach holy communion, without this implying an official authorization.

In these and similar cases it would be a matter of a tolerant and benevolent pastoral solution in order to do justice to the different situations of the divorced and remarried.

4. Even if analogous pastoral solutions have been proposed by a few fathers of the Church and in some measure were practised, nevertheless these never attained the consensus of the fathers and in no way came to constitute the common doctrine of the Church nor to determine her discipline. It falls to the universal magisterium, in fidelity to sacred Scripture and tradition, to teach and to interpret authentically the *depositum fidei*.

With respect to the aforementioned new pastoral proposals, this congregation deems itself obliged therefore to recall the doctrine and discipline of the Church in this matter. In fidelity to the words of Jesus Christ,[5] the Church affirms that a new union cannot be recognized as valid if the preceding marriage was valid. If the divorced are remarried civilly, they find themselves in a situation that objectively contravenes God's law. Consequently, they cannot receive holy communion as long as this situation persists.[6]

This norm is not at all a punishment or a discrimination against the divorced and remarried, but rather expresses an objective situation that of itself renders impossible the reception of holy communion:

> They are unable to be admitted thereto from the fact that their state and condition of life objectively contradict that union of love between Christ and his Church which is signified and effected by the eucharist. Besides this, here is another special pastoral reason: If these people were admitted to the eucharist, the faithful would be led into error and confusion regarding the Church's teaching about the indissolubility of marriage.[7]

The faithful who persist in such a situation may receive holy communion only after obtaining sacramental absolution, which may be given only 'to those who, repenting of having broken the sign of the covenant and of fidelity to Christ, are sincerely ready to undertake a way of life that is no longer in contradiction to the indissolubility of marriage. This means, in practice, that when for serious reasons, for example, for the children's upbringing, a man and a woman cannot satisfy the obligation to separate, they "take on themselves the duty to live in complete continence, that is, by abstinence from the acts proper to married couples."'[8] In such a case they may receive holy communion as long as they respect the obligation to avoid giving scandal.

5. The doctrine and discipline of the Church in this matter are amply presented in the postconciliar period in the apostolic exhortation *Familiaris Consortio*. The exhortation, among other things, reminds pastors that out of love for the truth they are obliged to discern carefully the different situations and exhorts them to encourage the participation of the divorced and remarried in the various events in the life of the Church. At the same time it confirms and indicates the reasons for the constant and universal practice, 'founded on sacred Scripture, of not admitting the divorced and remarried to holy communion.'[9] The structure of the exhortation and the tenor of its words give clearly to understand that this practice, which is presented as binding, cannot be modified because of different situations.

6. Members of the faithful who live together as husband and wife with persons other than their legitimate spouses may not receive holy communion. Should they judge it possible to do so, pastors and confessors, given the gravity of the matter and the spiritual good of these persons,[10] as well as the common good of the Church, have the serious duty to admonish them that such a judgment of conscience openly contradicts the Church's teaching.[11] Pastors in their teaching must also remind the faithful entrusted to their care of this doctrine.

This does not mean that the Church does not take to heart the situation of these faithful, who moreover are not excluded from ecclesial communion. She is concerned to accompany them pastorally and invite them to share in the life of the Church in the measure that is compatible with the dispositions of divine law, from which the Church has no power to dispense.[12] On the other hand, it is necessary to instruct these faithful so that they do not think their participation in the life of the Church is reduced exclusively to the question of the reception of the eucharist. The faithful are to be helped to deepen their understanding of the value of sharing in the sacrifice of Christ in the Mass, of spiritual communion,[13] of prayer, of meditation on the word of God, and of works of charity and justice.[14]

7. The mistaken conviction of a divorced-and-remarried person that he may receive holy communion normally presupposes that personal conscience is considered in the final analysis to be able, on the basis of one's own convictions,[15] to come to a decision about the existence or absence of a previous marriage and the value of the new union. However, such a position is inadmissible.[16] Marriage, in fact, both because it is the image of the spousal relationship between Christ and his Church as well as the fundamental core and an important factor in the life of civil society, is essentially a public reality.

8. It is certainly true that a judgment about one's own dispositions for the reception of holy communion must be made by a properly formed moral conscience. But it is equally true that the consent that is the foundation of marriage is not simply a private decision since it creates a specifically ecclesial and social situation for the spouses, both individually and as a couple. Thus the judgment of conscience of one's own marital situation does not regard only the immediate relationship between man and God, as if one could prescind from the Church's mediation that also includes canonical laws binding in conscience. Not to recognize this essential aspect would mean in fact to deny that marriage is a reality of the Church, that is to say, a sacrament.

9. In inviting pastors to distinguish carefully the various situations of the divorced and remarried, the exhortation *Familiaris Consortio* recalls the case of those who are subjectively certain in conscience that their previous marriage, irreparably broken, had never been valid.[17] It must be discerned with certainty by means of the external forum established by the Church whether there is objectively such a nullity of marriage. The discipline of the Church, while it confirms the exclusive competence of ecclesiastical tribunals

with respect to the examination of the validity of the marriage of Catholics, also offers new ways to demonstrate the nullity of a previous marriage in order to exclude as far as possible every divergence between the truth verifiable in the judicial process and the objective truth known by a correct conscience.[18]

Adherence to the Church's judgment and observance of the existing discipline concerning the obligation of canonical form necessary for the validity of the marriage of Catholics are what truly contribute to the spiritual welfare of the faithful concerned. The Church is in fact the body of Christ, and to live in ecclesial communion is to live in the body of Christ and to nourish oneself with the body of Christ. With the reception of the sacrament of the eucharist, communion with Christ the head can never be separated from communion with his members, that is, with his Church. For this reason, the sacrament of our union with Christ is also the sacrament of the unity of the Church. Receiving eucharistic communion contrary to the norms of ecclesial communion is therefore in itself a contradiction. Sacramental communion with Christ includes and presupposes the observance, even if at times difficult, of the order of ecclesial communion, and it cannot be right and fruitful if a member of the faithful, wishing to approach Christ directly, does not respect this order.

10. In keeping with what has been said above, the desire expressed by the Synod of Bishops, adopted by the Holy Father John Paul II as his own and put into practice with dedication and with praiseworthy initiatives by bishops, priests, religious and lay faithful is yet to be fully realized, namely, with solicitous charity to do everything that can be done to strengthen in the love of Christ and the Church those faithful in irregular marriage situations. Only thus will it be possible for them fully to receive the message of Christian marriage and endure in faith the distress of their situation. In pastoral action one must do everything possible to ensure that this is understood not to be a matter of discrimination, but only of absolute fidelity to the will of Christ, who has restored and entrusted to us anew the indissolubility of marriage as a gift of the Creator. It will be necessary for pastors and the community of the faithful to suffer and to love in solidarity with the persons concerned, so that they

may recognize in their burden the sweet yoke and the light burden of Jesus.[19] Their burden is not sweet and light in the sense of being small or insignificant, but becomes light because the Lord – and with him the whole Church – shares it. It is the task of pastoral action, which has to be carried out with total dedication, to offer this help, founded in truth and in love together.

United with you in dedication to the collegial task of making the truth of Jesus Christ shine in the life and activity of the Church, I remain yours devotedly in the Lord.

Cardinal Joseph Ratzinger
prefect

Archbishop Alberto Bovone
secretary
('CDF Letter to Bishops', *Origins*,
27 October 1994, pp. 337–341)

Note

During an audience granted to the cardinal prefect, the supreme pontiff John Paul II gave his approval to this letter, drawn up in the ordinary session of this congregation, and ordered its publication. Given at Rome, from the offices of the Congregation for the Doctrine of the Faith, Sept. 14, 1994, feast of the exaltation of the Holy Cross.

1. Cf. John Paul II. Letter to Families (Feb. 2, 1994), No. 3.
2. Cf. ibid., apostolic exhortation *Familiaris Consortio* (Nov. 22, 1981), Nos. 79–84: *Acta Apostolicae Sedis* 74 (1982) 180–186.
3. Cf. ibid., 84; Letter to Families, 5; Catechism of the Catholic Church, 1651.
4. Cf. Paul VI, encyclical *Humanae Vitae*, 29: AAS 60 (1968) 501; John Paul II, apostolic exhortation *Reconciliatio et Paenitentia*, 34: AAS 77 (1985) 272; encyclical *Veritatis Splendor*, 95: AAS 85 (1993) 1208.
5. Mk. 10-11-12: "Whoever divorces his wife and marries another, commits adultery against her, and if she divorces her husband and marries another she commits adultery."
6. Cf. Catechism of the Catholic Church, 1650; cf. also No. 1640 and the Council of Trent, Sess. XXIV: Denzinger-Schonmetzer 1797–1812.
7. *Familiaris Consortio*, 84.
8. Ibid; cf. John Paul II, Homily at the Closing of the Sixth Synod of Bishops, 7: AAS 72 (1980) 1082.
9. *Familiaris Consortio*, 84.
10. Cf. 1 Cor. 11:27–29.

11. Cf. Code of Canon Law, Canon 978.2.
12. Cf. Catechism of the Catholic Chnurch, 1640.
13. Cf. Congregation for the Doctrine of Faith, Letter to the Bishops of the Catholic Church on Certain Questions Concerning the Minister of the Eucharist, III/4, AAS 75 (1983) 1007; St. Teresa of Avila, *The Way of Perfection*, 35, 1; St. Alphonsus de Liguori, *Visite al SS. Sacramento e a Maria Santissima*.
14. Cf. *Familiaris Consortio*, 84.
15. Cf. *Veritatis Splendour*, 55.
16. Cf. Canon 1085.2.
17. Cf. *Familiaris Consortio*, 84.
18. Cf. Canons 1536.2 and 1679 and Eastern Canons 1217. 2 and 1365 concerning the probative force of the depositions of the parties in such processes.
19. Cf. Mt. 11:30.

THE THREE GERMAN BISHOPS' MESSAGE TO THEIR PEOPLE
(Comment on the CDF Letter, 14 October 1994)

A year ago we addressed a joint pastoral letter on the pastoral care of divorced and of divorced-and-remarried people to all the faithful of the Upper Rhine ecclesiastical province. At the same time we sent you 'Principles for the Pastoral Guidance of People from Broken Marriages and of Divorced-and-Remarried People.'[1] In both documents what we attempted to do was to arrive at joint solutions that would be both theologically and pastorally responsible with regard to this difficult and urgent question of present-day pastoral practice.

1 Reception of the Joint Letter

We have stressed several times that, from the start, it was not and could not be our intent to introduce doctrinal innovations or a new canon law. Rather, we have attempted, even while upholding the doctrine and discipline of the Church, to arrive at acceptable solutions in terms of their pastoral application. In this attempt we were able to base ourselves on the diocesan synod of Rottenburg-Stuttgart, the diocesan forum of the Freiburg Archdiocese and the diocesan assembly in Mainz as well as on a great number of theological and canonical publications. In addition, we had available statements of other bishops, along with a series of synodal texts from other dioceses which go in a similar direction.

We composed both our documents solely for the region of the Upper Rhine ecclesiastical province. Accordingly, as a matter of principle we refrained from publicizing our texts outside the area that falls under our jurisdiction. We have therefore, for example, turned down many requests for interviews. Nevertheless, our initiative found an unexpectedly wide resonance far beyond our dioceses, both in Germany and abroad. Translations appeared without our being involved in these in any way. Without our knowledge, these were sometimes abridged in part, to the detriment of the topic at hand. Many bishops in Germany and abroad also made statements, some of which were critical and negative, others supportive and thankful, still others expressing a 'wait and see' stance.

It was clear that with our pastoral letter we had picked up on an important challenge of contemporary pastoral practice. In so doing we could not and did not wish to claim that we had already found a solution that is satisfactory in every respect.

2 Discussion with the Doctrinal Congregation

At the end of December 1993, we received from the Congregation for the Doctrine of the Faith in Rome a letter in which we were informed that we had not 'fully upheld' Catholic doctrine in our pastoral letter and in the attached principles. Accordingly, this February we were in Rome for a thoroughgoing discussion with the Congregation for the Doctrine of the Faith, a discussion which was carried on in an atmosphere of objectivity. In this discussion we presented and offered supporting arguments for our position both orally and subsequently, in more detail, in writing. In this way various misunderstandings could be disposed of.

This discussion had as its presupposition the urgency of the pastoral problem. Our basic theological position was not contested in principle. No full agreement could, however, be reached on the question of the reception of communion. Since, however, various members of the worldwide episcopate were clearly calling for a clarification, the Congregation for the Doctrine of the Faith decided to issue its presentation of the Catholic position.

In June 1994 there was a further discussion in Rome with regard to this. The congregation's declaration, which had already been announced, came to our attention on 14 September 1994. We have conducted a very open dialogue. Above all, the congregation assured us that its declaration merely addresses in a general way current widely disseminated opinions in the Church as a whole rather than being directed at our position in particular.

We are sending you herewith the text of the declaration, dated 14 September, along with this our statement, and we ask that you give them conscientious attention. The declaration is titled: Congregation for the Doctrine of the Faith, 'Letter to the Bishops of the Catholic Church Concerning the Reception of Holy Communion by Divorced-and-Remarried Members of the Faithful.'

3 Fundamental points of agreement

It is with gratitude that we discern that, on fundamental points, the presentation of the above-mentioned letter of the Congregation for the Doctrine of the Faith agrees with our statements. It is also our conviction – and we have purposely noted this quite often – that the resolution of the complicated problems of the pastoral care of the divorced and remarried can come about only in unconditional fidelity to the witness of Holy Scripture and the binding tradition of the Church, not by adaptation to contemporary trends.

Our overriding concern was and is therefore, in fidelity to the word of Jesus, to emphatically highlight the existing and binding teaching of the Church concerning the indissolubility of marriage and to make this newly understandable. Hence, we quite deliberately devoted the first half of our pastoral letter to this fundamental theme. We are convinced that precisely in so doing we did people an important service. A series of polemical assertions have misconstrued this clear intent of our statement and thereby distorted the whole of it.

Like the Congregation for the Doctrine of the Faith, we also pointed out that the divorced and remarried are not excommunicated; rather they continue as before to belong to the Church and are invited to its liturgies and to participate in parish life. In view of their situation they even have need of special care and attention. Our basic concern – i.e., a helping pastoral practice for the divorced and remarried – should in no way be reduced to the question of the so-called admission to the sacraments.

Unfortunately, however, this is what has happened repeatedly in the discussion concerning our statements, with the result that the approach and intended goal of the pastoral letter and of the principles have been obscured. For it is also our view that re-marriage during the lifetime of the first marital partner of a valid sacramental marriage stands in objective contradiction to the divine order as renewed by Jesus Christ, which precludes official admission to the reception of holy communion, both generally and in the individual case. We have stressed this point several times.

It is of importance for us to point out that there is no disagreement whatever in all these fundamental questions of Church teaching. We are therefore requesting you from our hearts and with urgency to adhere to these binding principles of the universal Church in your pastoral practice. Intensive care for people from broken marriages and the divorced and remarried is and remains a major contemporary pastoral concern, one which is far from having been seriously undertaken and carried through up till now. This concern would not be fostered by an easygoing stance.

4 Our approach

It certainly cannot be overlooked that the cases of the divorced and remarried often involve delicate and highly complex human situations in which the concrete application of the above principles becomes pastorally difficult. We attempted to show why for various reasons these problems have enormously increased in our modern Western societies. They represent a pastoral challenge which stands in urgent need of an answer.

According to the traditional teaching of the Church, the general norm must in each case indeed be applied to concrete persons and their individual situations, without this doing away with the norm itself. 'Canon law can only posit a generally valid order of things; it cannot, however, regulate all individual cases, which are often very complex' (Catholic Catechism for Adults, *Das Glaubensbekenntnis der Kirche*, published by the German episcopal conference, p. 395). The Church's doctrinal tradition has developed for this purpose the concept of *epikeia* (equity), while canon law has come up with the principle of canonical equity (*aequitas canonica*). It is not a question here of doing away with the law that is in force or the valid norm. Rather, it is a matter of applying them in difficult and complex situations according to 'justice and equity' in such a way that the uniqueness of the individual person is taken into account. This has nothing to do with a so-called 'situational pastoral practice.'

We are, moreover, convinced that the sometimes arbitrary treatment of the divorced and remarried must be countered with a differentiated pastoral procedure. This is needed also with regard to the reception of communion, which in some places occurs with little thought and on occasion in a way that is not admissible. Taking this state of affairs as our starting point, we wanted to bring order and healing into it.

5 The difficult question of receiving communion

The controversy concerning our pastoral letter and the principles was ignited above all by the question of whether the concepts of *epikeia* and canonical equity could also be applied, in individual cases having a given character and under precisely circumscribed conditions, to the question of the reception of communion by the divorced and remarried. In other words, the question is whether in particular cases of the divorced and remarried it is thinkable and legitimate not, indeed, that they be officially admitted to holy communion, but that such individuals, after appropriate guidance by a priest who first recalls to them the Lord's word concerning lifelong fidelity in marriage, see themselves as justified by their truth-oriented consciences in approaching holy communion.

We saw no possibility of an official admission, but rather of an approach to the table of the Lord under precisely stated conditions, this being made possible on the basis of a reflective pronouncement by the individual's conscience. This distinction between *admission* and *approach* is fundamental for us. We also believed that we can and must adopt such a solution, which admittedly requires a high degree of readiness to assume responsibility by all concerned, in terms of the ever necessary balancing of justice and compassion (cf. the encyclical *Dives in Misericordia* of Pope John Paul II of Nov. 30, 1980, Nos. 4, 7, 12, 14, 40). Moreover, on the basis of our proposed model, it would not be a question here of the approval of such a step, but rather, following a clarification of the facts of the matter, of a toleration of this.

The 1980 Synod of Bishops, which led in November 1981 to the apostolic exhortation *Familiaris Consortio*, formulated in this connection the thesis that 'the synod, motivated by pastoral concern for these [divorced-and-remarried] faithful, desires that a new and still more thoroughgoing investigation be initiated – one that will also take into account the practice of the Eastern churches – with the goal of deepening pastoral compassion still further' (Proposition 14, No. 6, *Enchiridion Vaticanum* 7, 2nd ed. [Bologna,

1990], p. 686, No. 729). We were guided by this pastoral goal and wished to do justice both to the seriousness of the word of the Lord as witnessed to by the Church and to the seriousness of human destinies. In so doing we were aware that the Church still has much to learn at all levels in this regard and that in the process the danger of occasional abuses cannot be totally excluded.

As emerges from the letter of the Congregation for the Doctrine of the Faith, which we are now sending you, the congregation could not agree with our position on the above point with its appeal to the apostolic exhortation *Familiaris Consortio*. Hence, we must take note of the fact that as a result of the congregation's letter certain statements in our pastoral letter and in the principles are not accepted by the universal Church and therefore cannot be the binding norm of pastoral practice.[2]

6 Import of the 'Letter'

As individual bishops and also as those of an ecclesiastical province, we belong to a world-wide collegial communion of bishops with and under the successor of the apostle Peter. This does not dispense us from nor preclude our responsible seeking for viable pastoral solutions in difficult situations – as the many examples from church history to which we alluded show. This is how we have understood our 'initiative,' prompted by our concern for the persons affected but also for the right interpretation and application of the Gospel.

We wish therefore to emphasize explicitly that we do not find ourselves in any doctrinal disagreement with the position of the Congregation for the Doctrine of the Faith. The difference has to do with the question of pastoral practice in individual cases. According to the witnesses we cited from Church tradition (cf. pp. 20ff), there does, in light of newer research, exist room, beneath the threshold of the binding teaching, for pastoral flexibility in complex individual cases that is to be used responsibly. Such flexibility does not stand in contradiction to the indissolubility of marriage.[3]

Naturally, as with the document of the Congregation for the Doctrine of the Faith, it is also our primary concern to underscore indissoluble fidelity in marriage and to help people attain it. With this, however, many pastoral problems remain unsolved, especially today. It is not only we who must continue to reflect on the matter. A series of questions in biblical, historical and systematic theology and canon law also still remains open.

Ultimately, what is at stake in these questions is to rightly determine the relationship of generally valid norms to the personal decision of conscience. People of our time have a great sensitivity as to how the two poles are mediated. It is certainly often the case that the objective norm is minimalized and violated (against this tendency see the entire encyclical *Veritas Splendor* of Pope John Paul II). However, the force of the objective norm can only be brought to bear convincingly in the long run if we take into account not just people's very complex life situations, but also the individual person's unique personal dignity as it is expressed in an educated conscience. The Second Vatican Council states explicitly: 'It is through his conscience that man sees and recognizes the divine law' (Declaration on Religious Liberty, *Dignitatis Humanae*, 3). This statement points up in an exemplary way the indissoluble connection between conscience and norm. The purer the conscience becomes, the more it will be in a position to mediate the demands of the divine order and to apply these to the concrete situation without distortion.

This core problem of pastoral practice with the divorced and remarried is also the key to many other conflicts of contemporary pastoral practice. In another connection Pope Paul VI pointed out that the Church's magisterium should not only reject controverted doctrinal views in a negative or defensive fashion, but must also elucidate the matter itself about which questions have been raised in positive terms (cf., e.g., the apostolic letter *Integrae Servandae*, in *Acta Apostolicae Sedis* 37 [1965], pp. 952–955, esp. p. 953).

7 Appeal and request

As bishops we know ourselves to be bound both to the generally valid doctrine of the Church and its unity as well as to people in existentially difficult situations. From this arises our solidarity with you, our pastoral collaborators, who are often confronted in very concrete ways with these problems. In dialogue with other bishops and with the Apostolic See, we shall therefore continue to endeavour to come up with answers that are capable of generating a consensus and that are theologically and pastorally responsible. Of course, we shall continue to be in discussion with you on the matter. In priests' councils, in deanery conferences, in other diocesan councils and in pastoral conferences, we shall discuss the outstanding questions with you in detail. In addition, theological scholarship must continue to concern itself with these questions.

We can understand that many of you, and above all very many of the people affected, are disappointed now. We ask you, however, not to become discouraged or carried away with premature critical reactions, but instead to seek for responsible solutions for individual cases in fidelity to the message of Jesus and the faith of the Church as well as in solidarity with the people involved and in communion with the entire Church. We trust that you will act in a pastorally responsible way in light of the above-cited basic principles and will advise the people entrusted to you in a right way.

We thank you for all your efforts, and we ask for your prayers and God's blessing on our dioceses, and remain yours with heartfelt greetings.

('The Three German Bishops . . . ', *Origins*,
27 October 1994, pp. 341–344)

Notes

1 Published by the chanceries of the ecclesiastical province of the Upper Rhine, i.e., Freiburg, Mainz and Rottenburg-Stuttgart, August 1993.

2 Important statements of the congregation's letter in this respect are:

'If the divorced are remarried civilly, they find themselves in a situation that objectively contravenes God's law. Consequently, they cannot receive holy communion as long as this situation persists' (No. 4).

The apostolic letter *Familiaris Consortio* 'confirms the constant and universal practice, "founded on sacred Scripture, of not admitting the divorced and remarried to holy communion." The structure of the exhortation and the tenor of its words give clearly to understand that this practice, which is presented as binding, cannot be modified because of different situations' (No. 5).

'Members of the faithful who live together as husband and wife with persons other than their legitimate spouses may not receive holy communion' (No. 6).

3 On this see the letter from the Congregation for the Doctrine of the

Faith: 'Even if analogous pastoral solutions have been proposed by a few fathers of the church and in some measure were practised, nevertheless these never attained the consensus of the fathers and in no way came to constitute the common doctrine of the Church nor to determine her discipline. It falls to the universal magisterium, in fidelity to sacred Scripture and tradition, to teach and to interpret authentically the *depositum fidei*' (No. 4).

DIVORCE AND REMARRIAGE: CONFLICT IN THE CHURCH

Kevin T. Kelly

The headlines in some of the Catholic press in Britain last weekend would suggest that the recent letter to the bishops from the Congregation for the Doctrine of the Faith (CDF) imposed new and much harsher rules regarding the admission to the sacraments of divorced people who have remarried. In fact, the letter seems to be saying nothing new. It could be summarized briefly as 'no change'. It repeats the arguments heard in previous documents. Theologically it declares that the second marriage of a divorced person 'objectively contradicts' the union of love between Christ and the Church signified by the Eucharist, and pastorally it claims that the reception of the Eucharist by such a person would be a cause of scandal, since the impression would be given that the Church does not believe in the indissolubility of marriage. It also repeats the same practical solutions: separation or, when this is impossible, living together 'as brother and sister', without expressing love in sexual intimacy.

Most theologians who have studied this issue have some difficulties with all these arguments. Moreover, they are not alone in this opinion. I know many bishops, priests and lay men and women who think the same.

The assertion about an objective contradiction proves too much. It overlooks the fact there is 'objective sinfulness' in the lives of all of us. We all belong to a world shot through with many layers of structural injustice and inequality, and we are all members of a Church in which there has been grave 'objective sinfulness' over the centuries and right up to the present day. It is no wonder that we begin each Eucharist by remembering gratefully God's forgiveness which we all need so much and that our final words before actually receiving Communion are, 'Lord, I am not worthy'.

The pastoral argument about scandal is an argument from consequences. It asserts that the reception of Communion by someone who is divorced and remarried would weaken the witness of the Church to the indissolubility of marriage. No empirical evidence is offered to prove the truth of this assertion. Hence, it carries no more weight than the opposite assertion that an across-the-board denial of the sacraments to divorced people who have remarried gives scandal by weakening the witness of the Church to the compassion and forgiveness of Christ and its healing mission to those who have been wounded on their journey through life.

As for the two practical solutions suggested, these tend to be received by theologians with some incredulity and are rejected as impractical for the majority of couples concerned. Separation in most cases would simply create a further injustice since the second marriage carries with it new responsibilities. As for living together as brother and sister, modern-day family homes are hardly designed for such a lifestyle and couples in inadequate housing would be faced with an impossible situation, quite apart from the psychosexual unhealthiness that could result. Furthermore, to regard the brother and sister arrangement as an acceptable solution seems to imply that the heart of marriage lies in sexual intercourse rather than in the whole loving relationship of a shared life together. Unless a couple had a 'brother and sister' logo on their doorpost, neighbours and fellow parishioners would be none the wiser and so the alleged scandal would presumably still be given.

I have space only for the above brief and rather inadequate summary of some of the reasons why many moral theologians, bishops, priests and lay people find the arguments repeated in the letter of the CDF unconvincing. Even Cardinal Ratzinger himself, writing before his appointment as prefect of the CDF, held a similar position: 'Whenever in a second marriage moral obligations have arisen toward the children, toward the family and toward the woman, and no similar obligations from the first marriage exist; whenever also the giving up of the second marriage is not fitting on moral grounds, and continence does not appear as a real possibility in the practical order; it seems that the granting of full communion, after a time of probation, is nothing less than just, and is fully in harmony with our ecclesiastical traditions.'[1]

Where does all this leave divorced and remarried people who are currently receiving the sacraments, having arrived at this position as a result of a decision of conscience made in honesty and integrity before God, after careful consultation with a priest or spiritual director? It seems to me that there is nothing in this letter to make them alter their decision. After all, the letter merely reiterates very forcefully the teaching of Pope John Paul II in his apostolic exhortation, *Familiaris Consortio*. Presumably they will have already taken that teaching fully into consideration in arriving at their decision, with the help of their priest or spiritual director. Consequently, they should feel able to rest at peace with their decision of conscience reached so painstakingly. I think they should resist the temptation to go back over the whole agonizing process.

In the same vein, I hope that priests who support such people in receiving the sacraments will not change their pastoral practice. In fact, the exercise of pastoral responsibility by the German bishops which has occasioned this letter should affirm such priests in the pastoral approach they have been following. I feel that will also be true for theologians.

But although this letter says nothing new to the divorced and remarried, the same is not equally true of the bishops to whom it is addressed. This particular letter seems to have been occasioned by an exercise of episcopal pastoral responsibility on the part of three German bishops of very high standing in the Catholic Church: Bishop Karl Lehmann, president of the German Bishops' Conference and a highly respected moral theologian; Bishop Walter Kasper, a theologian of the highest international repute who is by no stretch of the imagination a left-wing radical or leader of dissent; and Archbishop Oskar Saier, vice-president of the German Bishops' Conference. These three carry weight ecclesiastically and theologically.

On 10 July 1993 they collectively issued very careful and prudent guidelines about the reception of the sacraments by divorced and remarried people. In no way were they suggesting *carte blanche* reception of the sacraments for all the divorced who have remarried. They recognized, however, that under clearly defined conditions some of them could arrive at a conscientious decision to receive the sacraments and they offered pastoral guidance to priests and lay people about this. Their statement was very carefully worded and the practical guidance was preceded by substantial theological grounding. I would suspect that their position would have the full backing of many other bishops – and, indeed, of most moral theologians.

In a sense, therefore, the CDF letter is directed both to the bishops of the world and implicitly, to the three German bishops. It is as though the CDF were saying to the bishops of the world: 'Three of your brothers have decided to exercise their episcopal pastoral responsibility in this way. We want to let you know that this is not acceptable. It is not part of your role as bishops.' I suspect, however, that very many bishops, in their heart of hearts, would believe this to be precisely how they should exercise their pastoral responsibility.

I think it unfortunate that the CDF letter has been made public. In the present climate this makes it difficult for individual bishops, or groups of conferences of bishops, to beg to differ from the CDF line without seeming to challenge the authority of the Pope himself. Yet one of the unresolved issues relating to collegiality – the doctrine that the college of bishops, with the Pope at their head, governs the Church – lies precisely in how the authority and pastoral responsibility of the local bishop relates to that of the other local bishops, and to the college of bishops presided over by the Pope, and to the Pope's unique personal authority as head of the college of bishops.

Collegiality is not simply the concern of bishops. It also involves local Churches. How local Churches respond creatively to their own pastoral needs within the wider context of the Catholic Communion as a whole pertains to the heart of collegiality. Consequently, this current source of tension could be a creative moment which might occasion an important growth in the life of the communion of local Churches within the worldwide Church. There could be a mutually enriching learning process between local Churches, including the Church of Rome and recognizing the primacy of its bishop.

Disagreement can play an important part in the growth of communion. The eminent German sociologist, Georg Simmel, taught his pupils to consider conflict as a creative force rather than as something destructive, since it was able to strengthen existing bonds and establish new ones. That is why he believed a 'conflict-free' society was neither healthy nor good. If this is true, our love for the Church as a communion of local Churches might lead us to pray that bishops who are dissatisfied with the CDF letter will be prepared to accept their own episcopal responsibility for what they believe to be the pastoral practice most helpful to their own local Church, even if this differs from the norm reiterated in the CDF letter.

It seems clear from the report in last week's *Tablet* that the

German bishops do not see the Vatican letter as closing down all discussion and ruling out the possibility of more open pastoral approaches. There could be far-reaching implications for the Church in the episcopal response to the German bishops' pastoral initiative.

(Kevin Kelly, 'Divorce and remarriage: conflict in the Church', *The Tablet*, 29 October 1994, pp. 1374–1375)

Notes

1 Quoted in Ladislas Örsy, *Marriage in Canon Law* (Michael Glazier, Delaware, 1986, p. 292). (Cf. pp. 173–174 below.)

SECTION B:
OTHER OFFICIAL CHURCH STATEMENTS SINCE THE FIRST EDITION OF THIS BOOK

RECONCILIATIO ET PAENITENTIA, JOHN PAUL II

The Pope's only direct reference to the divorced-remarried in this document is in the third paragraph of n. 34 where he gives a reminder that he has spoken clearly about them in his earlier Apostolic Exhortation, Familiaris Consortio. *Nevertheless, the context in which he discusses their situation is very significant. That context is defined by two principles. The first is compassion and mercy. The second is truth and consistency. Whether the Pope's pastoral conclusion based on these 'two complementary principles' is the only one which could be drawn from them is the precise point which is debated among many theologians and has been one of the issues under discussion in this book.*

34. I consider it my duty to mention at this point, if very briefly, a pastoral case that the Synod dealt with – insofar as it was able to do so – and which it also considered in one of the *Propositiones*. I am referring to certain situations, not infrequent today, affecting Christians who wish to continue their sacramental religious practice but who are prevented from doing so by their personal condition, which is not in harmony with the commitments freely undertaken before God and the Church. These are situations which seem particularly delicate and almost inextricable.

Numerous interventions during the Synod, expressing the general thought of the Fathers, emphasized the coexistence and mutual influence of two equally important principles in relation to these cases. The first principle is that of compassion and mercy, whereby the Church, as the continuer in history of Christ's presence and work, not wishing the death of the sinner but that the sinner should be converted and live,[197] and careful not to break the bruised reed or to quench the dimly burning wick,[198] ever seeks to offer, as far as possible, the path of return to God and of reconciliation with him. The other principle is that of truth and consistency, whereby the Church does not agree to call good evil and evil good. Basing herself on these two complementary principles, the Church can only invite her children who find themselves in these painful situations to approach the divine mercy by other ways, not however through the Sacraments of Penance and the Eucharist, until such time as they have attained the required dispositions.

On this matter, which also deeply torments our pastoral hearts, it seemed my precise duty to say clear words in the Apostolic Exhortation *Familiaris Consortio*, as regards the case of the divorced and remarried,[199] and likewise the case of Christians living together in an irregular union.

At the same time, and together with the Synod, I feel that it is my clear duty to urge the ecclesial communities, and especially the Bishops, to provide all possible assistance to those Priests who have fallen short of the grave commitments which they undertook at their ordination and who are living in irregular situations. None of these brothers of ours should feel abandoned by the Church.

For all those who are not at the present moment in the objective conditions required by the Sacrament of Penance, the Church's manifestations of maternal kindness, the support of acts of piety apart from sacramental ones, a sincere effort to maintain contact with the Lord, attendance at Mass, and the frequent repetition of acts of faith, hope, charity and sorrow made as perfectly as possible, can prepare the way for full reconciliation at the hour that Providence alone knows.

(John Paul II, *Reconciliatio et Paenitentia*,
2 December 1984, n. 34)

Notes

197 Cf. Ez. 18:23.
198 Cf. Is. 42:3; Mt. 12:20.
199 Cf. Apostolic Exhortation *Familiaris Consortio*, 84: *AAS* 74 (1982), 184–186.

CATECHISM OF THE CATHOLIC CHURCH

Both Parts One and Two of the Catechism contain passages dealing with marriage breakdown, divorce and remarriage.

Part One is entitled 'The Celebration of the Christian Mystery'. Chapter 3 of its second Section ('The Seven Sacraments of the Church') deals with Marriage. In that chapter divorce and remarriage are discussed under the heading of 'The fidelity of conjugal love':

1650 Today there are numerous Catholics in many countries who have recourse to civil *divorce* and contract new civil unions. In fidelity to the words of Jesus Christ – 'Whoever divorces his wife and marries another, commits adultery against her; and if she divorces her husband and marries another, she commits adultery'[158] the Church maintains that a new union cannot be recognized as valid, if the first marriage was. If the divorced are remarried civilly, they find themselves in a situation that objectively contravenes God's law. Consequently, they cannot receive Eucharistic communion as long as this situation persists. For the same reason, they cannot exercise certain ecclesial responsibilities. Reconciliation through the sacrament of Penance can be granted only to those who have repented for having violated the sign of the covenant and of fidelity to Christ, and who are committed to living in complete continence.

1651 Towards Christians who live in this situation, and who often keep the faith and desire to bring up their children in a Christian manner, priests and the whole community must manifest an attentive solicitude, so that they do not consider themselves separated from the Church, in whose life they can and must participate as baptized persons:

They should be encouraged to listen to the Word of God, to attend the Sacrifice of the Mass, to persevere in prayer, to contribute to works of charity and to community efforts for justice, to bring up their children in the Christian faith, to cultivate the

158 Mk. 10:11–12.

spirit and practice of penance and then implore, day by day, God's grace.[159]

Part Two is entitled 'Life in Christ'. Its second section covers the Ten Commandments. There divorce and remarriage come under the 6th Commandment and are dealt with under the general heading of 'Offences against the dignity of marriage':

Divorce

2382 The Lord Jesus insisted on the original intention of the Creator who willed that marriage be indissoluble.[173] He abrogates the accommodations that had slipped into the Old Law.[174]

Between the baptized, 'a ratified and consummated marriage cannot be dissolved by any human power or for any reason other than death.'[175]

2383 The *separation* of spouses while maintaining the marriage bond can be legitimate in certain cases provided for by canon law.[176]

If civil divorce remains the only possible way of ensuring certain legal rights, the care of the children, or the protection of inheritance, it can be tolerated and does not constitute a moral offence.

2384 *Divorce* is a grave offence against the natural law. It claims to break the contract, to which the spouses freely consented, to live with each other till death. Divorce does injury to the covenant of salvation, of which sacramental marriage is the sign. Contracting a new union, even if it is recognized by civil law, adds to the gravity of the rupture: the remarried spouse is then in a situation of public and permanent adultery:

If a husband, separated from his wife, approaches another woman, he is an adulterer because he makes that woman commit adultery; and the woman who lives with him is an adulteress, because she has drawn another's husband to herself.[177]

159 *FC* 84.
173 Cf. Mt 5:31–32; 19:3–9; Mk 10:9; Lk 16:18; 1 Cor 7:10–11.
174 Cf. Mt 19:7–9.
175 CIC, can. 1141.
176 Cf. CIC, can. 1151–1155.
177 St Basil, *Moralia* 73, 1: PG 31, 849–852.

2385 Divorce is immoral also because it introduces disorder into the family and into society. This disorder brings grave harm to the deserted spouse, to children traumatized by the separation of their parents and often torn between them, and because of its contagious effect which makes it truly a plague on society.

2386 It can happen that one of the spouses is the innocent victim of a divorce decreed by civil law; this spouse therefore has not contravened the moral law. There is a considerable difference between a spouse who has sincerely tried to be faithful to the sacrament of marriage and is unjustly abandoned, and one who through his own grave fault destroys a canonically valid marriage.[178]

(*Catechism of the Catholic Church*,
Geoffrey Chapman, London, 1994,
nn. 1650–1651 & 2382–2386)

178 Cf. *FC* 84.

THE 1983 CODE OF CANON LAW:
FOUR COMMENTARIES ON CANON 915

In the post-Vatican II 1983 Code there is no canon which explicitly forbids the sacraments to the divorced-remarried. Some canonists would interpret canon 915 as implicitly containing such a prohibition. However, other canonists do not accept that interpretation. Moreover, they go on to argue that, in case of doubt, the less restrictive view should be followed. To help readers get a flavour of this debate among canonists, I have included below the actual text of canon 915 along with the relevant (and divergent) passages interpreting it found in the two major English-language commentaries on the new Code. The same point is discussed even more fully by James Provost in his magisterial article, Intolerable Marriage Situations: A Second Decade, *in* The Jurist, *1990, pp. 575–612. The relevant pages (590–596) are also printed below. I have also included four helpful paragraphs from an important article which will be appearing in the delayed 1995.1 issue of* The Jurist, *Patrick J. Travers,* Reception of the Holy Eucharist by Catholics attempting Marriage after Divorce and the 1983 Code of Canon Law.

Canon 915

Those upon whom the penalty of excommunication or interdict has been imposed or declared, and others who obstinately persist in manifest grave sin, are not to be admitted to holy communion.

(a) The Code of Canon Law: a text and commentary

Canon 915, based on canon 855 of the 1917 Code, prohibits giving the Eucharist to anyone who obstinately perseveres in manifest, serious sin. A manifest sin is one which is publicly known, even if only by a few; obstinate perseverance is indicated when a person persists in the sin or sinful situation and does not heed the warnings of church authorities or adhere to church teachings. Clearly, those who are excommunicated or interdicted by an inflicted or declared sentence are regarded by the Church as grave and manifest sinners, and they are excluded from the sacraments by penal law as well (cc. 1331, §1, 2°; 1332). Other categories of manifest and grave sins are not so neatly discernible. The minister cannot assume, for example, that the sin of public concubinage arising from divorce and remarriage is always grave in the internal forum. Any prudent doubt about either the gravity or the public nature of the sin should be resolved by the minister in favour of the person who approaches the sacrament.

> *(The Code of Canon Law: A text and commentary,*
> Geoffrey Chapman, London, 1985, p. 653)

(b) The Canon Law: letter and spirit

This canon deals with those who are to be excluded from holy communion. 'Of its very nature celebration of the Eucharist signifies the fullness of profession of faith and the fullness of ecclesial communion'.[2] Those upon whom the penalty of excommunication or interdict has been imposed or declared are by definition no longer in full communion with the catholic Church and this is juridically a public fact. Their exclusion from eucharistic communion is a sign and consequence of this (see Can. 1331 §1 2°). Likewise excluded are those 'who obstinately persist in manifest grave sin'. In this third case, unlike the first two, there has been no public imposition or declaration of the person's state and so, before a minister can lawfully refuse the Eucharist, he must be certain that the person obstinately persists in a sinful situation or in sinful behaviour that is manifest (i.e. public) and objectively grave.

Those who are divorced and remarried find themselves in this situation.[3] Apart from 'the fact that their state and condition of life objectively contradict that union of life between Christ and the Church which is signified by the Eucharist', there is also the consideration of possible error and confusion in the minds of the faithful about the Church's teaching on the indissolubility of marriage.[4]

> *(The Canon Law: letter and spirit,*
> Geoffrey Chapman, London, 1995, p. 503)

---

2 SPUC instr *In Quibus Rerum Circumstantiis* IV 1: AAS 64 (1972) 518–525: Fl I 557.
3 Cf. Comm 15 (1983) 194 at Can. 867.
4 For a clear and practical appreciation of the Church's caring and sensitive attitude in this matter, the reader is earnestly referred to the relevant section of Pope John Paul II's ap exhort *The Christian Family in the Modern World* 22.XI.1981: FC 84: Fl II 888–889.

(c) Intolerable Marriage Situations: a second decade

James H. Provost

Admission of divorced and remarried persons to penance and the Eucharist is not addressed directly in the new codes.[66] Indirectly, however, they are considered to be included under the provisions of canon 915 in the Latin code: 'Those who are excommunicated or interdicted after the imposition or declaration of the penalty and others who obstinately persist in manifest grave sin are not to be admitted to Holy Communion.'[67]

The canon has several requirements. It is addressed to those who are administering the Eucharist, and directs them to exclude from Communion three classes of persons. The first two of these classes – excommunicated and interdicted persons, once their penalty has been declared (if it was incurred *latae sententiae*) or imposed – do not apply to divorced remarrieds as such. The third category has several requisites. First, the persons must be in a state of grave sin. Second, their status as grave sinners must be public and notorious (*manifestus* requires both characteristics[68]). Third, they must be obstinate in persisting in this state of grave

---

66 The same was true under the 1917 code.

67 Originally the *coetus* drafting this canon was not convinced it did apply to divorced and remarried Catholics. There was no explicit mention of them in the 1975 schema sent to the bishops, although an earlier version of the latter part of c. 915 was contained in that draft. When the *coetus* met to discuss the responses to the 1975 draft, they found a number of suggestions that provision be made for admission of divorced remarrieds to Communion. In response 'all the consultors agreed that it was not for the commission to decide this matter; the Holy See will have to respond to the question.' *Communicationes* 13 (1981) 412.

When the revised text of the canon (not yet so explicit as the final version) appeared in the 1980 schema for the code, Cardinals Florit and Palazzini considered it too vague. The commission secretariat replied that the text had all the requisites: grave act, publicity of the act, and contumacy. 'Certainly the text applies also to divorced and remarried persons.' *Relatio complectens synthesim animadversionum ab em.mis atque exc.mis Patribus Commissionis ad novissimum schema Codicis Iuris Canonici exhibitarum, cum responsionibus a secretaria et consultoribus datis* (Vatican City: Typis Polyglottis 1981) 214. There was no further explanation for why it was now considered to apply to divorced and remarried persons. Although the 1982 and final 1983 version of the canon is more detailed than its predecessors, it does not explicitly state divorced remarried Catholics are to be excluded from the Eucharist.

The corresponding canon in the Eastern code is worded quite differently: 'Publicly unworthy persons are to be prevented from (*arcendi sunt*) receiving the Divine Eucharist' (CCEO, c. 712). No further specifications are given.

68 See Frank J. Rodimer, *The Canonical Effects of Infamy of Fact*, Canon Law Studies 353 (Washington: Catholic University of America Press) 96–97.

sin. Obstinacy carries with it the connotation of having been told to stop doing something (even if it is the law itself which told them) but continuing to do it despite the warning; there is a certain hard-headedness about 'obstinacy'.

A number of commentators take for granted that this category of obstinate public sinners excludes divorced and remarried persons from the Eucharist. Most draw on *Familiaris consortio* as the basis for this interpretation.[69] Other commentators examine the question in greater depth and develop more nuanced positions. For example, Klaus Lüdicke analyzes all the elements of the canon carefully, pointing out that questions of 'sin' and 'grave' are not canonical notions and need to be dealt with by confessors, not by those dispensing the Eucharist. Thus, if a person is fulfilling all the conditions of *Familiaris consortio* for a brother-sister relationship, these would be known by the confessor not by the person administering Communion.[70] John Huels points out the difficulty of discerning manifest grave sins aside from the first two categories (excommunicated or interdicted persons) in canon 915.[71]

69 See Angel Marzoa in *Código de Derecho Canónico: Edicion anotada* (Pamplona: EUNSA, 1963) 560; Giuseppe Damizia in *Commento al Codice di Diritto Canonico*, ed. Pio V. Pinto (Rome: Urbaniana University Press, 1985) 555; Jan Hendriks, '"Ad sacram communionem ne admittantur . . ."' Adnotationes in Can. 915,' *Periodica* 79 (1990) 172–173; Tomás Rincon in *Manual de Derecho Canónico*, ed. Instituto Martin de Azpilcueta (Pamplona: EUNSA, 1988) 457; Ludwig Schick, 'Stellung der wiederverheirateten Geschiedenen in der Kirche nach "Familiaris Consortio,"' *Österreichisches Archiv für Kirchenrecht* 33 (1982) 433; Hartmut Zapp, *Das Kanonische Eherecht* (Freiburg-i.-Br.: Rombach, 1988) 59–62.

   On the other hand, in reaching the same conclusion Julio Manzanares in *Código de Derecho Canónico: Edición bilingüe comentada*, ed. Lamberto de Echeverriía, 5th ed. (Madrid: BAC, 1985) 459, makes direct reference to the *Relatio*; Johann Enichlmayr, *Wiederverheiratet nach Scheidung: Kirche im Dilemma versuch einer pastoralen Aufarbeitung* (Vienna: Herder, 1986) 183–184, relies on *Reconciliatio et Paenitentia*; and Adalbert Mayer in *Handbuch des katholischen Kirchenrechts*, ed. Joseph Listl et al. (Regensburg: Pustet, 1983) 680–681, merely cites the 1973 declaration of the Congregation for the Doctrine of the Faith and various scholarly studies in Germany.

70 Klaus Lüdicke in *Münsterischer Kommentar zum Codex Iuris Canonici*, ed. Klaus Lüdicke (Essen: Ludgerus Verlag, 1985-) c. 915/2–4. He considers the position of *Familiaris consortio*, and also analyzes the stand taken by Mayer in *Handbuch des katholischen Kirchenrechts*, and by Hans Heimerl and Helmuth Pree, *Kirchenrecht: Allgemeine Normen und Eherecht* (Vienna: Springer Verlag, 1983) 270–271.

71 Huels cautions that 'the minister cannot assume, for example, that the sin of public concubinage arising from divorce and remarriage is always grave in the internal forum. Any prudent doubt about either the gravity or the public nature of the sin should be resolved by the minister in favour of the person who approaches the sacrament.' In *The Code of Canon Law: A Text and Commentary*.

The Eastern code's wording of 'publicly unworthy' (*publice indigni*) is perhaps closer to the canonical tradition. Regatillo reports that the Roman Ritual prior to 1925 classified usurers, magicians, fortune tellers and blasphemers among those who are 'publicly unworthy.' Their very way of life could not be carried on without either habitually sinning or remaining in the occasion of serious sin. Regatillo includes in this category those who live in concubinage or adultery.[72] While the new codes do not contain the detailed description of public, notorious, and occult crimes (1917 code, c. 2197), these concepts may still help to understand the presuppositions underlying the new codes.

Both codes have a canon admonishing those who are in serious sin not to approach Communion until they have been absolved in the sacrament of penance.[73] The focus here is on the individual who seeks the Eucharist, not the one who is distributing it. But nowhere in the law is it stated that those who are divorced and remarried are necessarily sinning. This issue is not decided by the law but is left to moral theology.

What is remarkable is that neither code explicitly excludes divorced and remarried Catholics from the Eucharist, despite the attention given to this topic in the process of revising at least the Latin code, and in two apostolic exhortations by the pope who promulgated both codes. It is difficult to determine the significance of this silence with accuracy, but it can at least be observed that where the law leaves room for nuance, it is not inappropriate for those who interpret or apply the law to leave room for nuance also.

(James H. Provost, 'Intolerable Marriage Situations:
a second decade', *The Jurist*, 1990, pp. 594–596)

---

ed. James A. Coriden et al. (New York/Mahwah, NJ: Paulist Press, 1985) 653.

See Michael Knipe, 'Canon 915 and the Exclusion of the Divorced and Remarried Catholic from Reception of the Eucharist,' JCL dissertation, Catholic University of America, 1989, who concludes the canon is not the final answer on the question. See also Francois Reckinger, 'Die Sakramente im neuen Kirchenrecht,' *Theologisch-Praktische Quartalschrift* 135 (1987) 256–258.

72 Eduardus F. Regatillo, *Ius Sacramentarium*, 4th ed. (Santander: Sal Terrae, 1964) 202.

73 1983 code, c. 916; *CCEO*, c. 711. Both note the possibility of making an act of perfect contrition if it is not possible to receive the sacrament of penance at the time and there is a grave reason to receive the Eucharist; an act of perfect contrition is said to include the intention of receiving the sacrament of penance as soon as possible.

(d) Reception of the Holy Eucharist by Catholics attempting Marriage after Divorce and the 1983 Code of Canon Law

Patrick J. Travers

By the time this book is republished, this important and carefully rea-
soned article will have appeared in the delayed 1995:1 issue of The
Jurist. *Bearing in mind the fact that canon 912 states clearly that 'any*
baptized person who is not prohibited by law can and must be admitted
to Holy Communion', the author argues that the clear text of canons
915 and 916 does not automatically exclude all divorced and remarried
persons from Communion since they only envisage people who are con-
scious that they are in a state of subjective *grave sin and are stub-*
bornly persevering in that state of sin. This cannot be assumed to be the
case with everyone who is divorced and remarried. Moreover, he argues
that the clear meaning of the text of this canon should not be reinter-
preted in the light of the subsequent CDF Letter to the Bishops. Hence,
that Letter, despite its focus on the objective *gravity of the remarriage*
after divorce, should be interpreted in the light of the 1983 code. It
should not be seen as necessitating a pastoral practice which is more
restrictive than that found in the canons of that code. In the concluding
pages, the author explores some situations where a priest might legiti-
mately discern that the couple with whom he is in pastoral dialogue do
not fulfil the above-mentioned conditions of being conscious that they
are in a state of subjective *grave sin and are stubbornly persevering in*
that state of sin. One such situation is that which is brought about by
lack of full liberty and moral impossibility. Some readers might find the
following four paragraphs from the concluding pages of Travers' article
particularly helpful:

A Catholic who has attempted remarriage after divorce may
also fall outside the categories of persons excluded from Holy
Communion by canons 915 and 916 because he or she lacked the
liberty necessary for the deliberate consent required for a mortal
sin. In some cases, the person might have enjoyed this liberty at
the time of the attempted remarriage, but has subsequently lost
it with respect to the continuance of that union as a result of
changed circumstances.

A lack of liberty and deliberate consent with respect to an
attempted remarriage or its continuance may result from
economic and social factors, especially in those societies in which

the livelihood and social status of a woman derive primarily from those of her husband. It may result from emotional factors, such as overwhelming fear of loneliness or lack of sexual fulfilment. It may result from concern for the raising of children. And, especially when it is a question of a long-standing attempted remarriage, it may result from genuine love of and devotion to the second partner.

As the congregation's letter emphasizes, such factors do not of themselves generally exempt a Catholic who has attempted remarriage after divorce from exclusion from Holy Communion.[76] The nature and validity of these factors will vary from person to person, and must be explored with him or her by the priest through the process of reflection and discernment. In many cases, the duty of the priest will be gradually to help the person to realize that these limits on his or her freedom can be overcome, albeit with considerable sacrifice. It would be in this context, for example, that a 'brother and sister' arrangement might be proposed in circumstances that favoured its viability.

From time to time, however, the priest may find that the harm to be done by breaking up or limiting the scope of the second union far exceeds any foreseeable gain. If, for example, the attempted remarriage is of long standing, is marked by mutual Christian love and devotion at all levels, and has provided a sound environment for the education of the children; while the original spouses of the partners have no interest in the revival of their first marriages, and the current partner of the Catholic who has attempted remarriage after divorce refuses to agree to perpetual continence; the priest may be faced with a situation in which the disruption of the current union is a moral impossibility. If this is the case, then the Catholic who has attempted remarriage after divorce does not incur sin by continuing the union, despite the grave sinfulness of the matter involved.[77] If the priest finds a disruption of the second union to be morally impossible, he must, under canon 912, with appropriate safeguards against confusion and scandal, admit the Catholic who has attempted remarriage after divorce to Holy Communion. Where the attempted remarriage was a mortal sin when it was first contracted, such

---

76 CDF, nn. 3–4.
77 Eduard Génicot and Joseph Salsmans, *Institutiones Theologiae Moralis*. 17th ed., vol. 1, ed. A. Gortebecke (Brussels: L'Édition Universelle, 1951), 98–100; Arthur Vermeersch. *Theologiae Moralis Principia-Responsa-consilia*, 4th ed., vol. 2 (Rome: Pontificia Universitas Gregoriana, 1947), 185–186.

admission may take place only after the person has received absolution in the sacrament of penance.

(Patrick J. Travers, 'Reception of the Holy Eucharist by Catholics attempting marriage after divorce, and the 1983 Code of Canon Law', *The Jurist*, 1995, pp. 187–217 at 215–216)

STATEMENT BY THE BISHOPS' CONFERENCE OF ENGLAND AND WALES 1994, ON THE PASTORAL CARE OF MARRIAGES

Although this statement makes no specifc mention of remarriage, the bishops draw attention to the fact that 'many in the midst of the pain and trauma of marital breakdown have felt alienated and ostracized'. Presumably they would not want to be understood as saying that the divorced-remarried who have felt marginalized in this way are outside their pastoral concern. Is it fair to make the same presumption with regard to their apology ('We regret our failings') to those who have experienced hurt within the Church?

In this, the United Nations' International Year of the Family we, the Catholic Bishops of England and Wales, wish to renew our commitment and that of the Catholic community to the continuing support of marriage and family life. It is the firm belief of the Church that God's call to married couples is that they should live in permanent, stable, fruitful and peaceful relationships. We wish to encourage every Christian, political and social initiative designed to enable people to achieve these goals and recognize the sanctity of marriage and family life. We pay tribute to those whose marriages give witness to these values, sometimes in difficult situations. We also commend the work of all those who help to prepare people for the permanent commitment of married life, and those who offer them continuing support and guidance, particularly the Catholic Marriage Advisory Council.

We are heartened by the results of a recent study in the Catholic community, commissioned by the Committee for Marriage and Family Life, which indicate that these ideals are clearly understood and aspired to by the great majority of members of the Church. However, we also note with concern that among those Catholics whose marriages have failed, many have not experienced the 'solicitous care', which Pope John Paul II insisted they must receive when he wrote his Exhortation on 'The Role of the Christian Family in the Modern World' (*Familiaris Consortio*

84). We acknowledge that many in the midst of the pain and trauma of marital breakdown have felt alienated and ostracized. As pastors we feel a special sense of responsibility towards them and therefore we wish to reach out to the separated and divorced who have experienced hurt within the Church. We regret our failings and those of our communities in this regard, and encourage those in this situation always to seek help and support in their local parish community.

We acknowledge the pastoral care offered by many priests and people over the years. We thank those societies, like the Association of Separated and Divorced Catholics, the Beginning Experience and the Rainbow Groups, which have attended to this ministry in recent years: and we promise to ensure that as far as possible such pastoral care will be available in the future to all those in need.

We are aware of many of the difficulties of the present system for attending to marital breakdown in the Catholic Church. We will continue to seek ways of addressing them. At the same time we remind all our priests and people that upholding the Church's teaching on marriage and family life always includes the care and support of those who have suffered the pain of separation or divorce.

('The Pastoral Care of Marriages',
Briefing, 28 April 1994, p. 8)

SECTION C:
SOME OTHER RELEVANT ARTICLES OR EXCERPTS

I have selected for inclusion in this Appendix the following nine pieces of writing, all published since my book in 1982, in the hope that readers will find them helpful theologically and pastorally. I am very grateful to all the authors concerned and their publishers for their kindness in allowing me to reproduce their writing in whole or in part. By way of introduction, I offer a short word of explanation as to why I have chosen each item.

1. Kevin McDonald, 'Divorce and Remarriage', in *The Clergy Review*, 1983, pp. 193–198. This article was written by a fellow moral theologian as a considered critique of my book when it first appeared.
2. Ladislas Örsy, *Marriage in Canon Law*, (Michael Glazier, Delaware, 1986), pp. 288–294. A very clear and concise look at the issue of admission of the divorced-remarried to eucharistic communion by someone who has a keen theological mind as well as being one of the foremost canon lawyers writing in the English language.
3. Theodore Davey, 'The Internal Forum', in *The Tablet*, 27 July 1991, pp. 905–906. A very helpful article for people wanting to understand the background to the 'internal forum solution' and its practical application. This was one of a series of articles in *The Tablet* by different writers on the general theme, 'Dealing with Divorce'.
4. Cardinal Joseph Ratzinger, 'Letter to the Tablet', *The Tablet*, 26 October 1991, p. 1311. In this section of a much longer letter to *The Tablet*, the Prefect of the Congregation of the Doctrine of the Faith takes issue with part of Theodore Davey's article on the internal forum (cf. above). It is very encouraging to find the head of the CDF being prepared to enter into dialogue and open debate through a personal letter in the correspondence columns of *The Tablet*.
5. Kevin Kelly, 'Looking beyond failure: life after divorce', in *The Tablet*, 3 August 1991, pp. 935–937. This was another

contribution to the 'Dealing with Divorce' series in *The Tablet*. It explores the implications of the 'dying and rising' paradigm for the 'failure' experience of marriage breakdown and the 'new life' which some divorcees experience in a second marriage.

6. Margaret A. Farley, 'Divorce, Remarriage and Pastoral Practice', in Charles Curran (ed.), *Moral Theology: Challenge for the Future. Essays in honour of Richard A. McCormick*, (Paulist Press, 1990), pp. 226–239. The writer has published a major work on the notion of commitment, *Personal Commitments: Beginning, Keeping, Changing*, (San Francisco: Harper & Row, 1986). In these pages she wrestles with the difficult question of how a second marriage after divorce can in any way be reconciled with the life-long commitment made by a person in their marriage vows.

7. Anne Thurston, 'Living with Ambiguity', in *Doctrine and Life*, 1994, pp. 537–542. This article gives readers an opportunity to listen to the voice of experience. This writer offers a theological reflection on remarriage after divorce in the light of her own experience of being married to a divorced man.

8. John R. Donahue, 'Divorce: New Testament Perspectives', in *The Month*, 1981, pp. 113–120. Some Christians claim that the sayings of Jesus prohibiting divorce and/or remarriage, as found in the New Testament, do not allow the Church any freedom of movement with regard to its pastoral approach to the divorced-remarried. It has no option but to regard their situation as adulterous and, accordingly, refuse them the sacraments until they demonstrate effective repentance by giving up their sinful relationship. Many New Testament scholars do not accept this position. They claim that the case for greater flexibility is actually strengthened by these sayings attributed to Jesus when they are studied and interpreted with the help of the best tools of contemporary New Testament studies. Donahue's article and the following one by Mary Rose D'Angelo provide two excellent presentations of the most up-to-date scholarship on this issue. Because my book does not contain a thorough discussion of these sayings, I thought these articles might be helpful to readers.

9. Mary Rose D'Angelo, 'Remarriage and the Divorce Sayings Attributed to Jesus', in William P. Roberts (ed.), *Divorce and Remarriage: Religious and Psychological Perspectives*, (Sheed & Ward, Kansas City, 1990) pp. 78–106. Mary Rose D'Angelo's

article is rather long for inclusion as it stands. With her permission, I have abbreviated it by omitting her excellent detailed analysis and argumentation in its three main sections. Hence, in each of these sections the reader is led straight to her very thought-provoking and challenging conclusions.

DIVORCE AND REMARRIAGE

Kevin McDonald

The pastoral care of the divorced-remarried is one of the most worrying and difficult tasks facing priests today. The pressing nature of the problem has occasioned a lot of critical reflection both on our current pastoral practice and on the theology of marriage more generally. In this country, the Catholic Church has been aware of important developments in theology and practice in the Church of England, and there has been a lot of useful dialogue between the Churches on the whole matter. One of the most significant British Catholic contributions has been Kevin Kelly's book *Divorce and Second Marriage: Facing the Challenge.*[1] Fr Kelly's book draws on contemporary Anglican thinking, and on the writings of the influential Catholic psychiatrist, Jack Dominian; and his ideas have much in common with recent contributions to the debate from Catholics in the USA. But the book is very much his own, and what gives it unity and focus is his deeply-felt concern for people who are not fully involved in the sacramental life of the Church precisely because they have remarried after divorce. He argues that in the light of our growing understanding of the nature of marriage, there is no reason why the Church should not be able to recognize a second union as a perfectly real and valid Christian marriage. Central to his argument is a specific understanding of what marriage essentially *is*.

In this article I will seek to respond to Fr Kelly's initiative in opening this matter up. I wish to argue that there are important aspects of this question which are not dealt with in the book but which have real bearing on the general philosophy and on the particular conclusions. I would hope, therefore, to widen the context in which the problems of the divorced-remarried should be considered. I find the grounds on which Fr Kelly argues for his position too confined, and his conclusions not justified by them. But it is precisely because I acknowledge that *Divorce and Second*

1 Kevin T. Kelly, *Divorce and Second Marriage: Facing the Challenge*, Collins 1982.

Marriage is a very thoughtful and concerned contribution to this vexed problem that I agreed to give a critical reflection on it.

First, I will consider the place of the institution of marriage in Western society quite generally. Secondly I shall locate the contemporary discussion about marriage in the tradition of sacramental and moral theology.

Marriage and society

Alasdair MacIntyre's book *After Virtue* [2] contains a very power-ful diagnosis of the state of Western society. He takes issue with the theory of justice that has been proposed by the American philosopher John Rawls. Rawls takes it for granted that in our society people have values and ideals that vary: the purpose of his theory of justice is to try to secure a situation in which people are free to pursue their aims and objectives in a way that does not interfere with the freedom of other people to do the same. Rawls's ideas are very much in the spirit of liberal democracy. Indeed, one could regard it as the great achievement of Western society that it allows people to pursue the style of life they want to. MacIntyre's view is that we don't in fact enjoy this kind of freedom, but more importantly, the philosophy that suggests that we do is a formula for disintegration, and that disintegration is well under way. True justice can only come about in so far as people together pursue aims and objectives that are true. A society can only knit together and true social friendship can only be established when people draw together in the pursuit of shared values and shared ideals. The present social set-up in fact denies that there are any objective values and ideals whose pursuit can secure the well-being of society as a whole.

Stanley Hauerwas,[3] an American writer on Christian Ethics, is sympathetic to MacIntyre's views and has noted the place that the institution of marriage occupies in a liberal democracy. There are no universally-held beliefs about what marriage is for; about things like whether or not a couple living together *ought* to get married, whether married people ought always to stay together for life, whether having children is a necessary and integral part

2 Alasdair MacIntyre, *After Virtue*, Duckworth, 1981. cf. John Rawls, *A Theory of Justice*, Clarendon Press, Oxford, 1972.
3 Stanley Hauerwas, *A Community of Character*, University of Notre Dame Press, 1981.

of marriage. People are free to interpret marriage as they wish, and what has happened is that most people's view of marriage is shaped not by any deeply-held and shared convictions about the purpose of life but by the social and economic forces that dominate our lives. We live in a fiercely competitive society, a society that is threatening in all sorts of ways. It is a society in which we are forced to think of ourselves as individuals over against other individuals, and we have no real bond with our fellow citizens. Our local and national communities do not provide us with any real sense of belonging. There are, of course, parts of Europe where ties of blood or religion weld a community together. But as these forces lose their strength, people inevitably become more isolated and lonely. In this situation, marriage has tended to become a 'haven in a heartless world'.[4] It has become the context in which people seek the emotional satisfaction and stability which are necessary for human happiness. When young people grow up and leave home, they will need and seek emotional security, and a surprisingly large number of them still see marriage as the place where it is to be found. So marriage has become the arena for emotional fulfilment and personal happiness: those who marry expect marriage to provide them with those things.

If this is true – and broadly speaking, I think it is – we may start by asking: is this a good reason for getting married? Certainly in the past people have got married for a great variety of reasons. In previous generations marriage was often more about property than about emotional fulfilment, and in the days when children were an investment in the future rather than a financial liability the purpose of marriage must have seemed very different. Today's heightened awareness of the significance and potential of marriage as a personal relationship is clearly an advance. But a problem arises when marriage becomes the context in which one either succeeds or fails in finding happiness. When that is the case, marriage breakdown becomes inevitable and remarriage after divorce becomes a necessary part of life. If a marriage is not meeting someone's need for emotional fulfilment, and if a new relationship opens up that promise to provide it, then remarriage after divorce is the only solution.

In the CMAC bulletin a few years ago,[5] Martin Ward wrote a very perceptive article that pinpointed this problem well. We

4 This is the title of a book by Christopher Lasch quoted by Hauerwas.
5 Martin Ward, *How many of us are really married?* (CMAC) *Bulletin*, 19th January 1979.

have come to accept today a specific ideology of marriage. We put great store on subject-to-subject relationships, and we assess the quality of these relationships on the basis of how people *feel* about one another. A marriage is good or bad depending on the depth of emotional satisfaction experienced within it, and this is most clearly the case in the more developed of the world's economies. His perception is roughly similar to that of Hauerwas: we live in a society where people are isolated and have been manoeuvred into a situation in which we must obtain all our emotional satisfaction from isolated relationships; relationships between two people in which the only bond is how they feel about one another. Martin Ward expresses surprise at the fact that the Church has tended to approve, even baptize this development. And elements of this philosophy have found their way into the Church's nullity procedures. Marriage annulments are given to people who at the time of their marriage were not competent to sustain a marriage. But our understanding of that which has to be sustained has become more sophisticated and has been built up by the kind of personalist thinking I have outlined. Ward remarks:

> I cannot see why we will not eventually adopt a position where the fact that a couple were not able to sustain a relationship will be sufficient evidence to show that they could not.[6]

Our deeper appreciation of personal relationship has greatly enriched both moral theology and Church teaching on marriage. And it is not my intention to underestimate the great emotional fulfilment that some people find in marriage today. But if the Church is to develop its teaching and practice on marriage, it must do so on the basis of a comprehensive and critical grasp of the social context from which the call for those developments is arising. Moreover, when the personal relationship does become the key focus for reflection on the nature of marriage and the ethics of marriage, wider issues are likely to be obscured. And that is my feeling about Fr Kelly's book.

In the first chapter of the book, entitled *A Fresh Look at Marriage and Indissolubility*, he states his view as follows:

> In entering marriage today, a couple are making a greater investment in their personal relationship than was ever done in the past. This is very healthy because the human reality of marriage at the present day

6 Martin Ward, p. 16.

is such that unless the personal relationship is firmly based, there is little hope that the marriage will survive, at least in a form that would be regarded as desirable. It is not realistic to say that contemporary expectations of marriage are too high and that if couples would only lower their sights they would have no problem with their marriage. These expectations do not concern some incidental benefit which they hope to draw from marriage. They touch the very heart of what the couple believe their marriage to be. Consequently, if these expectations are not fulfilled, their marriage is experienced by them as something which does not make sense, as something which is self-contradicting and a lie.[7]

The kernel of Fr Kelly's argument is that marriage is essentially a human reality and if the Church is to respond adequately to the needs of married people she must listen to their testimony about the nature of that human reality. In the past we have tended to see marriage as a contract, a legally binding contract that two people enter into on their wedding day. But the perceptions of married people today do not go along with this. The bond between the two people does not come into being automatically when they marry. It grows gradually in the course of their life together and reaches the point at which they are no longer two individuals but a couple. Indissolubility, therefore, if it is to mean anything at all, is an espect of the human reality of marriage. It is not something that happens automatically with marriage vows. The consequences of this line of thought are far-reaching. Some people, when they marry, commit themselves to what turns out to be an empty shell. They do not grow together in their marriage; indeed, their marriage withers and dies. It is about people in this position that Fr Kelly is concerned: he says that for some people whose marriages break down, a second union does provide all the fulfilment that eluded them in their first marriage. Should not the Church therefore see its way to blessing second marriages, rather than excluding the divorced-remarried from the sacramental life of the Church?

My first difficulty with this way of thinking is that it rather suggests that the integrity of a marriage can be judged by the depth of fulfilment it yields to the couple involved. Surely it is possible to have a perfectly real marriage in which the partners do not particularly find this kind of mutual fulfilment and where their mutual fidelity is differently motivated?

7 Kevin T. Kelly, p. 22.

This bears on my second point which I will make by referring to Fr Kelly's section on the teaching of Jesus on divorce. Fr Kelly does not build up his case for divorce and remarriage on the basis of the 'exception clause' in Matthew's account. Rather, he takes it that Christ's prohibition of divorce was absolute. But he comments:

> Fidelity to the teaching of Jesus does not oblige the Church to remain locked within the thought categories of his time and culture. In fact the Church today can only be truly faithful to his teaching by presenting it enriched by the best insights of our own age and culture.[8]

Fr Kelly fully agrees that life-long fidelity in marriage is both the will of God and the command of Christ. But for some people, a second marriage will in fact turn out to be the context in which they can respond to Christ's call. Now my difficulty here is with the implication that the ideas marshalled in the first part of the book can be taken to constitute the 'best insights of our own age and culture'. I think these ideas need to jostle with a wide range of other ideas. On its own Fr Kelly's reading of the 'human reality' of marriage represents too uncritical an acceptance of a particular ideology of marriage with roots in a particular culture. Certainly the insights that originate in our own culture are indispensable in any discussion of the nature of marriage and for an adequate theology of marriage. But the meeting of culture and tradition is a more complex process than the book suggests, and that meeting must involve openness to the Word as it transcends culture and challenges it.

Marriage and theology

One of the Anglican reports on marriage contains the following proposition:

> There is no such entity as Christian marriage, except in the sense of the marriage of a Christian man and woman.[9]

But in Catholic theology, marriage is a sacrament, and in the celebration of the sacrament of matrimony the true nature and meaning of every marriage is preached and revealed. The Council's decree on the Church saw the Church as the primordial sacrament:

8 Kevin. T. Kelly, pp. 57–58.
9 *Marriage, Divorce and the Church*, London SPCK, 1971, p. 14.

The Church is the sacrament or instrumental sign of intimate union with God, and of unity for the whole human race.[10]

In the Church, the truth about the world, about human community, and about the future is celebrated and revealed. All men are called to make this truth their own. The sacraments are not simply God's blessing on the various phases or areas of human life. The eucharist is not a divine blessing on a human meal. Rather, within the eucharist we may discover the truth about all the sharing and coming together that make up our lives. The same is true of marriage.

In the context of a very illuminating analysis of the Christian understanding of the nature of time, Hans Urs Von Balthasar considers the place of marriage in 'Christ's mode of time':

> The sacrament of marriage is not some sort of supernatural blessing on a 'natural institution'; rather, it contains within itself the true meaning, the true substance of marriage, made living by Christ himself as the subsistent covenant; and this reality of marriage draws men into that relationship between the Lord and his Church which is the foundation and justification of every marriage.[11]

This is important when we are wondering how to understand the true nature of marriage. Our starting point for understanding anything at all must be experience enlightened by the understanding that is bestowed in prayer, in the sacraments, and in the preaching of the Word of God. The theology of marriage, like all theology has taken shape through sustained reflection on the mystery of Christ. And the fruit of that reflection has been the conviction and teaching that it is through their life-long commitment to one another that married people grow into Christ. Marriage becomes the context in which people may give themselves to Christ in total fidelity.

In a very crisp analysis of the problem in hand, Oliver O'Donovan sounds a salutary note that clarifies what marriage must be in the life of a Christian. He compares the vocation to marriage with the vocation to singleness:

> Singleness, the ascetic vocation, *confronts* the pains of loneliness, directly, welcoming and exploiting the eschatological possibilities for freer service of the Lord . . . Marriage on the other hand *contains* the sufferings that are likely to arise in the course of a long relationship by forging, from the joy and delight that marks the beginning of it, a

10 *Lumen Gentium, 1.*
11 Hans Urs Von Balthasar, *A Theology of History*, Sheed and Ward, 1963, p. 93.

bond of loyalty which will hold firm in the face of them. As it were, marriage takes precautionary action against suffering in the future, while singleness goes onto the offensive against suffering in the present.[12]

So the decision to marry is a ratification and a deepening of the decision of faith. It involves a readiness to die and rise with Christ in the context of a life-long relationship with another person. So marriage is not just a human reality, particularly if by that we mean a reality whose nature and purpose can be adequately defined by our present experience of it. Those who marry in the Lord are taken into the mystery of Christ, and that mystery is precisely something more than the insights and feelings of the present moment. I do not wish to draw any simplistic moral or ethical conclusions from these theological premises. What I do say is that this level of reflection must form a critical part of the basis on which moral arguments and pastoral practice are built.

Marriage and morality

Fr Kelly is fully aware of the evil of divorce and makes the very fair point that no one is more aware of the evil of divorce than those who have been through the trauma of divorce themselves. Moreover those who remarry after divorce often do so in search of that precious gift of life-long fidelity that eluded them in their first union:

> When a second marriage does happen, it must surely be God's healing touch which is being experienced, since all genuine healing comes from him. Someone who was lost has now found himself. The Christian is called to rejoice at this, rather than resent it after the manner of the elder brother.[13]

The justification of a second marriage, then, lies with the happiness and well-being it restores to someone who has become isolated and alone through divorce. While this may well be a true record of people's experience, it needs to be seen both in the context of the theological vision I have outlined, and in the context of Christian teaching on sexuality and chastity. As I have said, the theology of marriage has grown up through reflection

12 Oliver O'Donovan, *Marriage and Permanence*, Grove Booklets on Ethics no. 26, p. 15.
13 Kevin T. Kelly, p. 40.

on the mystery of Christ. Within that reflection there has been a growing perception of the moral dimension of Christian marriage. In the Latin tradition the most significant development has been the conviction and teaching that a consummated sacramental marriage demands unconditional life-long fidelity.

Karl Lehmann has said about this:

> It is hardly possible to overestimate the human and religious importance of this victory of the principle of unconditional fidelity in marriage as something that has to be carried out in real life.[14]

St Augustine defined the three goods of marriage as *fides, proles* and *sacramentum*: fidelity, offspring, and sacrament. This account of the three 'goods' of marriage, or three reasons for marriage was the fruit of a rational analysis of marriage conducted in the light of the gospel. And this reflection has continued within the Church. Partly because of the influence of St Augustine, there has been a tendency to focus on procreation as being the true reason for marriage. In this century the Church has moved clearly, if rather laboriously, beyond this and in *Humanae Vitae* we find an affirmation of the deep value of the union of husband and wife:

> By means of the reciprocal personal gift of self, proper and exclusive to them, husband and wife tend towards the communion of their beings in view of mutual personal perfection, to collaborate with God in the generation and education of new lives.[15]

The good of offspring and the good of the union of husband and wife are placed side by side by *Humanae Vitae*.

For an elucidation of what has been established in Christian reflection on the moral dimension of marriage, we may draw on the present Pope's book *Love and Responsibility*.[16] His approach is specifically personalist, but it is a personalism coherent with traditional conceptions of marriage and chastity. In this book, first published in 1960, the Pope argues that true love between people must be governed by the 'personalist norm'. This means that I may never see another person as a *means* to my happiness. To think in that way inevitably (albeit unconsciously) reduces the other person to something I use. Marriage must be based on a

---

14 Karl Lehmann, 'Indissolubility of Marriage and Pastoral Care of the Divorced who Remarry', *International Catholic Review*, July/August 1972, p. 244. This article is also contained in a useful collection entitled *Ministering to the Divorced Catholic*, ed. James J. Young, Paulist Press, 1979.

15 *Humanae Vitae*, CTS, p. 8.

16 Karol Wojtyla, *Love and Responsibility*, Collins, Fount Paperbacks, 1982.

shared choice of a common aim and that common aim must be something that is good in itself (in classical terms, *bonum honestum*) and not simply something that is good for me (in classical terms, *bonum utile*). The common aim in marriage must be a shared life and the procreation that may be the fruit of that shared life. The pursuit of a common aim brings into being a type of reciprocity which is the true basis of marriage and it necessarily eliminates the possibility of utilitarianism, that is, of using or discarding another person.

The conclusion, of course, is that divorce and remarriage are symptoms of a utilitarian attitude towards the person. Clearly, this is a way of thinking that runs counter to a good deal of contemporary moral philosophy. But it is also a way of thinking that matches the theological vision of marriage that I presented earlier. Offspring and union are goods that are *objective*, and it is by choosing them that we choose to be drawn into the mystery of Christ. Someone who chooses to marry is choosing the framework in which they are to enter into Christ's death and resurrection. So marriage is a calling, a vocation, and this vision provides key elements of an answer to Stanley Hauerwas's statement of the question confronting society today: why marry at all? The fact that no terribly clear answer to that question is available to our society lies at the root of a good deal of its sexual and marital problems. This account of marriage puts it in the context of a life of unconditional love of God and neighbour. And that context is the source of the mosaic of values and beliefs which provide the true basis and justification for every marriage, every family and every community.

Conclusion

Fr Kelly's book is subtitled *Facing the Challenge*. In the book he opens up the whole problem of the divorced-remarried and confronts the issues head on. Throughout he is sensitively aware of the tension that exists between upholding the value of life-long fidelity on the one hand, and a realistic pastoral practice on the other. That tension is inevitable and can never be resolved entirely. I would maintain that for the Church to bless the re-marriage of divorced people would be to resolve the tension at the wrong point. In terms of the total mission of the Church in the world, it would constitute a breakdown of teaching and of witness. So how is the Church to address itself to the problem? Many of the people who are divorced and remarried are the victims of circumstances; many more are victims of the moral vacuum in modern society. Many Catholics do not feel part of a community that can give shape and direction to their lives, though the challenge of the gospel is precisely a challenge to a community. Fr Kelly analyses the question of allowing divorced people who have remarried outside the Church to receive the sacraments. As he rightly points out, it is possible to be open to this without going along with his main thesis about the nature of marriage. Sacraments for the divorced-remarried raises its own set of questions: the difference between human disorder and human guilt, scandal and Church order, the tension between mercy and judgment, and what it means to belong to the Church. I believe that some resolution of the tension between upholding indissolubility and pastoral care of the divorced-remarried is most likely to issue from deeper exploration of these questions. The tension between mercy and judgment is a tension that exists in the Word of God itself. Our problem is that many priests feel unable accurately to mediate that tension within the discipline of ministry that is available to them at the moment.

(Kevin McDonald, 'Divorce and Remarriage',
Clergy Review, 1983, pp. 193–198)

MARRIAGE IN CANON LAW

Ladislas Örsy

Question 13: Could persons living in irregular marriages be admitted into eucharistic communion?

The terms of the question should be clarified. Clearly, we are speaking of Catholics, otherwise in communion with the church. A marriage could be irregular for several reasons; the point here being that it cannot be rectified in canon law, in most cases, because there has been a previous marriage that remains valid. Eucharistic communion here means the reception of the eucharist, which is the fullness of communion in the Christian church.

It seems not, *videtur quod non*: The International Theological Commission summed up the arguments against it in their Statement on Marriage, 1977:

> The incompatibility of the state of remarried divorced persons with the precept and mystery of the paschal love of the Lord makes it impossible for these people to receive the sign of unity with Christ in the Eucharist. Access to eucharistic communion can only come through penance, which implies detestation of the sin committed and the firm purpose of not sinning again. (5.2; *see* in CPM, p. 32)

This seemingly severe position, however, is further qualified in the same statement:

> They are not dispensed from the numerous obligations stemming from baptism, especially the duty of providing for the Christian education of their children. The paths of Christian prayer, both public and private, penance, and certain apostolic activities remain open to them. (5.4; CPM, p. 32)

John Paul II in his Apostolic Exhortation *Familiaris Consortio* upheld the prohibition:

> ... the Church insists on the custom, rooted in the very Sacred Scriptures, not to admit to the eucharistic communion those faithful who after divorce entered into a new marriage. In fact, they impede themselves, because their state and their condition of life are objectively

opposed to that union of love between Christ and the Church that is signified and made present by the eucharist. There is also a particular pastoral reason: if such persons were admitted to the eucharist, the faithful would be misled and confused about the doctrine of the Church concerning the indissolubility of marriage. (84: AAS 74 (1982) pp. 185–186)

He, too, however, qualified his statement:

Together with the Synod we strongly exhort the pastors and the whole community of the faithful to help those who failed through divorce: to be careful with solicitous charity not to regard them as separated from the church because they [*the divorced*] can, even must, as baptized participate in its life. Moreover, they should be exhorted to hear the Word of God, to be present at the sacrifice of the mass, to persevere in prayer, to help the charitable works and the under-takings of the community for justice, to instruct their children in the Christian faith, to cultivate the spirit and the works of penance, to implore thus the race of God every day. (*Ibid.*, p. 185)

The two documents are clearly not on the same level; one is a statement issued by a group of theologians with no formal authority, the other is an apostolic exhortation by the pope who has authority. The form he has chosen for his document has its own theological significance: it is an exhortation. There is no doubt, however, that the position taken by the commission and the pope are virtually identical.

From a theological point of view both see the divorced and remarried as constituting a special group in the Church, with their own rather well defined status. They are not separated; therefore they are in communion. Their communion appears as full, except for the actual reception of the eucharist, although they are entitled to be present at its celebration. They are bound by their baptismal promises, and they are exhorted to share in the prayer life and the charitable works of the community.

This status of the divorced and remarried appears new and unusual. It would be difficult to find a precedent for a group of faithful to be invited to participate in the devotional, charitable, even apostolic life of the Church and at the same time to be barred from the reception of the eucharist because they are public sinners. Further, ordinarily we assume that the gift of life received at baptism must be nourished by the eucharist; now this group of persons is called to lead a full Christian life in every way, but without the strength that normally is given through the eucharist.

Further, again and again it is hinted that, once repentant, the grace of God may be with such persons. If that is true, they can hardly be stubborn sinners who do not want to mend their ways.

Clearly, the two documents testify that the Church is moving away from a severe and rigid stance, judging the divorced and remarried as public sinners, and is moving toward appreciating them, provided they are of contrite heart, as recipients of God's grace. The very content of the documents indicates that we are in the midst of a development that has not reached its final goal yet. The status of such a couple, participating in everything in the life of the community, except in the reception of the eucharist, appears so anomalous that one wonders if it could be sustained for any length of time, without causing serious tensions to both the persons involved and the community.

A seemingly obvious advice to remedy this situation is sometimes given: the couple should separate, and then they will be able to receive the eucharist.

In some cases, however, a genuine conflict-of-duties situation may have developed. From the second marriage children may have been born; children who have a natural right to be educated, not just in the abstract, but in a warm and loving home. Such education cannot be accomplished without the loving union of the parents. There is just too much evidence to show what happens to children of broken homes. So, the parents may have a duty to stay together for the sake of the children.

An answer to this problem can also be found in manuals of moral theology and canon law: the parents should commit themselves to live as brother and sister. A thoughtful psychologist, however, is likely to find fault with this answer; he will point out that the truth is different: they are not brother and sister, and nature does not tolerate false pretences. The natural dynamics, physical and psychological, between a brother and sister are unique and different from any other relationship between a man and a woman.

The authors who advocate this solution are simply using a euphemism to say that a couple should commit themselves not to have sexual relations. But then logically, if they are not married, they should not be allowed to enjoy any *consortium* either; after all consortium and procreation together are the specific ends of marriage, and of marriage only. How could a couple be allowed to have one part of true marriage, the *consortium*, but not the other, the procreation? After all, we are consistently told that sexual union should be an expression of a deeper spiritual union. There seems to be a built-in logical inconsistency in the so-called brother-and-sister solution, apart from all the problems that it may cause psychologically to those involved.

There are therefore arguments to the contrary, *sed contra est*:

Weighing the complex problems involved, a significant number of scholars reached the conclusion that there are circumstances in which divorced and remarried persons could and should be admitted to the eucharist. Although such writings appeared in many countries, the arguments and conditions were perhaps most carefully presented by a number of German theologians, especially by Walter Kasper (University of Tübingen), Franz Böckle (University of Bonn), and Joseph Ratzinger (*then*, University of Regensburg). Their positions are virtually identical; none of them advocates a wholesale pardon, all of them plead for granting communion to individual couples provided that they are of contrite heart.

Böckle states this succinctly in the form of a thesis:

> The eucharistic communion must not and should not be denied to those who, after having lived in a marriage that legally and sacramentally appears valid, divorced, and now live in a second marital union, provided they have repented of their fault and in a spirit of faith they proved themselves and are doing what they can by way of reparation.[23]

Ratzinger describes the conditions, and does it in the context of ancient traditions:

> The demand that a second marriage must prove itself over a longer period as the source of [*container of*] genuine moral values, and that it must be lived in the spirit of faith, corresponds factually to that type of indulgence [*leniency*] that can be found in Basil's teaching; there it is stated that after a longer penance, communion can be given to a *digamus* (= to someone living in a second marriage), without the suspension of the second marriage; this in confidence in God's mercy who does not leave penance without an answer. Whenever in a second marriage moral obligations have arisen toward the children, toward the family and toward the woman, and no similar obligations

23 Franz Böckle, 'Die gescheiterte Ehe,' in *Ehe und Ehescheidung* (München: Kösel, 1972), p. 130.

from the first marriage exist; whenever also the giving up of the second marriage is not permissible [*not fitting*] on moral grounds, and continence does not appear as a real possibility in the practical order (*magnorum est*, says Gregory II [*that is, it is beyond the ordinary strength of the parties*]); it seems that the granting of full communion, after a time of probation, is nothing less than just, and is fully in harmony with our ecclesiastical traditions. The concession of communion in such a case cannot depend on an act that would be either immoral or factually impossible.[24]

The same conditions can be put more systematically:

1 the previous marriage cannot be retrieved any more;
2 the present invalid union produced and supports important human values which would be destroyed by separation;
3 the couple has repented and shown visible signs of 'conversion' for a fairly long time;
4 perpetual abstinence is not a practical possibility;
5 the couple has shown willingness to participate in the life of the Christian community; to which one more condition should be added:
6 the community is properly instructed to receive the couple without being unduly disturbed or confused about the evangelical precept of life-long fidelity.

So much for the stance of these theologians. But how do they support their proposal?

All of them state that what they propose in no way conflicts with the doctrine of indissolubility. On that point they stand firm. Rather, they all make an appeal to a radical power in the Church that can go beyond the ordinary rules and can provide forgiveness and healing when most needed. Kasper puts it in this way:

> A broken marriage is not simply cancelled out. It continues to exist, even though it can be compared with a ruin. It is therefore not possible to replace it with a second marriage equal to the first. What is possible, however, and in many cases necessary for survival, is some kind of emergency accommodation. This image would seem to be in accordance with the way in which God acts in the history of human salvation. He often writes straight on crooked lines.[25]

24 Joseph Ratzinger, 'Zur Frage nach der Unauflösigkeit der Ehe,' in *Ehe und Ehescheidung* (München: Kösel, 1972), p. 55.
25 Walter Kasper *Theology of Christian Marriage* (New York: Seabury, 1980), pp. 67–68.

Ratzinger is more mindful to put his proposed solution into the context of our traditions:

> The anathema [*of the Council of Trent*] against a teaching that claims that foundational structures [*forms*] in the church are erroneous or that they are only reformable customs remains binding with its full strength. Marriage is a sacrament; it consists of an unbreakable structure, created by a firm decision. But this should not exclude the grant of ecclesial communion to those persons who acknowledge this teaching as a principle of life but find themselves in an emergency situation of a specific kind, in which they have a particular need to be in communion with the body of the Lord.[26]

These approaches are very close to the Eastern practice of *oiko-nomia*, a mysterious and undefinable power given by Christ to his Church, which empowers it to heal and redress a situation that cannot be helped in any other way.

An Eastern theologian would prefer to rest the issue there and not to inquire any further. The Western mind, however, being much more analytically inclined, will want to know the nature of the second union: is it a marriage? Could it be a sacramental marriage?

There is no way of answering such questions with precision in our present state of knowledge; nor is it necessary to answer them before action can be taken. Many times in history the Church has taken positions relying on its own grace-filled instinct; the explanations arrived later, sometimes centuries later. This is a sound enough position.[27]

(Ladislas Örsy, *Marriage in Canon Law*, Michael Glazier, Delaware, 1986, pp. 288–294)

---

26 Joseph Ratzinger, *ibid.*, pp. 55–56
27 Nonetheless, a search for some explanation can be attempted, perhaps by simply raising a few questions.

   Is it conceivable that after human sinfulness destroyed a union destined to be permanent in the plan of God, the Church can accept the fact of failure (as God has accepted the Fall) and out of the power given to it by Christ, authorize a new beginning? (Tibor Horvath, a Canadian theologian, holds this view, noting that before the second union can be allowed, serious penance must be done.)

   Is it conceivable that after the first marriage became irretrievably lost, its capacity to be a sign of the union of Christ to his Church is lost as well? Ordinarily a sign must operate in the concrete order, it must be real and not nominal; it must be addressed to a determined public, which should be able to read it. But a lost marriage speaks to no one, the union is purely nominal and so is the sign; no one can read its meaning. (Horvath draws a comparison between the eucharist and marriage: if the eucharistic symbols, the bread and the wine, are destroyed, there is no eucharist anymore; if there is no unity between the man and woman, the sign is destroyed, therefore, there cannot be any marriage either.)

Is it conceivable that after a consummated sacramental marriage has been destroyed a non-sacramental marriage could come into existence? (There have been speculations in earlier times that when the nuptial blessing was not given, as in the case of a second marriage after the death of the first partner, the second marriage was natural and not sacramental.

Such questions are, of course, not affirmations, no less than the questions of Thomas Aquinas above each chapter of his *Summa* are affirmations. The mark of good research is that in the beginning it abounds in questions, until gradually the bad ones are discarded and the few that remain lead to the right answers. But how can a question be proved bad, unless it is raised and examined?

THE INTERNAL FORUM

Theodore Davey

In 1973 the then prefect of the Congregation for the Doctrine of the Faith, Cardinal Seper, issued a statement which was highly critical, to say the least, of 'new opinions which either deny or attempt to call into doubt the teaching of the magisterium of the Church on the indissolubility of marriage'. It is not my recollection of the 1970s that the venerable tradition of the Church with regard to the permanence of marriage was under serious attack from any quarter, be it from the magisterium of the bishops or that of the theologians. What was happening, however, was the emergence of a pastoral problem of considerable magnitude, marital breakdown, affecting unbelievers and believers alike throughout the Western world.

The interesting thing about Cardinal Seper's letter, though, was the final paragraph, which addressed the pastoral problem of divorced and remarried Catholics:

> In regard to admission to the Sacraments, the Ordinaries [bishops] are asked on the one hand to stress observance of current discipline and, on the other hand, to take care that the pastors of souls exercise special care to seek out those who are living in an irregular union by applying to the solution of such cases, in addition to other right means, the Church's approved practice in the internal forum.

This final remark about an approved practice in the internal forum was somewhat perplexing, since few bishops at that time seem to have realized such a practice existed. What was clear, however, was that the use of the internal forum was to enable people who were divorced and remarried to receive the sacraments – primarily Reconciliation and the Eucharist – again. It was not concerned, nor could it be, with any formal or canonical recognition of the second marriage.

On behalf of the American hierarchy, Archbishop Bernardin of Cincinnati wrote to Rome in December 1974, asking what the approved practice was. The secretary of the Congregation for the

Doctrine of the Faith, Archbishop Hamer, replied three months later in the following terms:

> I would like to state now that this phrase must be understood in the context of traditional moral theology. These couples may be allowed to receive the sacraments on two conditions, that they try to live according to the demands of Christian moral principles and that they receive the sacraments in churches in which they are not known so that they will not create any scandal.

This was a very reasonable reply to a complex and fast growing problem, bringing in, so it seems to me, the ministry of the confessor as a valuable source of practical theology, and at the same time pointing out the very real risk of scandal in its theological sense: that the People of God might be led to conclude that the Church was weakening in its commitment to the evangelical teaching with regard to permanence of marriage.

That exchange of correspondence took place over fifteen years ago, and while the rate of marital breakdown, from which Christians are not exempt, has continued unabated, another factor has intervened to make the problem even more acute. This springs from the overwhelming success of a pastoral initiative begun slowly in the years following the Second Vatican Council and known by the ugly acronym RCIA – the Rite of Christian Initiation of Adults, a process of gradual reception into the Church over a period of many months, which has now become mandatory in every parish.

More and more of the people who are seeking admission into the Church come from a society where divorce and remarriage are the acceptable norm. They are often totally unaware of divorce and remarriage as possible obstacles to full Eucharistic communion with the Church, and, as many priests and catechists will confirm, very often it has been the trauma of divorce and a successful second marriage that has brought them to seek admission. So, faced with the dilemma of either receiving people into the Church, and immediately forbidding them the Eucharist, or refusing to allow them to enter the Church at all, many priests have expressed renewed interest in the possibility of dealing with this serious pastoral problem by means of 'the Church's approved practice in the internal forum'.

When we use the word 'forum' in reference to the Church, we are alluding to the ambit within which the Church exercises her saving, and in this context, her healing ministry. And we are considering the individual approaching God in the privacy and depth of conscience, or that same individual relating to God publicly as a member of the Church.

The exercise of that ministry, as it has evolved down the centuries, has taken either of two forms, public (or external), private (or internal). When a bishop administers his diocese by ordaining priests and appointing them to parishes, he is acting, as the canonists say, in the external forum. Two believers marrying in the presence of the priest and the community make a statement in the external forum. When however, a person makes manifestation of conscience – known to God alone – and receives absolution and healing from the confessor, then it is obvious that the 'power of the keys' is being used privately – in the internal forum. When a mother vows to God to make a pilgrimage to Lourdes in thanksgiving for the recovery of her sick child she is acting in the internal forum – as is a parishioner consulting the parish priest privately about a marriage problem.

The distinction, however, does not imply that only the internal forum has effects in conscience. In the case of a man and woman committing themselves to each other for life before the Church, they are surely bound in conscience, and not just subject to the legal requirements of the canon law.

Ministry in the internal forum is exercised directly and immediately in favour of individual persons, or, as the final canon (1752) of the 1983 code puts it, 'having before one's eyes the salvation of souls, which is always the supreme law of the Church'. Ministry in the external forum is exercised directly and immediately for the good of the Christian community as a whole; it is the ambit of the common good. But another factor emerges, namely the need to keep the two forums distinct, in the sense that what is said and done in the internal forum will not be recognized in the external forum. That is not to say that the magisterium necessarily disapproves of the course of action a priest takes in the internal forum, but simply that a bishop may not think such a course of action suitable or pastorally beneficial to be given public approval in the external forum.

As regards the Church's 'approved practice', two distinct situations present themselves. First, that of the person who, although he has gone through an apparently valid wedding ceremony, is convinced that factually it never was a marriage in any human or Christian sense of that term. Pope John Paul II refers to this in his Exhortation on the Christian Family (1981):

'There are those who have entered into a second union for the sake of the children's upbringing, and who are sometimes subjectively certain in conscience that their previous and irreparably destroyed marriage had never been valid'.

But that person may not be able to go to a marriage tribunal for a variety of reasons. For example, he has no witnesses to the fact, which the external forum rightly insists upon; or he is unwilling to involve his former spouse for what he considers serious reasons; or it is morally impossible for him to begin what he considers a most formidable undertaking; or the marriage tribunal is inoperative in his diocese. For any or several of these perfectly sound reasons, seeking a declaration of nullity in the external or public ambit of the Church is not open to him.

The second situation commonly experienced today is that of the person who, unlike the first, is convinced of the validity of the previous marriage, and could not in conscience state it was otherwise. Again the Pope's comment is apposite: 'Pastors must know that, for the sake of truth, they are obliged to exercise careful discernment of situations. There is in fact a difference between those who have sincerely tried to save their first marriage and have been unjustly abandoned, and those who through their own grave fault have destroyed a canonically valid marriage'.

In either of these cases the confessor, or preferably the parish priest, is consulted privately about the possibility of the parishioner receiving the sacraments. To help such a decision, an evolving pastoral practice has elaborated several guidelines in this matter:

- there is no possibility of reconciliation between the spouses since the first marriage has irreparably broken down;
- acknowledgement of any responsibility for the failure of the first union, and where necessary reparation is made;
- the second marriage has been in existence for some time, morally speaking it is impossible to separate because of new obligations arising from the second union, and the partners to it are genuinely doing their best to live an authentic Christian life;
- such Eucharistic sharing should in no way be seen as a questioning of the teaching on indissolubility, and by preaching and teaching, such a practice must be regarded as entirely exceptional.

I mentioned above that the parish priest should be consulted, not only because of his general responsibility for the spiritual and sacramental life of his parish, but also because he will be better placed to make judgements about scandal were some divorced and re-married parishioners admitted to the Eucharist. In a curious reverse way it often happens that scandal does arise in a parish where the re-married are forbidden the Eucharist.

It should be noted that among the pastoral theologians who have helped to formulate these norms by their writing, the most distinguished is the present prefect of the Congregation for the Doctrine of the Faith, Cardinal Ratzinger.

(Theodore Davey, 'The Internal Forum',
The Tablet, 27 July 1991, pp. 905–906)

LETTER TO *THE TABLET*

Cardinal Joseph Ratzinger

Sir: Please permit me to correct two misrepresentations of my positions which appeared in your publication.

The first concerns the doctrine of papal primacy . . . The second misrepresentation concerns the problem of divorce and remarriage as presented by Theodore Davey in the issue of 27 July 1991. Fr Davey cites me as having contributed to the formulation of 'norms' of 'an evolving pastoral practice' whose application could permit divorced and remarried Catholics to receive the sacraments. The 'norms' Fr Davey refers to, accurately recounted in themselves, are not norms in any official sense at all. They formed part of a *suggestion* ('*Vorschlag*') I made as a theologian in 1972.[4] Their implementation in pastoral practice would of course necessarily depend on their corroboration by an official act of the magisterium to whose judgment I would submit. Incidentally, unlike Fr Davey, as a Catholic theologian I could never subscribe to the notion of dual magisteria, 'the magisterium of the bishops or that of the theologians' (Davey, p. 905).

Now *the* magisterium subsequently spoke decisively on this question in the person of the present Holy Father in *Familiaris Consortio*.[5] Since the *Tablet* series on divorce nowhere cites the pertinent passage, please allow me to (no. 84):

> . . . the Church reaffirms her practice, which is based upon Sacred Scripture, of not admitting to Eucharistic Communion divorced persons who have remarried. They are unable to be admitted thereto from the fact that their state and condition of life objectively contradict that union of love between Christ and the Church which is signified and effected by the Eucharist. Besides this, there is another special pastoral reason: if these people were admitted to the Eucharist, the faithful would be led into error and confusion regarding the Church's teaching about the indissolubility of marriage.

There are other errors and distortions in Fr Davey's position amounting to an all but rhetorical repudiation of the doctrine of the indissolubility of marriage. These would require too much space for me to deal with here. I would, however, at least like to correct Davey's misinterpretation of statements of Cardinal Seper and Archbishop, now Cardinal, Hamer since they concern my predecessors at the Congregation for the Doctrine of the Faith.

First, Cardinal Seper's mention in his letter of 1973 of the 'approved practice in the internal forum' which Fr Davey cites was not referring to the so-called internal forum solution which properly understood concerns a marriage known with certainty to be invalid but which cannot be shown to be such to a marriage tribunal because of a lack of admissible proof. Cardinal Seper for his part was not addressing the question of the validity of a prior marriage, but rather the possibility of allowing persons in a second, invalid marriage to return to the sacraments if, in function of their sincere repentance, they pledge to abstain from sexual relations when there are serious reasons preventing their separation and scandal can be avoided.

By the way, as far as the 'internal forum solution' is concerned as a means for resolving the question of the validity of a prior marriage, the magisterium has not sanctioned its use for a number of reasons, among which is the inherent contradiction of resolving something in the internal forum which by nature also pertains to and has such important consequences for the external forum. Marriage, not a private act, has deep implications of course for both of the spouses and resulting children and also for Christian and civil society. Only the external forum can give real assurance to the petitioner, himself not a disinterested party, that he is not guilty of rationalization. Likewise, only the external forum can address the rights or claims of the other partner of the former union, and, in the case of the tribunal's issuance of a judgment of nullity, make possible entering into a canonically valid, sacramental marriage. I might add, moreover, that the numerous abuses committed under the rubric of the internal forum solution in some countries attest to the practical unworkability of the internal forum solution. It is for reasons such as these that the Church in recent times, most notably in the new Code of Canon Law, has broadened the criteria for the admissibility of testimony and evidence in marriage tribunals so that the need to appeal to an internal forum solution would not arise. Of course in some extremely rare case where appeal to the Church's canonical practice has not availed and a matter of conscience is at stake, recourse can be had to the Sacred Penitentiary.

Finally, Archbishop Hamer's stipulation in his letter of 1975 that divorced and remarried couples, whose first marriages were not declared null and void, could be allowed to receive the sacraments if 'they try to live according to the demands of Christian moral principles' means nothing more again than abstaining, as Pope John Paul II would later write in *Familiaris Consortio*, 'from the acts proper to married couples' (no. 84).

In closing, echoing the words of the International Theological Commission, I would underscore that what is at stake in respect to the teaching of the indissolubility of marriage is nothing less than the Church's fidelity to the radicalism of the Gospel. 'This severity does not derive from a purely disciplinary law or from a type of legalism. It is rather a judgment pronounced by Jesus himself (Mk. 10:6ff.). Understood in this way, this severe norm is a prophetic witness to the irreversible fidelity of love that binds Christ to his Church. It shows also that the spouses' love is incorporated into the very love of Christ (Eph. 5:23–32).'[6]

(Cardinal Joseph Ratzinger 'Letter to *The Tablet*,'
The Tablet, 26 October 1991, p. 1311)

---

4 Cf. *Ehe und Ehescheidung* (Kösel-Verlag, Munich, 1972), pp. 54f. I say there as follows: 'I would like to attempt, with all due caution, to formulate a concrete suggestion which seems to lie within these parameters.'

5 Contrary to what is said in the *Tablet* editorial of 10 August 1991, I made exactly this point in remarks at Cambridge when my earlier position was held up to me.

6 Cf. 'Propositions on the Doctrine of Christian Marriage', in *International Theological Commission: Texts and Documents 1969–1985* (Ignatius Press, San Francisco, 1989), pp. 163–174. Cf. also 'Christological Theses on the Sacrament of Marriage' in the same volume, pp. 175–183.

LOOKING BEYOND FAILURE: LIFE AFTER DIVORCE

Kevin Kelly

The death-resurrection paradigm is central to Christian living. Hence, it must colour a Christian approach to morality. Moral theology needs to be sensitive to all occasions when the death-resurrection paradigm seems to be at work in human life. Moral theology is quite at home, therefore, with our growing understanding that the development of a lasting relationship in marriage seems to follow this death-resurrection paradigm, because of the high degree of dying-to-self on the part of both partners. Our appreciation of what this entails has been heightened since Vatican II encouraged us to think of marriage in personalist rather than contractual terms.

Can moral theology feel equally at home with the suggestion that the death-resurrection paradigm might also be at work in the case of marriage breakdown, with or without subsequent remarriage? It is certainly true that many men and women who have suffered the trauma of marriage breakdown and divorce speak of their experience in terms of dying or bereavement. If this description accurately expresses the experience of marriage breakdown for many couples, there would seem to be something here that moral theology should be paying special attention to. It might be that somewhere in this dying experience of marriage breakdown lies the seed of resurrection and new life. The aim of this article is to offer a few tentative thoughts on this possibility.[1]

Statistics for divorce are often quoted as cause for alarm – one in three marriages break down in the United Kingdom and (West) Germany, one in two in the United States. The conclusion usually drawn from these statistics is that moral standards are declining and that young people today lack any sense of commitment. The validity of that conclusion can at least be questioned. Moral

---

1 Some of the ideas expressed here owe much to two articles in the May 1990 issue of *Concilium* on 'Coping with Failure': Dietmar Mieth, 'The Ethic of Failure and Beginning Again: a forgotten perspective in theological ethics'; and Elisabeth Bleske, 'Failure in the Lifelong Project of Fidelity'.

theology, with its special sensitivity to signs that the death-resurrection paradigm might be operating, needs to look more carefully at what is going on with regard to marriage in contemporary society. It is possible that these 'alarming' statistics are distracting our attention from more hopeful signs with regard to faithful and responsible human sexual relationships.

It could be argued that 'no success without failure' is simply another way of presenting the 'good news' brought by Jesus. One could even paraphrase one of the well-known sayings of Jesus as: 'I have not come to call the successful, but failures.' After all, Jesus kept open table for people whom the religiously successful dismissed as failures. In fact, they flocked to hear him because he brought them the 'good news' that in the eyes of God they were not failures at all.

This 'good news' challenges our normal criteria for success and failure. The story of Jesus is not that of a successful man who dedicated his life to empowering the world's 'failures' to become 'successes' like him. Jesus deliberately chose a path which he knew was doomed to 'failure'. The passion and death of Jesus was not an accident. Jesus purposefully set his face for Jerusalem and even the baffled apostles could see the inevitable outcome of such a decision.

Deliberately to opt for failure seems crazy. Either Jesus had taken leave of his senses or else there was something very mysterious going on. What we view as success is challenged by the freely-accepted, dishonourable death of Jesus. The failure we are dealing with here is the same painful and shattering experience men and women have always found it to be. The 'good news' lies in the realignment of the relationship between failure and success, in which success itself is redefined.

Failure, for all its pain, is no longer seen as the end of the road, a cul-de-sac leading nowhere. Death is no longer the final full-stop in the last chapter of life, after which the story is ended and there is no more to be said. What is being suggested is that the losing of self which is involved in accepting these experiences is the route – the only route – to finding our selves in a fuller and richer way. This is the Gospel meaning of success. What does it profit one to gain the whole world and yet fail to find one's own self?

Dorothy Sölle, reflecting on her own experience of marriage breakdown, comments: 'I noticed that all those who believe limp a little' (quoted by Mieth in *Concilium*). This is a penetrating remark. For me it throws light on something I have noted from my own very limited experience. It is that the common denominator linking many people whom I would consider men and women of deep personal faith is not the style or frequency of their religious practice. Rather it is that they have been through some kind of 'rock-bottom' experience which has left them feeling weak and powerless, their helplessness totally exposed to themselves and others. Whatever complex array of defence and escape mechanisms they had built up as a mask hiding their real selves from others and, even more so, from themselves, had been stripped away. When this rock-bottom experience has been the failure of their marriage, it has shattered whatever semblance of self-esteem they may have had. The person who had made an act of faith in them when they pledged their marriage vows is now saying: 'I no longer believe in you. I can no longer be with you as you now are.'

Stripped naked like this, a person encounters self with no possibility of self-deception. In a very real sense such a person is alone before God. Their instinctive cry is: 'I am worthless. Lord, have mercy on me, a sinner.' Such a cry into the darkness seems to make their antennae specially sensitive to the still voice of the Lord: 'Do not be afraid, have faith. Believe in me – and believe in yourself too.' Paul Tillich describes this experience very power-fully in a celebrated sermon where he speaks of a voice welling up from the depths of a person at such a moment. 'You are accepted', it says. Dorothy Sölle mentions that the Bible passage which brought her light when she was at rock-bottom was the message Paul heard in his time of weakness: 'My grace is enough for you: my power is at its best in weakness'. This led Paul him-self to comment: 'For it is when I am weak that I am strong' (2 Cor. 12:9–10).

It is in her account of the beginnings of her resurrection that Sölle makes her remark about the limping characteristic of believers. It is worth quoting this whole passage as given by Mieth:

> I began to an infinitesimal degree to accept that my husband was going another way, his own way. I had come to the end and God had torn up the first plan. He did not comfort me like a psychologist, who would have explained to me that this was foreseeable. He did not offer me the usual social consolations; he threw me face down on the floor. It was not death that I wanted for myself, nor was it life either. It was another death. Later I noticed that all those who believe limp a

little, like Jacob after he had struggled with the angel. They have already died once. One cannot wish this on anyone. but one cannot attempt to spare them the lesson either. There is as little substitute for the experience of faith as there is for the experience of love.

Faith-provoking failures can come in all shapes and sizes. That is only to be expected, since the unreal selves imprisoning us also come in all shapes and sizes. The question facing moral theologians is whether divorce, with or without remarriage, might be one possible shape of faith-provoking failure. This need not be as shocking as it sounds. After all, a 'successful marriage' does not seem to feature in the New Testament among the basic criteria for Christian living. In fact, a successful marriage could be part of that 'whole world' which it would be pointless to gain if it was to be achieved only through the loss of one's true self.

All human relationships are threatened by the basic selfishness which seems to be so deeply rooted in all of us. This comes out in a whole variety of ways – our tendency to recognize no agendas save our own, our inability to listen to each other, especially at the deeper level of feelings, our refusal to make the kinds of compromise needed if we are to share life together and so on. These general factors no doubt contribute towards the breakdown of many marriages today. So too do the unhealed wounds we bring in from our earlier upbringing and childhood and adolescent experiences. These often set an unconscious agenda for the marriage relationship, with the result that when this agenda is completed, the relationship loses its purpose and becomes destructive rather than life-giving.

It is too easy to blame the increase in marriage breakdown on a decline in moral standards and a lack of commitment among young people today. This is part of the 'good old days' syndrome. It may be true that 'life is not what it used to be', but the change that has taken place is very complex and is falsified by the simplistic 'good old days' comparison.

According to Elisabeth Bleske, the underlying reason why so many marriages are breaking down today is because in present-day Western society excessive demands are being placed on the marriage relationship or its equivalent. Previously a 'good enough' relationship was sufficient to keep a family together. The extended family was always at hand to give support when needed and neighbours provided a natural network of support and advice. With such a support base the 'good-enough' quality in the relationship needed for a marriage to survive could be fairly minimal. Furthermore, it was not emotional security that was looked for in the marriage. It was more a matter of home-and-family security based on functional competence – the father as bread-winner, the mother looking after the home and caring for the children. Hence, the psychological demands on the relationship were not great since the emotional expectations were low.

Today in most places this natural network of support has gone. Neighbourhoods are no longer havens of security. Neighbours are even seen as a threat to one's privacy. Whatever security is on offer tends to be social security. Even if this meets financial, housing and health needs, it does not provide the same personal and emotional support which was bound up with the extended family and the close neighbourhood.

Consequently, couples today look to their marriage relationship for this personal and emotional support. However, as Bleske notes, there are features of contemporary life that affect the marriage relationship in a way that reduces its ability to provide the level of security and support needed. So many couples enter marriage today with expectations that are excessive and unrealistic.

Marriage is expected to be a 'partnership marriage'. This brings all sorts of new demands with it, such as shared decision-making and equal rights in resolving conflicts. Yet very often the partners' upbringing has not equipped them with the skills needed to handle the inter-personal relationships such a partnership marriage involves. The partners are then likely to make excessive emotional demands on each other, suffocating each other's individuality and stifling their psychological growth into fuller maturity. The result is that many marriages turn out to be a life-denying prison sentence rather than a life-enhancing partnership in love. This might seem particularly true of women rather than men, since the healthy development of their personal self-esteem can be seriously arrested or distorted by the second-class image of women they have absorbed from their upbringing and education, as well as from the patronizing attitude of chauvinistic men and the patriarchal structures of society.

Even if a couple are fortunate enough to have a basic grounding in the inter-personal skills needed for their demanding relationship, many features of life today which are extrinsic to their marriage can undermine its success. For those lucky enough to have a job, unsocial work schedules can turn the home into a transit camp; and excessive working hours, or the need for one partner to work away from home, can mean that they do not share sufficient common time and space to develop the depth of personal relationship needed in a partnership marriage. Obversely, too much living on top of one another due to unemployment, or the home-confinement imposed by poverty and ill-health, can deny them the time and space needed to develop their individual selves. If a partnership marriage is to succeed it needs two persons sufficiently confident in their own self-identity.

In his letter *Octogesima Adveniens* Paul VI writes about the role of utopias in social thinking. He notes that utopian thinking can be a form of escapism from wrestling with the nitty-gritty of life in the real world. Nevertheless, he is willing to accept a role for utopian thinking in so far as it serves the positive function of encouraging us to believe that we are capable of greater things than we sometimes give ourselves credit for. Positive utopian thinking encourages us because it is based on the belief that the seeds of growth are already alive within us. It helps us see the positive side of even our most crucifying experiences.

Negative utopian thinking, on the other hand, is destructive. It sets impossible standards before us and hence only serves to further consolidate the negative self-image most of us are prone to. Negative utopian thinking aggravates the failure feeling in us, since its criteria for success cannot be met. It operates judgementally and by way of self-condemnation. As such it is anti-Gospel.

The Christian theology of marriage should be utopian in the positive sense. Sadly, in the practical life of the Church it often operates in a negative way, crushing people through the imposition of standards which have no bearing on the reality of their lives. This is particularly true with regard to the situation of many couples who are now stably settled in a loving and life-giving second marriage after divorce.

Some people would argue that, at a practical level, 'positive' utopian thinking about marriage breakdown operates in the Roman Catholic Church through the nullity procedure. A nullity decision enables the persons involved to feel that their marriage was not a failure since there was no real marriage there in the first place. However, this often runs counter to their own experience. The declaration of nullity does not automatically erase the painful experience they have been through. They also know that the pain has sent shock-waves through the circle of significant persons in their lives – their families, friends and neighbours, not to mention their own children. Whatever may be said in favour of the nullity procedure, it is hardly true to say that it removes the 'failure' dimension from marriage breakdown and divorce.

A theology of marriage and human relationships which is sensitive to the death-resurrection paradigm at work in human affairs should not only be open to the 'signs of the times' at a general level. It should also be able to speak a positive word of hope to men and women who have been through the 'dying' experience of the failure of their marriage relationship. The death-resurrection message that can help to release new life in them is not the deadly reiteration of the bad news that they have failed. To interpret the Gospel in terms of an obligation to remain faithful to a partnership which in reality has ceased to exist is to impose a burden which cannot but dishearten and crush a person. since it is impossible of fulfilment in any meaningful sense. It is refusing to face up to the reality so clearly expressed by Dorothy Sölle: 'I began to an infinitesimal degree to accept that my husband was going another way, his own way. I had come to the end and God had torn up the first plan.'

The painful experience of the failure of some marriages would suggest that a crucial act of faith for a couple can be the moment when they finally commit themselves to leave the false security of a marriage which has in reality been imprisoning and destroying them and take a major step into the unknown. Elisabeth Bleske writes: 'The way of divorce and remarriage . . . can in fact be a bold decision of life and further development.'[2]

The death-resurrection message of the Church is not a consolidation of the experience of failure. Rather it offers a positive interpretation of that negative experience. It could perhaps be paraphrased somewhat along the following lines:

You are shattered by your failure. You may feel worthless. This painful experience might lead you to believe that you are not capable of taking on a commitment of life-long fidelity and sustaining it. Do not believe all that about yourself. The Lord invites you to believe in him and to believe in yourself. You are not alone. He is with you to strengthen you as you continue your journey through life. Arise! Come forth and live. Leave behind your old self, that half-truth you were living. You have

2 Bleske, ibid.

lost that old self and are now en route *towards finding a richer and fuller self.*

Live your new and true life by loving as I have loved you. Have confidence to follow that love wherever it leads you. If your new life turns out to be a life lived in the single state, whether alone or as parent to your children, live it out with complete belief in your own dignity and that of those around you. Live out your singleness as the gift of the richness of yourself to the present and the future. Refuse to let all the love you can share as a single person be devalued by negative utopian thinking. That would turn it into a life-denying noose placed round your neck by the restraining obligation of a partnership which no longer exists.

If your new life eventually leads you to a new life-giving relationship, accept that with gratitude and live it out in faith – faith in yourself, in your partner and in your God who is entrusting his gift of love to you in this new chapter of your life.

(Kevin T. Kelly, 'Looking beyond failure: life after divorce',
The Tablet, 3 August 1991, pp. 935–937)

DIVORCE, REMARRIAGE AND PASTORAL PRACTICE

Margaret A. Farley

Marriage as 'commitment': another try at the impasse?

There are three perspectives from which the absolute indissolubility of sacramental consummated marriages has been and is today understood – juridical, moral, and ontological. When the sacramental dimension of marriage is appealed to as the ultimate ground of indissolubility, it, too, is considered from these three perspectives. The categories here of 'juridical,' 'moral,' and 'ontological' are not completely discrete, nor is their meaning univocal for everyone who uses them.[47] One way to take account of all three perspectives – avoiding in a sense, but perhaps shedding light on, disagreements among those who use them – is to consider the obligation of indissolubility in terms of marriage as a 'commitment.' Everyone, no matter where they are on the spectrum of positions regarding indissolubility, presupposes that marriage entails an initial and ongoing covenant (a concept and term now in favour over the traditional 'contract') to which the parties come in freedom and in which they are bound because of the obligation they have themselves assumed.[48] Indissolubility as a requirement of Christian marriage is part of the content of the marriage commitment, but it also specifies the way in which one is to be committed (that is, unconditionally or with very few conditions). The moral meaning of the marriage commitment

---

47 E.g. Örsy interprets the marital 'bond' as a legal relationship which gives rise to and is characterized by moral obligations, in *Marriage in Canon Law* 202–05, 270–72. McCormick argues against a juridical interpretation of the indissolubility requirement in favour of a moral interpretation, but he clearly does not rule out institutional considerations (at least as a safeguard for the social dimension of marriage). John Paul II offers an ontological perspective on marriage, but in the last analysis this is protected by law.

48 See e.g. *Gaudium et Spes* no. 48; 1983 Code of Canon Law, Canon 1055; McCormick, *Critical Calling*, chap. 13 (McCormick's theological 'adjustments' are in the direction of viewing marriage as a commitment); John Paul II, 'Apostolic Exhortation on the Family,' no. 12; Curran, *Ongoing Revision* p. 106.

bears examination first, and juridical considerations can be incorporated into it.[49]

Like any other explicit, expressed, interpersonal commitment, marriage involves the giving of one's word in a way that gives to another a claim over one's self. It is a promise which, like any other promise, includes an intention regarding future action and a placing of oneself under a moral claim regarding that action. In the case of marriage, the intended action includes interior actions (of respect, love, trust, etc.) and exterior actions (a way of sharing a life together). Marriage, of course, is a mutual commitment – two persons' words given one to the other, two persons yielding and receiving a claim, two persons establishing by their commitments a new form of relationship intended to move into the future.

There are good reasons why marriage involves commitment as such. Love can desire it; experience can show its need. All commitments in the human community imply a state of affairs in which there is doubt about our future actions; they imply the possibility of failure to do in the future what is intended in the present. Commitments are made (claims given, obligations undertaken, bonds embraced) precisely to assure others and to strengthen ourselves – to give assurance that our word will endure and to strengthen ourselves in keeping our word. This is especially true of profound commitments like marriage, where commitment is a way of safeguarding our desire to do what we deeply want to do not only now but in the future. By committing ourselves we give, as it were, a law to ourselves; we bind ourselves by the claim we give to another. A Christian commitment to marry involves a commitment to more than one person.[50] That is, in a marriage not only is a commitment made by each partner to the other, but both partners also commit themselves to God and to a community of persons (to the Church and to society, however that is construed in terms of family, community, and wider society). In each of these directions a word is given, intentions and expectations are clarified, an obligation is undertaken, and a newly qualified relationship is formed.

---

49 The general theory of commitment that follows is based on my analysis in *Personal Commitments: Beginning, Keeping, Changing* (San Francisco: Harper, 1986) esp. chaps 2 and 7.

50 What I say here would, I believe, apply to a great extent to so-called 'natural' marriages as well as Christian marriages.

A marriage commitment is made to persons, but its content includes a commitment to a certain framework of life in relation to persons. While those who marry commit themselves to love one another, they do so (precisely in marrying) by committing themselves to whatever is understood to be the institution, the framework of life, that is marriage – not for its own sake but as the form of their life together.[51] This 'framework' can have different levels of specification. There is a kind of generic understanding of 'marriage' as a social institution that crosses cultures and religions. But 'marriage' will also always have a particular framework in particular societies and religious traditions. Finally, there is a level of framework which is the particular structure of the marriage of two individuals – informed by but not necessarily limited to the institutional frameworks of their own historical context. The commitment to marriage as a framework of life and a way of loving at all of these levels is not necessarily explicit in every marriage, but it is nonetheless there.

In our own culture, and certainly in the Roman Catholic tradition, an intention of permanence in the relationship of marriage is included in marital commitment. Given massive historical changes in social contexts, some of the reasons for incorporating the notion of permanence in the framework of marriage have changed, though many remain the same. The importance of interpersonal reasons has grown, and institutional reasons have receded. Yet there have always been reasons intrinsic to the marital relationship itself and reasons of social utility beyond the relationship. Love itself can want to give its whole future, to bind itself irrevocably to the one loved and to express itself in this way. Some interpreters of the possibilities of human sexuality have also argued that sex is best served by being activated in a context of commitment and of commitment that intends to be permanent.[52] Insofar as marriage is a social institution, permanence can serve the good of children (who need a stable context in which to survive and mature), the general good of society (which depends on the institutions within it for

---

51 Even if the persons marrying wish to resist the cultural forms of marriage as an institution, their understanding of marriage will somehow be influenced by these.

52 See my treatment of this in 'An Ethic for Same-Sex Relations,' in *Challenge to Love*, ed. Robert Nugent (New York: Crossroad, 1983) pp. 103–04. See also Paul Ricoeur, 'Wonder, Eroticism, and Enigma,' in *Sexuality and Identity* ed. H. Ruitenbeck (New York: Delta, 1970) pp. 13–24; and John Paul II, 'Apostolic Exhortation on the Family,' no. 11.

its own stability and growth), and the good of the Church (in which marriage can function as a way of Christian life and a sign of God's presence to all).

If an intention of permanence is intrinsic to the meaning of marriage, and if marriage as a commitment is self-obligating, can it ever be justified to end a marriage short of the death of one's spouse? In other words, can the claim that is given to another in the commitment of marriage ever be released? This is the central moral question for both divorce and remarriage. It is the central moral question even when the context is a Christian sacramental and consummated marriage (though there are complexities here that we must still address).

We are used to acknowledging release from a marriage obligation when it can be determined that some basic flaw marked the original marrying – a flaw in the procedure, or a lack of capacity to commit to marital life on the part of either partner, or a situation of unfreedom. Strictly speaking, however, this kind of release from obligation is not a 'release' but a recognition that no marriage obligation was ever truly undertaken; the marriage did not exist. The much more difficult question is whether or not a truly valid marriage (and even one that is genuinely sacramental and consummated) may no longer bind.

My own position is that a marriage commitment is subject to release on the same ultimate grounds that any extremely serious, nearly unconditional, permanent commitment may cease to bind.[53] That is, an obligation to sustain a marriage ceases when (1) it truly becomes *impossible* to sustain it; (2) the marriage no longer serves the purposes, or has the *raison d'être*, it was meant to have; (3) another obligation comes into *conflict* with, and takes priority over, the marriage commitment. It is a difficult matter to discern when such conditions actually come to be, but that they do and that they can be identified seems to me to be without doubt. Some brief observations about each of these may help to make this clear.

---

53 I do not mean to imply here that there can be no commitments that are absolutely binding (for example, commitments to love God and to love one's neighbour as one's self); but any that are absolutely binding are so because they are not vulnerable to the conditions I outline here. Also, it should be noted – though without opportunity to elaborate – that the unconditionality of the marriage commitment is sufficient to rule out simple release by the agreement of the partners – or, for that matter, by the advent of circumstances other than the ones I identify here.

First, then, when it truly becomes impossible to sustain a marriage relationship, the obligation to do so is released. Impossibility has long been accepted as a general justifying reason for release from the obligation of a promise. The kind of impossibility that is relevant for marriage commitments is not, of course, physical but psychological or moral impossibility. Hence, recognizing it is less like perceiving an incontrovertible fact than like making a judgment or even a decision. Still, examples can be given (of irremediable rupture in a relationship, or utter helplessness in the face of violence, or inability to go on in a relationship that threatens one's very identity as a person); and it seems true that a threshold of real impossibility does exist.

Interestingly, while McCormick and Curran do not construe marital obligation in just the way I have, they both appeal to a kind of impossibility as justification for releasing the requirement of indissolubility. The irretrievable death of a marriage relationship is that point at which, according to McCormick, resuscitation of it is no longer possible; it is at this point that the obligation of indissolubility is discontinued.[54] And Curran argues that precisely where it is impossible 'for pilgrim Christians to live up to the fullness of love' – whether because of the limitation of creation, or sin, or the lack of the fullness of grace – there the obligation of indissolubility meets its limit.[55]

The second condition under which a marriage obligation may no longer bind is when it has lost its point, its *raison d'être*, its own intrinsic meaning. It is meant to serve love for spouses, for family, for society, for God. In order to do this it includes a commitment to a 'framework' for loving, providing love with a way of living. But if the framework becomes a threat to the very

54 McCormick, *Notes on Moral Theology 1965 through 1980*, p. 558; 'Indissolubility and the Right to the Eucharist' 82.

55 Curran, *Ongoing Revision* 105. My way of construing here the justifiable end of a valid marriage can be related to the debate in moral theology about the guilt or innocence of the spouses whose marriage ends. Surely there are instances where the death of a marriage comes through the fault of one or both of the partners (as McCormick insists and Curran allows). When this is the case (though I believe with Curran that it is not always so), it is accurate to say that the fault of the partners brings the marriage to the point of impossibility (the death of 'capacity' in McCormick's terms); but once this has happened, then the marriage obligation as such no longer holds. The end of a marriage comes finally in a *decision* by the spouses (it does not, strictly speaking, as a marriage just 'die'); and it is this decision that can be morally justified and necessary (however unjustified it may have been to reach the point where this decision must be made).

love it is to serve, if it weakens it or contradicts it or blocks it, then the very commitment to love may require that the commitment to marriage as a framework must come to an end. Marriage has multiple meanings and purposes, but all of them may be undermined by the marriage itself (or some of them so gravely as to jeopardize them all). If so, the obligation to the marriage commitment is released.

Closely related to this is the third condition under which a marriage obligation may end – that is, when another obligation conflicts with and takes priority over it. Given the seriousness of the commitment to marriage, there are not many other obligations that can supersede it, for it is made with the kind of unconditionality that is meant to override other claims almost without exception. Still, there are times when other fundamental obligations can take priority – fundamental obligations to God, to children, to society, even to one's spouse (when, for example, commitment to the *well being* of the spouse conflicts with continued commitment to relationship within the framework of marriage). It is also possible for a fundamental obligation to one's own self to justify ending a marriage (not because love of self takes priority over love of another, but because no relationship should be sustained that entails, for example, the complete physical or psychological destruction of a person – including oneself).[56]

When under certain conditions a marriage commitment ceases to bind, are there no obligations (human and Christian) that remain in relation to one's spouse? Clearly there are. Though commitment to a framework for loving (to a relationship as an ongoing marriage) is not completely unconditional or absolute, there are unconditional requirements within it. For example, there is never any justification to stop loving someone altogether – not a marriage partner any more than a stranger or even an enemy. When it is no longer possible or morally good to love someone within the framework of a married love, it is still possible and called for that we love that individual at least with the love that is universally due all persons. It may even be that an obligation continues to a particular love that is faithful to the relationship that once existed. But here we come to the most

56 This does not mean we are not called to great and noble loves that are self-sacrificing in a radical sense. But to sacrifice oneself is morally unjustifiable if it means violating one's very nature as a person.

difficult (for the Roman Catholic tradition) question of all: When the commitment to marriage no longer binds as such, when a true divorce is morally justified,[57] is it also justifiable to remarry? This question will ultimately take us to a consideration of the ontological perspective on divorce and remarriage.

The traditional Roman Catholic position has been and is, as we have seen, that even if an end must come to a marriage in the sense of a separation from shared 'bed and board,' there remains nonetheless an obligation not to remarry. The reason for this lies ultimately in a conviction that the original marriage in some sense still does exist.[58] Against the position I have just been outlining, the issues might be joined in the following ways: (1) Christian sacramental marriage is unlike other commitments in that it is under the command of God and the decree of Jesus Christ; hence, whatever our reasoning about the release of commitments the indissolubility of marriage remains an absolute obligation. (2) The 'framework' or institution of Christian marriage is regulated by the law of the Church. Herein is a special stipulation whereby there will always be a juridical 'remainder' of the covenant of marriage – to the effect that even if every other aspect of a marriage has become impossible (or without meaning or in conflict with greater obligations), it is still possible not to marry anyone else. This much of the marriage commitment still holds. (3) A commitment to marriage, when it is consummated as a sacramental reality, changes the partners in their very being. No longer is their union only a matter of moral or juridical bonding, but an ontological or mystical, indestructible, new reality. However it is lived out – with or without an actually shared life and love – it remains, and it makes impossible another commitment to marriage. All of these arguments have in one form or another been sustained in the tradition, but it is the third that currently is key.

One should not, of course, dismiss the first two of these arguments too quickly, though the limitations of this essay prohibit more than a brief response. Roman Catholic biblical scholars have effectively shown in recent years the exegetical

---

57 By 'true divorce' here I mean as distinguished from an annulment or a separation .

58 There are, of course, other arguments in the theological tradition as well – as e.g. McCormick's argument that even though the first marriage does not continue to exist, considerations of social utility ground a *prima facie* duty not to remarry.

difficulties of using New Testament texts as evidence of an absolute requirement of indissolubility. Indeed, if the various 'sayings of Jesus' show us anything clearly it is that the Christian community from its beginnings believed it was responsible to modify these 'sayings' in their application to different contexts.[59] But even if this were not the case – even if we could find in the biblical traditions a clear command in regard to divorce and remarriage – it is difficult to see how the logic of its application would not require the sort of analysis I have proposed. That is, for example, if something is in fact impossible, it cannot in the concrete be obligating.[60]

On the other hand, should the basis of a prohibition against remarriage be a purely juridical requirement, it can be questioned for its appropriateness to life, and it can also be changed. This is in part why the tradition has not appealed to a purely positive law as the basis for its ban on remarriage after divorce. Similarly, social utility arguments for the positive law are subject to empirical verification and to the challenge that the laws sanction the misuse of individuals for the sake of the common good.

The third argument – that indissolubility finally rests on an ontological union between spouses – is strongly entrenched in the Roman Catholic tradition. It has not gone away by the mere insistence on the part of moral theologians that (a) the bond of marriage is obviously not a reality independent of the relationship of spouses, and (b) insofar as the bond is in the 'objective order' it is only a juridical or a moral reality. These theses serve as correctives to some popular misunderstandings and some unusual claims made here and there in the tradition. But they do not finally meet the position of those who, recognizing quite well that there is no ontological bond separate from the relationship of spouses, nonetheless find in this relationship an indestructible binding of being.

The most important spokesperson for an ontological perspective on the permanence of marriage today is John Paul II. The International Theological Commission serves as a careful

---

59 See Mary Rose D'Angelo, 'Remarriage and the Divorce Sayings Attributed to Jesus,' in William Roberts (Sheed and Ward, 1990); cf. pp. 229–236 below.

60 I am presupposing here the fact that the Roman Catholic tradition, unlike some Christian traditions, has never held that God asks the impossible of human persons.

supporter and explicator of the themes he has so painstakingly developed. The substance of the position, as we have already seen, is this: When two persons marry they yield themselves to one another in a kind of ultimate gift, a gift of self that changes them at the core of their being. By a mutual commitment they become so one with each other that they can no longer be separated. They belong to each other, are joined with each other as 'two in one flesh.'[61] Indissolubility is a consequence as well as an obligation of their mutual exchange. 'For the gift of self, which engages one at the core of the person, transcends any change of mind. It is final.'[62]

Both anthropological and sacramental foundations are offered for this view. Human persons are essentially intersubjective and essentially complementary as male and female.[63] Even their bodies have a 'nuptial meaning' which incarnates the complementarity of their gendered persons and mirrors the relationship between Christ and the Church. When a man and a woman come together in the covenant of marriage they are sealed in the grace of Christ's covenant with the Church – imaging it, empowered by it, one with it. So transformed are they that even though their union is in process, or even though they choose at some point to violate their own new reality, they are nonetheless absolutely joined. 'There is no separation between them in spirit or flesh.'[64] This now is the way of their salvation, since it is thus that their sexual union can be redeemed: In being 'converted' to one another, they transcend the selfishness in their bodily love.[65] So important is their sexual union that 'the sacramental sign is determined, in a sense, by "the language of the body,"'[66] though it is the whole of two lives that become one.

Here is a position with great appeal. It takes account of persons (and not only laws), whole lives (and not only bodies or spirits), the transforming power of grace (and not only a theology of

61 John Paul II, *Original Unity of Man and Woman* (Boston: St. Paul, 1981), pp. 75, 106, 110.
62 International Theological Commission, quoted in Mackin, 'The International Theological Commission and Indissolubility.'
63 John Paul II, ibid.
64 John Paul II, 'The Apostolic Exhortation on the Family' no. 13. John Paul II here quotes Tertullian favourably.
65 John Paul II, *Love and Responsibility* (New York: Farrar, Straus & Giroux, 1981) p. 215.
66 John Paul II, Audience January 5, 1983, quoted from *Osservatore Romano* in *Moral Theology Today: Certitudes and Doubts* (St. Louis: The Pope John Center, 1984) p. 277.

marriage as an image of the relationship between Christ and the Church). Yet the picture it offers of marriage as a bond in being, settled once and for all by freedom and grace, is finally misleading and potentially harmful to individuals and to the Church. There are at least three grave problems with the position which I can only point to here (though they deserve a much fuller response).

First, while this position depends on a description of Christian marriage as a covenant, it takes no account of the limits of human freedom in the making and keeping of commitments. Our power of choice, self-determining in profound ways as it is, is not a power that can finish our future before it comes. Commitment is indeed a way to influence our future; by it we are changed in the present so that a new relationship can have both a history and a future. But even with the power of grace, the bonds that we forge are simply not completely indestructible. And while it is true that freedom may fail only in the sense that we betray, rather than fulfil, our promises, nonetheless it is also true that we can thereby destroy the relationships our promises have made. Moreover, there is surely what philosophers call 'moral luck,' and situations beyond our control that also have the terrible power to undo the projects of our freedom. A view of marriage that borders on a new mysticism can burden marriage more than liberate it, crush it even while it aims to inspire.

Second, the theological anthropology assumed into this position is not benignly separable from its core; and it is an anthropology that has already harmed persons in its consequences for centuries. The complementarity asserted between women and men, structured on a problematic understanding of the relationship between Christ and the Church, perpetuates a cultural 'framework' for marriage that (for all its protests to the contrary) is essentially a union between unequals. Today this framework is more likely to contribute to divorce than to the sustaining of marriage.

Third, the ontological union that this position depicts is itself cause for question, if not alarm. Drawing on the traditional metaphor of 'two in one flesh,' it risks violating the human nature it wants to affirm. The unqualified emphasis on 'total self-giving' yields a view of the fusion of selves that entails loss of autonomy in person and body. Nothing has been more dangerous in marriage, especially for women, than ideals of self-giving that mean loss of identity and self-agency. Efforts to explain the meaning of this in terms of mutuality of giving only make it more problematic, since they are joined still to a view of a husband as active and a wife as passive.[67]

All of this is not to say that there is no ontological union effected in and by marriage. I am not myself inclined to dismiss this possibility – nor even the consequence that some bond remains after the breakdown of a marriage and a justifiable divorce. In fact, when two persons commit themselves to one another in a profound sense, and when they share their lives together for whatever period of time, they *are* somehow changed in their beings. There are many ways in which this change continues – call it a bond or a residue or whatever. What remains after the radical rupture of a marriage may even include a 'bodily' bonding (now experienced positively or negatively) as a result of the sexual relationship that once was a part of the marriage. It may also include a spiritual bonding (now experienced positively or negatively) as a result of months or years of a shared history together. If the marriage resulted in children, their lives will be held together for years in the ongoing project of parenting. In any case, the lives of two persons once married to one another are forever qualified by the experience of that marriage. The depth of what remains admits of degrees, but something remains.

The question becomes, then: Does a remaining bond from a first marriage disallow a second marriage? My own opinion is that it does not (or at least in some situations it does not). Whatever ongoing obligation a residual bond entails, it need not include a prohibition of remarriage. Indeed, it may be that only a view of marriage that sees it primarily within an economy of sexuality and purity can sustain an absolute prohibition of remarriage after a justifiable divorce. The formulations of a position heavily dependent on extrapolations from a metaphor like 'two in one flesh' are at least likely to provide such an inadequate view.

These considerations remain incomplete. That is as it should be while we continue the task of moving beyond an impasse on the issues. Everyone shares a concern to reduce the misery in people's lives and to nurture the possibilities for well-being and love. How theology and law and social responsibility can converge to do these things is part of our question. We know ways in which we cannot go. We cannot solve the suffering of

67 See John Paul II, *Love and Responsibility* p. 275.

divorce by restoring patrilinear societies, by returning women to situations of economic dependence, by using law simply to coerce or condemn, by crushing expectations of worthwhile shared lives. In a culture where the earth quakes beneath us with the massive shifts in social institutions, discernment cannot be easy. What is certain is that the wisdom we need must come from a communal effort. That is why a serious impasse must be broken.

(Margaret A. Farley, 'Divorce, Remarriage and Pastoral Practice', in Charles Curran (ed.), *Moral Theology: Challenge for the Future. Essays in honour of Richard A. McCormick*, Paulist Press, 1990, pp. 226–239)

LIVING WITH AMBIGUITY

Anne Thurston

The pastoral approach of the German bishops is very welcome and signals the right direction for the debate (cf. Section A above). The letter shows sensitivity and realism, it recognizes the complex and different situations within which people find themselves and emphasizes the process of discernment alongside due respect for conscience.

I would like to respond from a different perspective. I should start by declaring my personal interest: seventeen years ago I married my husband, a divorced Anglican with one daughter, in a civil ceremony. Like many other couples in these situations the process of Church annulment was neither appropriate nor desirable. What follows is not a personal history but some comments and questions derived from my experience. It would however be dishonest not to admit that the analysis which follows conceals a great deal of pain, tension and struggle. All human relationships are immensely complex, all human experience is marked by ambiguity; in certain situations the complexities and ambiguities are intensified, this is one such example.

The official position of the Roman Catholic Church is that divorced and re-married people cannot be admitted to the Eucharist because 'their state and position in life objectively contradict that union of love between Christ and the Church which is signified and effected by the Eucharist.' There follows the requirement for careful discernment to distinguish between different situations in order to determine what persons may be readmitted to the Eucharist.

The problem with this approach is that it remains, in principle at least, very much a single issue approach to a moral problem. Behind it lies the good to be protected – the indissolubility of the marriage union. The question which needs to be asked here is whether this is the greatest good? There is a much wider context within which the process of discernment could take place.

Bernard Häring, in his very useful book on this subject *No Way Out*,[1] takes as his first principle the primacy of grace over the law and then looks at the practice of the Eastern Church with its vision of 'the economy of salvation'. Explaining what this means with reference to marriage Häring describes the 'moral death' of a marriage 'Briefly, moral death is accepted as having taken place when there is no longer within this marriage any potential of salvation, indeed when living together in fact works against the salvation and integrity of the other partner' (p. 45). As Häring points out the concept of sacramentality is integrated into 'an all-embracing vision of the total sacramentality of the Christian economy of salvation'. After such a 'death' has occurred there follows a period of mourning and healing before a second union is contemplated. This process remains very close to what people actually experience.

Covenantal process

One of the problems in the practice of the Roman Catholic Church is that the move towards a description of marriage as covenant rather than contract has not sufficiently penetrated pastoral practice when it comes to the breakdown of marriages. The important question is not whether a marriage is validly contracted – and most marriages are – but whether it has developed into 'a human relationship with potential for salvation' in other words whether the contract has become a covenant. This is a process, it happens over time, or not at all.

If we allow for the concept of marriage as process and not 'state' then we can accept that some marriages do not, cannot realize their potential. There are relationships which become destructive for all involved and where without stretching language far beyond what words can bear it is not possible to talk of such marriages as 'symbolizing the union between Christ and the Church'. Paradoxically the second union which is regarded as the sign of contradiction may in fact be the means of restoring faith, of renewing hope and of embodying love. Indissolubility is misunderstood if it is seen as an externally imposed law, it is rather a law written in the human heart: human relationships reach for permanence, long for communion.

There is, or need be, no contradiction between support for this deep human need – life-long commitment to one partner – and the recognition that people fail, that relationships fail. The attempts to extend the concept of nullity seem to me inappropriate here.

The fragile nature of all human relationships is not sufficiently recognized in a process which requires ultimately that the failed marriage is negated rather than taken up in the human experience of the gap between what we desire and what we realize. What we long for, what we most deeply desire shapes our lives. This is the framework within which we can speak of the ideal of indissolubility.

We need rituals

Compassionate and graced pastoral care for those whose marriages have broken down and a discerning and sensitive approach to all involved in second relationships will enhance and not detract from marriage as a sign of grace, as a sign of God's covenant.

Again the Eastern Church offers us a model. The liturgical celebration of a second marriage includes an expression of sorrow for the failure of the first relationship. In every case of marital breakdown it is possible and desirable to express sorrow without appropriating blame. The plea for forgiveness, for mercy acknowledges our dependence on God's grace. The second union can then be celebrated without denial and with a fuller understanding of ambiguity, of failure, of sin and of grace.

We need such rituals here. Without them the pastoral solutions as suggested by the German bishops remain too much in the private sphere and fail to recognize the full ecclesial dimensions of separation and divorce, except in negative terms – no official liturgical acts are considered appropriate. A ritual which allowed both lament and celebration would speak very deeply to the human experience and would allow it to become a source of grace for the whole Christian community. Those who have suffered the pain and trauma of divorce are not just in need of the compassionate understanding of the Christian community but may themselves be bearers of wisdom for that community. The present procedures see the pastoral work as a one-way process; but those who have experienced failure are also those who have had the opportunity to grow in faith. Many involved in second relationships bring a deepened sense of commitment to those relationships. They may bring a richer understanding of the process of marriage. They may also be involved in caring for children of the first union and through that may gain insights which need to be shared.

What is required is a nuanced discussion which takes account of all the complexities involved. But such a discussion is not possible if there is an insistence on divorce in terms of an absolute evil and if indissolubility becomes an absolute good. The indissolubility of the marriage union should be seen as a good which flows from the grace of marriage and cannot be imposed legally upon it. A marriage which becomes a sacrament carries within it the seeds of its own indissolubility; separation from one's partner becomes unimaginable. The Christian tradition provides both a vision and a story which help to protect that fidelity. Following from that it should be possible to argue that divorce is never a good *in itself* and is always tragic, but in a broader context of the whole economy of salvation it may become a 'necessary evil' and in that limited sense a 'good', relative to a greater good.

Like all moral issues this is extremely complex, and the context into which I want to place this debate is far wider than any notion of personal self-fulfilment. There is a whole web of relationships here and so there are no purely individual decisions of conscience. The Christian Churches have a valuable contribution to make towards a renewed understanding of the place of marriage in contemporary society but they can make such a contribution only if they recognize that some marriages do fail and if they approach the question of divorce and remarriage with realism and thus with credibility.

I suggest that the way forward is not to extend the remit of the marriage tribunals but to continue to develop the pastoral approach learning from the experiences of the married and of the divorced. The language of nullity does not do justice to the complexities and ambiguities of lived experience. If we listen to those whose marriages have failed, for whatever reason, the language used always refers to the existence of a marriage in however fragile a condition. Particularly when children are involved it is essential to affirm the union even while lamenting its failure. For all of us it is possible to move forward only if we are able to accommodate past experiences and not deny them.

It is possible, as evidenced in the Eastern Church, to continue to support lifelong commitment and to help to heal marriages and finally to recognize failed marriages without searching for the 'fatal flaw' which might prove that there was in fact no marriage. Marriage can be supported in a context which recognizes that we are all flawed and limited and that this is the human condition. The sayings of Jesus in relation to divorce cannot be isolated from the total thrust of his message and above all of his practice which demonstrated the primacy of grace over the law. Bernard Treacy talks about holding two truths together with Church bodies giving a strong support for marriage and also providing a healing and helping community for those whose marriages have broken down. Laws are necessary but clumsy and limited ways of organizing human affairs; they never absolve us from the exercise of discernment or from the exercise of making responsible and conscientious decisions.

The table of healing love

So far, I have not referred to the question of exclusion from the sacraments. If we reject the nullity approach and operate instead with the concept of affirmation of the ideal of lifelong fidelity alongside a recognition of human fragility and failure, then exclusion from the table of healing love makes no sense. It is particularly ironic when one observes the table-practice of Jesus: 'He has gone in to be the guest of a man who is a sinner...'; 'Now if this man were a prophet, he would have known...' The Pharisees who are astonished that Jesus has not washed before the meal have their notions of purity overturned and the lawyers are admonished for loading people with burdens hard to bear. It seems clear that those who cannot take the radical inclusiveness of the practice of Jesus are the only ones excluded from his fellowship; in fact they exclude themselves. These are the texts which need to be read alongside the words of prohibition on divorce.

The exclusion of this particular group also raises the deeper question about our theology of Church and of Eucharist. What does it mean to insist that the divorced and remarried are to share in the life of the Church, in its liturgy, its prayer and its works while remaining excluded from the sacraments? This proposal appears to be a contradiction in terms and implies a reduced and impoverished understanding of sacrament. It is difficult to see how one can be welcomed as a member of the Church and excluded from the symbolic celebration of that membership. Francis Moloney, addressing this topic, speaks of a problem with the Church's understanding of itself as 'the perfect society rather than a pilgrimage of sinners'.[2]

On a different level, the exclusion of the divorced and re-married from the sacraments creates a situation of enormous tension for those who experience their 'irregular unions' as a sign of grace, as a source of life and are denied the possibility of publicly acknowledging that grace.

Perhaps it is in this context that we might speak of scandal – for many who have lived through these situations, or who have observed others struggling with the contradiction between their interpretation of their own experience and official Church pronouncements, it is truly a scandal that they are not admitted to the sacraments. It is important also to acknowledge that the current teaching of the Church causes much anguish and pain not alone to those caught up in these situations but also to those who are ministering to them. For this reason it is necessary to hear all the voices in any debate on the issues.

I have attempted to argue here without the support of emotional factors which are bubbling just below the surface. My main thesis is that the context in which we discuss these issues must be broadened and that the perspective within which we view this and other moral issues is that God has created us in love and for freedom, and desires our good. What structures can we put in place to make it most likely that we can live this good? Finally, I quote Häring again:

> What is primarily and ultimately involved is whether the Church in its entire existence, in its dealing with the law of Christ and in its turning to those who have been hurt or who have failed, can ever more strongly be experienced as the sacrament of Christ's reconciling mercy.

(Anne Thurston, 'Living with Ambiguity', *Doctrine and Life*, 1994, pp. 537–542)

1 Bernard Häring, C.Ss.R., *No Way Out: Pastoral Care of the Divorced and Remarried*, St Paul Publications, 1989.
2 Francis Moloney, *A Body Broken for a Broken People: Eucharist in the New Testament* Collins Dove 1990, p. 136.

DIVORCE: NEW TESTAMENT PERSPECTIVES

John R. Donahue SJ

In presenting a picture of unity amid diversity in the Church St Paul writes to his community at Corinth:

> There are varieties of gifts, but the same Spirit. There are varieties of service, but the same Lord. There are varieties of working, but it is the same God who inspires them all in every one (1 Cor. 12:4–6).

Such a vision of diversity with simultaneous interdependence is true in no area of church life today more than in reflection on divorce. The problem posed to church life by the increasing divorce rate calls for mutual co-operation of different kinds of service, and different gifts. In this spirit I offer some reflections on divorce in the New Testament, always conscious that my reflections form only a part of a communal quest.[1] What I propose is a summary of some of the recent exegetical studies on divorce in the New Testament, along with an attempt to locate the New Testament divorce texts in their historical context, as well as some concluding reflections on how these texts bear on our present context.

I. New Testament divorce texts

A. Introductory remarks

An initial caution guides our remarks. What the New Testament says about divorce is disappointingly little. We have four sayings of Jesus from the gospels, one from Paul's first letter to the Corinthians, and some indication from these same sources of how the early Church addressed the question of divorce.[2] In

---

1 These reflections were originally presented as an address to the Midwestern Canon Law Society meeting in Nashville, TN, April 21, 1980.
2 There has been no corresponding dearth of exegetical studies of these limited

comparison with other aspects of Jesus' ethical teaching such as his polemic against legalism, his warnings about the danger of wealth, or his teaching on non-violence and forgiveness of enemies, what Jesus said about divorce is surprisingly meagre and often has been interpreted with a literalness and rigour which has not been applied to such other aspects of his teaching.

Also, almost four decades of New Testament research since *Divino Afflante Spiritu* (1943) have shown us that much of what we have in the gospels on the lips of Jesus bears adaptation to the early Church's theology, so that in assessing a teaching of Jesus one must both reconstruct its original form and context and assess the later context in which it is found. This principle will guide our presentation. We will attempt first to reconstruct and locate the teaching of Jesus on divorce and then assess its adaptation to the Matthean and the Pauline contexts.

B. The teaching of Jesus

From the perspective of tradition history there are three relatively independent sources for Jesus' teaching on divorce; the Q tradition represented by Luke 16:18 and Mt. 5:32; the Markan tradition of 10:1–12 (followed by Mt. 19:1–12); and the Pauline citation of a command of the Lord in 1 Cor. 7:10–11. No one of these sayings agrees exactly with any other and all appear in different contexts. The methods and arguments by which biblical scholars attempt to reconstruct the most original form of Jesus' teaching are complex and demand more attention than the present time allows, so I will present the conclusions adopted by Joseph Fitzmyer in a recent and important article.[3]

Fitzmyer suggests that the most original form of a saying of Jesus on divorce is Luke 16:18.

texts. The major monographs are: H. Baltensweiler, *Die Ehe Im Neuen Testament* (Zurich: Zwingli Verlag, 1967); J. Borsirven, *Le Divorce dans le Nouveau Testament* (Paris: Desclée, 1948) and J. Dupont, *Mariage et divorce dans l'Evangile* (Bruges: Desclée de Brouwer, 1959). A fine bibliography of recent works is: A. Myre, *Dix ans d'exègése sur le divorce dans le Nouveau Testament – Le Divorce: L'Eglise catholique ne devrait-elle pas modifier son attitude séculaire à l'égard de l'indissolubilité de mariage?* (Montreal: Fides, 1973), pp. 139–163. There is a lack of significant monographs in English. A recent popular study is M. & R. Kysar, *The Asundered: Biblical Teaching on Divorce and Remarriage* (Atlanta: John Knox, 1977).

3 J. Fitzmyer, 'The Matthean Divorce Texts and Some New Palestinian Evidence', *Theological Studies* 37 (1976), 197–226. This article and the article by B. Vawter 'Divorce and the New Testament', *Catholic Biblical Quarterly* 39 (1977), 528–542 provide the most up-to-date exegesis on the New Testament divorce texts.

Every one who divorces his wife and marries another commits adultery, and he who marries a woman divorced from her husband commits adultery.[4]

This saying has the flavour of Old Testament casuistic law. It is similar in form to Mt. 5:32 (without the exceptive clause), and is derived from Q. It mirrors the Palestinian environment where the right of divorce existed only for the male.

This saying appears in Luke in a rather isolated context and in Matthew in the antitheses of the Sermon on the Mount. While neither of these contexts may be the historical context, Fitzmyer again is of help in suggesting that the Markan version of the prohibition of divorce may be the more original context. In Mark 10:2–12, Jesus is in controversy with the Pharisees who question whether divorce is in accord with the law of Moses. Scholars until recently have often viewed this context as secondary to the Matthean context where the question is not the licity or non licity of divorce, but the grounds under which divorce was allowed. Since divorce was presumably permitted by all first-century Jews, the only possible historical context was thought to be a debate about its grounds, not its possibility.

The argument runs, then, that Jesus would never have had the occasion to make an absolute prohibition of divorce, but only to have passed judgment on a rabbinic dispute, as we find in Matthew. The recently discovered Temple Scroll and Fitzmyer's analysis of it makes one question this view.[5] The pertinent section from this scroll on the law of the king reads:

And he shall not take in addition to her another wife, for she alone shall be with him all the days of her life and if she dies he shall take for himself another wife (11Q Temple 57: 17–19).

The key phrase is 'she *alone* shall be with him *all the days of her life*'. We have then a text from a first-century Jewish group which rejects not only polygamy, but divorce, and affirms the permanence of monogamous marriage.

While this text does not change *radically* our understanding of the New Testament texts, it is important in a number of ways. First, it shows that Jesus need not be pictured in radical discontinuity with his Jewish environment since there were Jewish

---

4 Translations follow the Revised Standard Version.
5 Fitzmyer, 'Matthean Divorce Texts', 213–221 and 'Divorce Among First-Century Palestinian Jews', in *Eretz Israel: Archaeological, Historical and Geographical Studies*, Vol. XIV (Jerusalem: Israel Exploration Society, 1978).

groups who read the Torah as prohibiting divorce. Secondly it suggests that the Markan context may be close to the original context, that is, does Jesus *prohibit* divorce. Thirdly it suggests that the Matthean exceptive clause may well be Matthew's adaptation of Jesus' teaching to his own community.

At this point our conclusions are rather minimal. The earliest reconstructed tradition of the sayings of Jesus leaves us with a saying in which Jesus prohibits divorce and calls remarriage after divorce adultery. It tells us little about what Jesus meant by this prohibition. For example, all the sayings (except Mt. 5:32) are in the form of statements which forbid divorce and remarriage to the one who obviously initiates the process. There is little said about the innocent victim of divorce. Problems such as abandonment and desertion, which would have been rare in Palestinian society, are scarcely in the purview of Jesus' sayings. We also know too little about the context in which the sayings of Jesus were uttered: Some guidelines for reconstructing this context come from two directions: (a) Jesus' prophetic proclamation and; (b) his eschatological consciousness.

The kingdom proclamation

Virtually every New Testament scholar admits that Mark accurately summarizes the kingdom proclamation of Jesus early in his gospel when Jesus arrives in Galilee preaching the good news of God:

> The time is fulfilled, and the kingdom of God is at hand; repent and believe in the Gospel (Mk 1:14–15).

Jesus is the one who proclaims that in his life and teaching the power or rule of God draws near. This presence of God calls for the most radical of responses, a change of heart and a commitment of the total person in faith. What Jesus proclaims, he enacts. His offer of mercy to tax collectors and sinners, his disdain of ritual laws and his new teaching all scandalize and shock his hearers and summon them to open their hearts to a new way of viewing the world. His summons to discipleship or 'to follow' him invites people to enact in their own lives the commitment of faith.[6]

---

6 An excellent summary of the kingdom proclamation of Jesus can be found in W. Kasper, *Jesus the Christ* (New York: Paulist, 1977, pp. 72–88).

Jesus' prohibition of divorce must be seen in this light. It is a symbol of that most radical kind of conversion to which the kingdom summons. The sayings on divorce all appear in those contexts where Jesus is teaching his disciples the meaning of the kingdom. The Matthean context of 5:32 is in terms of radicalization of the old Torah where even a lustful look is adultery (5:27–28). In Mark, Jesus teaches about divorce in a special instruction to his disciples where he is explaining in hidden fashion the meaning of the cross and the need to lose one's life in order to find it in following Jesus – a teaching which, by the way, the disciples in Mark consistently misunderstand. The sayings on divorce in Mark follow closely on the command to self-mutilation rather than to give scandal, (9:43–50) and are followed by the commands to forsake riches and positions of power and prestige in order to follow Jesus (10:13–31).

To isolate the sayings of Jesus on divorce and make them into moral maxims or illustrations of the moral law is to soften their radicality.[7] They are symbolic ways of affirming that the demands of the kingdom touch the most intimate aspects of human life. At the same time to make these sayings uniquely normative for subsequent church life, is not to do justice to their original prophetic context.

The eschatological context

The second major context of Jesus' teaching on divorce is that of eschatology. Though there is a major debate on whether Jesus felt that the end of human history was actually beginning with his ministry or would arrive in the very near future, few scholars would doubt that Jesus was influenced by the intense

---

7 In the history of the Church the New Testament divorce texts have more often been interpreted in the context of natural law than in their biblical context. A major problem underlying not only the problem of these texts but of many New Testament texts dealing with ethical issues is a lack of a consistent theory of hermeneutics for bridging the gap between moral theology and exegesis. Some exploratory studies on this problem are: B. C. Birch and L. Rasmussen, *Bible and Ethics in The Christian Life* (Minneapolis: Augsburg, 1976); R. Collins, 'Scripture and the Christian Ethic', *Proceedings of the Catholic Theological Society of America*, 29 (1974), 215–241; C. E. Curran, 'Dialogue with the Scriptures: The Role and Function of the Scriptures in Moral Theology', *Catholic Moral Theology in Dialogue* (Notre Dame, Ind.: Fides Publishers, 1972), 24–64; and J. Gustafson, 'The Place of Scripture in Christian Ethics: A Methodological Study', *Interpretation* 24 (1970), 430–455, also in his *Theology and Christian Ethics* (Philadelphia: Pilgrim, 1974), 121–145.

eschatological expectation of his time.[8] Part of this expectation was that the end of history would be the restoration of the pristine state of the world as intended by the creator. It is this context which the gospel of Mark captures when Jesus roots the prohibition of divorce in Genesis 1:

> From the beginning of creation, 'God made them male and female'. For this reason a man shall leave his father and mother and be joined to his wife and the two shall become one flesh so they are no longer two but one flesh. What therefore God has joined together, let no man put asunder (Mark 10:6–8 = Gn 1:27, 5:2; 2:24).

Though these verses from Mark represent a conflation of Old Testament texts and provide evidence of early Church theology, they doubtless reflect Jesus' words. The collection of the texts from Genesis affirms that the possibility of easy divorce is counter to what marriage was intended to be. They attribute two essential aspects to marriage: Unity – the two shall become one; and complementarity or mutual interdependence – neither man alone nor woman alone is the fullness of God's creative design, but that man and woman in union mirror the mystery of God.

The saying of Jesus means in effect that the Jewish divorce laws preclude such an image-ing of God. Allied to this is the fact that the absolute prohibition of divorce on the lips of Jesus is in effect a prophetic defence of the innocent victim of divorce, the woman, since in some interpretations of the Torah at the time of Jesus, the woman had minimal rights in the area of divorce.[9] By negating the interpretation of that portion of the Torah which allowed easy divorce, Jesus undercuts the religious and social basis of this treatment of woman. He also says in effect that

---

8 Often the discussions of the eschatology of Jesus and of the early Church centre on the question of temporality. The argument is then made that since Jesus and the early Church expected the imminent end of history, the ethical teaching of both was an 'interim ethic' or practicable only in a period of intense religious expectation. Rather than pursue the question of temporality I have centred on another aspect of eschatological thought, the view that there was to be a correspondence between the beginning and the end of the age. In this sense Jesus' 'eschatological' teaching can be seen as offering a vision of God's intention for a restored creation. For an excellent short critique of the 'interim ethic' view see W. D. Davies, 'Ethics in the New Testament', *Interpreter's Dictionary of the Bible* 2 (Nashville: Abingdon, 1962), 167–171.

9 See C. R. Taber, 'Divorce', *Interpreter's Dictionary of the Bible Supplement* (Nashville: Abingdon, 1976), 245. Taber points out that though the law permitted easy divorce, 'It is generally agreed that divorce was never frequent among the Hebrews'.

where such a possibility of injustice and inequality exists in marriage there can be no true marriage according to the intent of Genesis. Jesus sees that marriage in which husband and wife are no longer two but one, living in unity and interdependence, as a symbol of a restored creation.

Jesus' teaching on divorce, then, should be viewed in this double context. On the one hand Jesus has a vision of a restored creation where unity and mutuality in marriage mirror God's design. On the other he summons one to a discipleship which recognizes the radical demand of God by precluding divorce, just as in some cases it precludes marriage. To emphasize the radical and eschatological character of Jesus' teaching is not to state as some scholars often do that Jesus proposes simply an impossible ideal. The demands of the kingdom and the fruits of the new creation are to be made concrete in human life. At the same time the social context of Jesus' prohibition of divorce is an intense religious ethic for a group with strong religious identity and support, who felt that the end of history was relatively soon.

What we will see in our next major section is that the teaching of Jesus left the Church with a dialectical legacy. On the one hand the Church continues to affirm the absolute quality of Jesus' prohibition; on the other it admits that this absolute prohibition does not translate always into absolute practice, and is adapted to changing historical and cultural circumstances.

Before leaving the context of Jesus' teaching, one aspect of it must be mentioned which, though not bearing directly on divorce, has significant indirect bearing. In contrast to what I would call the prophetic eschatological context of Jesus' ethical teaching, one must be attuned to what could be called the 'pastoral' context of Jesus' own activity. While the gospels portray Jesus as summoning people to unstinting personal commitment and show him in opposition to hypocrisy and false religiosity, they portray him as having a special penchant for those groups in his society caught in ambiguous moral situations, such as the tax collectors, ritual sinners and prostitutes.[10]

Significant in this light is that there is no word of actual condemnation on the lips of Jesus of 'the divorced' and the

---

10 Cf. R. McCormick, 'Notes on Moral Theology: April–September, 1974' *Theological Studies* 36 (1975), p. 117: '. . . when marriage is concerned, the church has a double mission: to be a prophetic teacher and a healing reconciler'.

gospel of John, in both the canonical (but non-authentic) *pericope de adultera* (7:53–8:11) and the story of the woman at the well (4: 7–42), portrays Jesus, on the one hand, giving special concern to an adulterous woman and on the other giving a special mission to an often married one.[11] A Church which follows the prophetic mandate of Jesus, must also incorporate in its life his pastoral mandate.

C. *Adaptation of the teachings of Jesus*

A few moments ago I suggested that the absolute prohibition of Jesus was adapted to new circumstances. Two such adaptations took place in the early Church and it is to these that we now turn.

The Matthean exceptive clause (Mt. 5:32 and 19:9)

Very few phrases in the New Testament have received the attention of Mt. 5:32 ' . . . everyone who divorces his wife, except on the ground of unchastity' and Mt. 19:9, ' . . . whoever divorces his wife except for unchastity'.[12] The array of technical discussions on the meaning of *porneia* (often translated as 'unchastity' or 'immorality') is staggering, as is the question of whether there is a true 'exception' in the texts.[13]

B. Vawter, followed by D. Crossan has isolated at least six major interpretations:[14] (a) the traditional interpretation, that *porneia* does mean adultery and that the divorce permitted is *separatio a mensa et thoro* – the Greek text supports neither this interpretation of *porneia* nor the translation of 'divorce' as separate; (b) the 'Protestant' (and Orthodox) interpretation that 'adultery' constitutes a ground for divorce – neither the Greek text nor church tradition supports this view; (c) the translation of

---

11 In his article, 'Roles of Women in the Fourth Gospel', *Theological Studies* 36 (1975), 688–699, R. Brown points out that the Samaritan woman becomes a missionary to the Samaritans.

12 See L. Sabourin, 'The Divorce Clauses (Mt. 5:32; 19:9)', *Biblical Theology Bulletin* 2 (1972), 80–86; and B. Vawter, 'The Divorce Clauses in Mt. 5, 32 and 19, 9', *Catholic Biblical Quarterly* 16 (1954), 155–167.

13 J. Jensen, 'Does *porneia* mean Fornication? A Critique of Bruce Malina', *Novum Testamentum* 20 (1978), 161–184; B. Malina, 'Does *porneia* mean Fornication?' *Novum Testamentum* 14 (1972), 10–17. On p. 180 of his article Jensen lists different meanings of *porneia*.

14 Vawter, 'Divorce Clauses', pp. 155–164; D. Crossan, 'Divorce and Remarriage in the New Testament', in *The Bond of Marriage*, ed. W. Bassett (Notre Dame, Ind.: University of Notre Dame Press, 1968), 1–40.

the phrase as 'not even in the case of uncleanliness' – an explanation which involves exegetical gymnastics; (d) the 'interpretative'
interpretation: Jesus while affirming the prohibition of divorce
wanted to favour the school of Hillel (divorce only for adultery)
rather than that of Shammai (divorce for any reason), and
the (e) 'preteritive' interpretation: Jesus wanted to exclude the
question of adultery from the discussion, so that the statement
could be paraphrased, 'Whoever divorces his wife – I don't want
to go into the question of adultery right now . . .', and (f) finally
the 'rabbinic' interpretation.

While all these interpretations have some cogency and
doubtless the combination of exegetical obscurity and human
ingenuity will produce more interpretations, the rabbinic interpretation seems to be gaining the most ground. According to this
interpretation, first popularized by Bonsirven and recently
confirmed by Fitzmyer, *porneia*, which in Greek has a wide variety
of meanings for all kinds of sexual immorality as well as for
ritual pollution and idolatry, translates or reflects in Matthew the
Hebrew term *z^enut*. *Porneia / z^enut* is then said to denote those
kinds of marriage which are within the forbidden degrees of kinship, an example of which would be Leviticus 18:7–18. Bonsirven
showed this usage to be true of rabbinic writings, many of which
are later than the New Testament period; Fitzmyer has shown it
true of the Temple Scroll, a document roughly contemporaneous
with Jesus.[15] In the rabbinic interpretation, then, Jesus would
be saying 'no one should divorce his wife, except in those
cases where the marriage was prohibited from the beginning by
kinship laws'.

The question posed to this rabbinic interpretation is whether it
constitutes a true exception or not. If in effect it says that 'divorce
is prohibited except in those cases where there is no marriage
in the first place', then the situation is simply analogous to
declaring a marriage null and void from the beginning.

There are two major arguments against this view. First, the
kinship laws of Leviticus and later rabbinic interpretation are
based on positive law and are *de facto* not those same kinship
laws followed by the Church in its subsequent history.[16]
Secondly, the term *z^enut* even in the rabbinic interpretation is not
used simply for marriages within the forbidden degrees of

15 Fitzmyer,'Matthean Divorce Texts', pp. 213–221.
16 Crossan, 'Divorce and Remarriage'.

kinship, but also for marriages between a Jew and a proselyte prior to conversion, a freed slave, or a woman guilty of cohabitation outside of marriage (a situation mirrored in the story of Joseph and Mary, Mt 1:18–19).[17] If *porneia* has these connotations in Matthew's exceptive clause then Matthew is giving a number of grounds by which divorce may take place even after the marriage was in existence.

The question remains: what is the meaning of this 'rabbinic exception' in the historical situation of Matthew's gospel? (All we can do here is offer a few hints, since adequate explanation would demand a separate paper). Matthew's gospel dates from the end of the first century, A.D. It is heavily Jewish in flavour with an ambivalent attitude toward Judaism. On the one hand Matthew wants to show that Christianity is the true heir of the promises to Israel and the fulfilment of prophecy; on the other Matthew engages in bitter polemic against Jewish groups. Matthew's gospel is simultaneously a missionary and an apologetic document. Matthew's community may, then, be faced with a number of pastoral problems associated with marriage. Potential Jewish converts living in the diaspora may be in those kinds of marriages which would have been called $z^e nut$/*porneia*.

When they wanted to become Christians, they may have been faced with the same kind of situation as the Gentiles in Corinth – a spouse who did not want to live as a Christian. Gentile converts entering the community may have found that their previous marriages were under the forbidden degrees of kinship of Lev. 18:6–18.[18] Matthew's exceptive clause could say to either group that divorce from one's spouse is permitted in order to become a Christian if the previous marriage was a case of *porneia*/$z^e nut$. The attached logion (Mt 19:12) on those who are eunuchs for the kingdom of heaven might suggest that there are some who are not covered by $z^e nut$ exception and, in this case, must remain unmarried in their lives as Christians.[19] Therefore,

17 M. Geldard, 'Jesus' Teaching on Divorce: Thoughts on the Meaning of *porneia* in Matthew 5:32 and 19:9', *Churchman* 92 (1978), 134–143: F. Hauck and S. Schulz, '*Pornē*, etc.,' *Theological Dictionary of the New Testament* 6 (Grand Rapids: Eerdmans, 1968), 589. These authors list the wider meanings of *porneia*.
18 Fitzmyer, 'Matthean Divorce Texts', p. 211.
19 Current exegetical opinion suggests that the eunuchs for the kingdom of God is not a reference to those who have chosen voluntary celibacy, but refers to those in 19:9 who would commit adultery through remarriage. See Q. Quesnell, 'Made Themselves Eunuchs for the Kingdom of Heaven', *Catholic Biblical Quarterly*, 30 (1968), 335–358; F. J, Maloney, 'Matthew 19, 3:12 and

Matthew's position on divorce represents a dialectic of handing on and affirming the apodictic prohibition of divorce which he received from the tradition and at the same time adapting it to pastoral conditions. While the details of my historical reconstruction would doubtless be debated by New Testament scholars, virtually all would admit that Matthew represents some kind of exception to an absolute prohibition of divorce.

D. The witness of Paul

Though the Synoptic Gospels provide the primary evidence for the teaching of the historical Jesus on divorce, the letters of Paul offer the earliest datable evidence of such teaching of Jesus and the adaptation of this to an historical community. In chapter seven of the first letter to the Corinthians, written around A.D. 57, from Ephesus, Paul addresses a series of questions on marriage and sexuality posed to him by the Corinthians.[20] The first set (7:1–8) seems to be addressed to those who would demand a celibate life of the Christian. While he affirms the value of celibacy as a charism from God and indicates his own preference for it, Paul rejects obligatory celibacy for Christians and portrays marriage as a relationship of mutuality and interdependence especially in the area of sexuality (7:3–6).

In the following sections Paul addresses different groups in the community. Noteworthy about the whole chapter as V. Furnish states is 'a recognition that individual cases may be different and that different circumstances may require different actions'.[21] Paul allows many varied patterns of action in this chapter, celibacy, marriage, re-marriage of widows, and re-marriage of the divorced. The first group addressed are the unmarried and the widows who are counselled to 'remain as I am' (7:8–9). Paul indicates his usual personal preference for the unmarried state, and for the idea that one should not change states (cf. 7:24). Later on in the chapter he will state that the overriding reason for this preference is that 'the time is short' (7:29).

In 7:10–11 Paul addresses those in the state of marriage. Only here does he carefully root the authority of his teaching in a

Celibacy: A Redactional and Form Critical Study', *Journal for the Study of the New Testament* 2 (1979), 42–60, traces the logion to the historical Jesus as a defence of Jesus' own celibacy.

20 V. Furnish, *The Moral Teaching of Paul* (Nashville: Abingdon, 1979), 30–51.

21 *Ibid.*, p. 49.

command of the Lord (Not I, but the Lord, 7:10), which he states as follows:

10b A Wife should not separate from her husband
11a (But if she does, let her remain single or else be reconciled to her husband) – and that
11b the husband should not divorce his wife

Though cited as a command of the Lord, the saying corresponds to no other version of the saying of Jesus. Like Mark, it mirrors the Hellenistic world where both the wife and husband had the ability to divorce; unlike Mark the woman is mentioned first. Unlike Q and Mark there is no explicit mention of adultery in conjunction with a second marriage. Since there is no saying of Jesus which speaks of the need for reconciliation and since the term is distinctly Pauline, many authors feel that the vs. 11[a], the 'advice' to the divorced woman, is a Pauline commentary on a saying of the Lord.[22] The original saying of the Lord is then a simple prohibition of divorce which has been adapted like that of Mark, to the Hellenistic environment. It is independent evidence that the saying without the exceptive clause of Matthew 19:9; 5:32 is the more original saying.

E. *The Pauline exception (1 Cor. 7:12–16)*

Our major concern is with the situation envisioned in vss. 12–16. Paul addresses this section to 'the rest', a different group from the married of vss. 10–11, and presumably those in mixed marriages, between believers and unbelievers. In contrast to his citation of a saying of the Lord in vs. 10, Paul bases the following verses strictly on his own authority ('I say, not the Lord'). Paul first sets down his general principle in regard to such marriages. Since there may have been some in the community who wanted to forbid Christians to retain their pagan spouses, Paul sets down the general principle that such marriages are permissible.[23] It is rather interesting that Paul seems to recognize the right of the Christian brother or sister to initiate divorce proceedings, for his exact advice reads:

22 Baltensweiler, *Die Ehe*, p. 191 states that the original saying of the Lord comprised 10b and 11b. 11a is an insertion by Paul evoked by an actual situation in Corinth. He is followed by D. Dungan, *The Sayings of Jesus in the Churches of Paul* (Philadelphia: Fortress, 1971), p. 41.
23 Furnish, *Moral Teaching*, p. 41.

> If any brother has a wife who is an unbeliever and she consents to live with him, he should not divorce her.
>
> If any woman has a husband who is an unbeliever and he consents to live with her, she should not divorce him (7:12, 13).

The English translation does not always capture the force of the Greek here. 'Agrees to live' could better be expressed as 'co-operates in forming a home'.[24] Paul is not talking about a life of minimal cohabitation, but, as the next verse shows, a union where there is some harmony, freedom and peace. The theological reason for this continued union is that there is a communication of holiness from the believer to the unbeliever and to the children of the marriage (7:14). Paul evidently sees marriage as that kind of union in which the faith and holiness of the Christian is such that it sanctifies the non-Christian spouse.

The Pauline exception appears in very condensed form in vs. 15:

> If the unbelieving partner desires to separate, let it be so; in such cases a brother or sister is not bound (lit. enslaved). For God has called us to peace.[25]

While Paul gives no explicit reasons for the departure there are certain hints in the text which suggest the reasons for the failure of the marriage and why Paul approves remarriage for the Christian partner. The first hint is the phrase that the Christian brother or sister is 'not to become a slave in these matters'. This emphasis given to freedom suggests other aspects of Pauline theology. In the letter to the Galatians, Paul writes: 'For freedom Christ has set us free', (5:1). Since the phrase 'in these matters' may refer to the situation prior to the divorce as well as after it, it may well be that the whole marital situation was for the believer a situation of virtual slavery where the Christian partner can no longer during the marriage or subsequent to its break-up experience the freedom of the gospel. Such a situation is for Paul contrary to the deepest meaning of the gospel and hence should not exist.

24 The Greek reads *syneudokei oikein*. The verb *oikein* is stronger than the English 'live with'. It is cognate to *oikia*, house or household and can also mean 'have an abode', settle. See, Bauer, Arndt, Gingrich, Danker, *A Greek-English Lexicon of the New Testament and Other Early Christian Literature* (Chicago: Univ. of Chicago Press, 1979), p. 557.

25 The RSV and NAB translation, 'Is not bound', is too weak. The Greek *dedoulōtai*, the perfect passive of *douloō*, is best understood as 'enslaved' or subjected to slavery. See Gal. 4:3 and 2 Pet. 2:19.

The second major reason for permission of divorce, is 'in peace God has called you'. One should not understand this 'peace' simply as domestic harmony which would be shattered by bitter disputes over matters of religion. It is primarily a theological and eschatological concept. Paul begins his letters most often by wishing his communities 'grace and peace' which are the *bona messianica*, the presence of God's graciousness and right order and harmony which is to characterize the new creation. In Romans Paul says that peace is the result of Christ's redemptive work (5:1). In his picture of the life in the Spirit consequent on baptism, Paul says that 'the mind controlled by the Spirit is life and peace' (8:6). In Romans he also says that the kingdom of God is a matter of 'righteousness, peace and joy' in the Holy Spirit and counsels his community 'to make every effort to do what leads to peace' (14:17, 19). In 1 Corinthians Paul allows divorce because the presumed unharmonious marriage creates a situation where that peace or *shalom* which is characteristic of the new age and the fruit of Christ's saving work cannot exist.[26] In terms taken from later theology we might say that for Paul this marriage has ceased to be a sign and a source of grace.

Finally, the third reason of vs. 16 is really quite obscure:

How do you know, wife, if you will save your husband
And how do you know, husband if you will save your wife.

The most general explanation is that Paul is saying that there is little reason for a marriage to continue where the kind of sanctification hoped for in vs. 14 is impossible. It is clear Paul thinks of marriage less as a bond or a contract than as a process where mutual sanctification should be taking place.

In 1 Corinthians 7:13–16 Paul presents a clear exception to an explicit command of the Lord. He does this on his own authority but with theological grounding inherent in his understanding of the total Christ event. He allows for divorce (and presumably remarriage) in those situations where disharmony and absence of faith destroy that union where sanctification is to occur. Such a marriage spawns a situation of slavery which is in opposition to his gospel of Christian freedom and creates a state without that peace which is to characterize the vocation of the Christian.

26 See W. Byron, '1 Cor. 7:10–15: A Basis for Future Catholic Discipline on Marriage and Divorce', *Theological Studies*, 34 (1973), 429–445. Byron argues for a Pauline exception to the absolute prohibition of divorce, an exception which is not equated with the later Pauline privilege.

II. Summary and conclusion

Though limitations of time have not allowed a full exegetical treatment of the New Testament divorce texts, I would like now, to offer a brief summary of the New Testament evidence and suggest more implications of this for church life today.

(1) The earliest tradition of the sayings of Jesus attested by Mark, the Q source and Paul discloses a saying of Jesus against divorce. Divorce is counter to that created order for man and woman intended by God, 'What God has joined together let no human put asunder'. Having said this we must add certain cautions. As L. Wrenn stated in 1973 and R. McCormick in 1975 we must not too quickly equate the language of Jesus with the canonical or legal language about indissolubility. In 1973 Lawrence Wrenn voiced this caution in the following terms:

> The distortion, I think, is not in seeing a bond where there is none but in seeing the bond as indissoluble whereas in fact it is quite fragile.[27]

and in 1975 R. McCormick in his address to the Canon Law Society argued against thinking of indissolubility only in the juridical sense and stated that 'indissolubility ought to be thought of above all and primarily as an absolute moral precept, a moral ought inherent in the marriage union'.[28] The teaching of the historical Jesus is cast in the form of such a 'moral ought', but it is not in the legal form of a declarative pronouncement about a bond which cannot be broken.

(2) The teaching of Jesus must be evaluated always according to its context. In his ministry Jesus was the proclaimer of the kingdom who confronted people with the presence of God in his ministry and teaching. The proclamation of Jesus presents a radical ethic in major areas of life such as non-resistance to evil, renunciation of wealth, the breaking of family ties, and the giving of life for another. One cannot relativize some of the teaching of Jesus while absolutizing other aspects of it, without doing injustice to the New Testament and its interpretation. The teaching of Jesus is also in the context of a prophetic defence of marriage in the face of easy divorce laws which prevented marriage from being that kind of life between man and woman in

27 L. G. Wrenn, *Divorce and Remarriage in the Catholic Church* (New York: Newman Press), p. 134.
28 R. A. McCormick, 'Indissolubility and the Right to the Eucharist – Separate Issues or One?' *Proceedings of the Canon Law Society of America, 37th Annual Convention*, 1975, p. 35.

mutual interdependence and harmony intended by the creator. It is also a protest against the innocent victim of such divorce laws, the woman spouse in the marriage.

(3) The handing on of the tradition of Jesus in the early Church involves a twofold movement. On the one hand, the Church continues to reiterate Jesus' prophetic defence of marriage. On the other hand, in its application of this defence to concrete instances the Church mirrors the 'pastoral' concern of Jesus.

In the early Church the Apostle Paul provides the clearest example of this double focus. He defends marriage against those who would force celibacy or separation upon would-be Christians and says that where separation does occur reconciliation is to take place. At the same time, he sees marriage as a dynamic process and in the case of the marriage between the unbeliever and the believer where sanctification freedom and peace can not arise, he allows for divorce.

Both Mark and Matthew defend marriage against easy divorce, and Mark adapts this defence to a Hellenistic environment, while Matthew allows divorce to members of his community whose first marriages did not meet the demands of Jewish law.

Despite disagreement on details there is a growing consensus among Catholic exegetes that Matthew and Paul present both an exception to the absolute prohibition of divorce and represent adaptation of Jesus' teaching to their own church situation. There is also consensus that these exegetical findings should bear on church life and practice today. Three significant figures illustrate this.

At the end of his most careful study of the Matthean divorce texts, Joseph Fitzmyer writes:

> If Matthew under inspiration could have been moved to add an exceptive phrase to the saying of Jesus about divorce that he found in an absolute form in either his Marcan source or in 'Q', or if Paul likewise under inspiration could introduce into his writing an exception on his own authority then why cannot the Spirit-guided institutional Church of a later generation make a similar exception in view of problems confronting Christian married life of its day or so called broken marriages (not really envisaged in the New Testament) as it has done in some situations.[29]

In similar vein George MacRae writes:

> We must discern the process by which the teaching of Jesus was remembered, communicated, interpreted, adapted and enshrined in

29 'Matthean Divorce Texts', pp. 224–225.

the practice of the early Christian communities. That process, we have seen, is one of accommodation to circumstances that were not the context of the preaching of Jesus himself.[30]

And most recently (1977) Bruce Vawter, who has studied the New Testament divorce texts for over twenty years writes:

> The Christian communities which have accepted divorce as a deplorable but an inevitable fact of life have taken some guidance admittedly from New Testament exegesis, but far more they have taken their guidance from other indices to the realities of the human condition in their times, and this is perhaps partly as it should be. I speak here not particularly of the Protestant churches, for of no Christian community is this fact truer than of the Roman Catholic church, which despite its reputation for an adamantine opposition to divorce in any form yet has asserted to itself more than any other Christian body the prerogative of dissolving – that is divorcing – practically every conceivable bond of marriage save one; and that one, as it happens, which should be the chief focus of its pastoral concern, the sacramental marriage *ratum et consummatum*.[31]

In a most basic sense the New Testament does sanction what is in fact church teaching and pastoral practice today. The Church stands in prophetic opposition to that divorce which destroys that love and life together which was intended by God for man and woman. At the same time through its marriage tribunals, through continued reflection on 'the pastoral solution' and through a ministry to the divorced, the Church is continuing that 'pastoral dimension' of the ministry of Jesus and the missionary practice of Matthew and Paul. While bearing in its life the prophetic teaching of Christ, the Church must also present to the world that Christ who defended the innocent victims of different forms of oppression and who was ever present to sinners and tax collectors and whose offer of love was closer to the religiously marginal than to the pious and just. Any step backwards to a simple 'adamantine opposition' to divorce without adaptation of this opposition and the questioning of its absolute application would not be faithful to the New Testament.

(John R. Donahue, SJ, 'Divorce: New Testament Perspectives',
The Month, 1981, pp. 113–120)

30 'New Testament Perspectives on Marriage and Divorce', in Wrenn, ed. *Divorce and Remarriage*, p. 12.
31 'Divorce and the New Testament', p. 542. A. Ambrozic, 'Indissolubility of
 . Marriage in the New Testament: Law or Ideal?' *Studia Canonica* 6 (1972), 269–288, argues against this 'consensus' and holds that neither Paul nor Matthew constitute a true exception to an absolute prohibition.

REMARRIAGE AND THE DIVORCE SAYINGS ATTRIBUTED TO JESUS

Mary Rose D'Angelo*

Recent Catholic theology has sought in the Jesus of history a critique and a source of guidance for the Church's theologizing, frequently in the expectation that Jesus' mission and teaching will provide either a more liberating and less rigid or a more stable and certain source of faith and practice than the diverse and sometimes ossified history of tradition. But this approach has only enhanced the status of the prohibitions of divorce and remarriage. 'Sayings of Jesus' have played a significant role in defending the Church's prohibition of remarriage after divorce.[1] This role has actually been reinforced by the use of historical-critical methods for retrieving the teaching of Jesus. Because sayings on divorce and remarriage are 'multiply attested,' that is, appear not only in Mark but in Paul, and may also have been handed down in Q, a large number of scholars have insisted that the prohibitions of divorce, or of divorce and remarriage, must be counted among a very few sayings that can be traced back to Jesus.[2] This has been taken to imply that they therefore have a special status in church legislation. Seeing the prohibitions of divorce and remarriage as a teaching of the historical Jesus has placed these prohibitions beyond the power of the Church to change or modify.[3] They are understood to express 'not merely an ideal but a norm' for Christian life.[4]

In recent years, there have been numerous studies of the sayings on divorce and remarriage attributed to Jesus and of issues and texts related to them. Catholic biblical scholars have argued that the early communities that used the sayings and the gospel authors who incorporated them into their narratives felt free to modify and adapt the sayings. The variety of decisions made in these sayings suggests that their collective message may be quite different than the one that is frequently drawn from them. Careful examination of the various versions of the sayings about divorce and remarriage attests to a common context, but to

---

* This article is summarized on pp. 157–158, n. 9.

quite different functions of the prohibitions. Thus the sayings themselves show that they mediate not unchanging teaching but rather a series of adaptations and revisions of practice. They demonstrate precisely the communities' prophetic authority to understand, apply, rethink, even suppress the prohibitions in response to their own situations.

This essay will build upon this observation, but will attempt further to change the grounds on which the sayings are discussed by bringing the experience of prophetic authority in the community from the background into the foreground of discussions of these sayings. It will make three major points. The first point will be that by preserving the variety of sayings that were used in the early communities, the New Testament itself manifests the early communities' belief that the authority of the Spirit permitted them to modify and to apply these sayings of the Lord.

Secondly, the essay will call into question the attribution of the prohibitions to the Jesus of history. It is certainly true that prohibitions of either divorce or remarriage appear in at least five different contexts and perhaps three different sources. But multiple attestation shows only their antiquity, not their origin with the historical Jesus. Indeed, the texts themselves offer evidence that the source of the prohibitions may be not the Jesus of history, but the experience of early Christian prophecy. I do not wish to argue that this experience is less authoritative than words of the historical Jesus, but rather to stress its authority in the early community.

Third, I shall argue that the common context in which these sayings occur is the context of early Christian asceticism. In each of the documents in which they are found, they function either to modify or to enforce the demands of sexual asceticism. In their New Testament contexts, the sayings do not express an ideal but rather a variety of expedients; thus they can not provide an adequate basis for reflection on marriage or remarriage.

These points can only be made by examining the sayings in very considerable detail. This essay will review the sayings three times, from different perspectives. It will first give a brief description of the sayings and their relation to one another, stressing the variations among the sayings. Next it will review them a second time in order to raise the question of their origin. A third review of the sayings will look at their function in the context of the various works in which they appear, underlining their function in early Christian sexual asceticism.

Sources, documents and the variety of rulings

After describing the various occurrences of sayings on divorce and how she understands the relations between these sayings, Professor D'Angelo summarizes her conclusions as follows:

Thus the early Christian rulings on divorce and remarriage exhibit a very considerable variation in the issues which the different versions address and the ways in which the sayings are applied. Paul prohibits divorce on a commandment of the Lord, and requires that a woman who divorces remains unmarried or be reconciled to her husband. On the other hand, he seems to permit a Christian who is divorced by a non-believer to remarry. Mark forbids divorce, and equates remarriage with adultery in the case of the one who divorces, whether man or woman, but makes no ruling about the party who is divorced. Matthew and Luke both rule that the man who divorces commits adultery and the man who marries a divorced woman commits adultery. Matthew also rules that the man who divorces a woman makes her an adulterer. Matthew forbids divorce in all cases except fornication. Hermas requires divorce, or at least separation, in the case of a spouse who commits sexual immorality.

These differences should not be looked upon as trivial, or as apparent only. How then are they to be interpreted? Some might argue that the differences should become the basis of current law or theology. For instance one might argue that because versions in Paul and Mark, the earlier writers, do not forbid a person who has been divorced to remarry, we should permit remarriage to the 'innocent party.'

But a more thoroughgoing conclusion can and should be drawn from the variations in the commands. Joseph Fitzmyer S.J.[19] and the late George MacRae S.J.[20] both have remarked upon the variety of rulings articulated in early Christianity[21] and have suggested that the lesson that ought to be learned from them is that the Church does indeed have the right and even the obligation to reinterpret and reapply the teaching of Jesus. The early communities which used the sayings and the gospel writers who interpreted them in their narratives acted with prophetic authority in appropriating and adapting the sayings. In the words of George MacRae,

> . . . we must discern the process by which the teaching of Jesus was remembered, communicated, interpreted, adapted and enshrined in

the practice of the early Christian communities . . . The matrix of modern discernment is, as it was in the churches of Paul and of Matthew, the dwelling of the Holy Spirit among God's people.[22]

In recognizing the variations in the sayings, we already acknowledge that words of Jesus are mediated to us by the prophetic authority of the early communities and the gospel authors. I wish to argue that the prophetic authority of the primitive communities not only lies behind the variations but also is the source of the prohibitions themselves.

The question of origin: Paul and the risen Lord in the Prophets

Professor D'Angelo argues that the original source of the various prohibitions of divorce and/or remarriage need not have been the Jesus of history but that it is possible, even likely, that they are sayings of the risen Lord speaking in the Prophets of the Jesus movement and/or the early Christian mission. After developing this line of argument, she concludes as follows:

In concluding this part of the discussion, I wish to clarify the intent of my argument in two ways. First, I have not shown (and have not intended to show) that Jesus could not have been the origin of the prohibitions of divorce and remarriage. But I have shown that it can no longer be taken for granted that they originated with Jesus, and have suggested an alternative origin for them in the experience of early Christian prophecy. Second, in arguing that they may derive from the Lord speaking in the prophets rather than from the historical Jesus, I am not simply attempting to call into question the authority of the sayings. I do not necessarily believe that the teaching of Jesus should be regarded as more authoritative than the teaching of the spirit in the Church. My concern is to illuminate the experiential context of the sayings. Seeing the sayings as the product of early Christian prophecy gives a new context and I hope new force to a case that has already been made by such scholars as MacRae and Fitzmyer: the case that sees the variety of stipulations as the precedent which authorizes the voice of the spirit in the life of today's Christian communities. This view of the sayings and their variety invites us to abandon attempts to reconstruct a single unequivocal intention of Jesus and ultimately of God that lies behind the differing stipulations. It requires us to value the differences, to take seriously the context to which they belong, and look to the prophetic authority in our own communities, asking how these sayings should interact with our context.

Some attempts to ask and answer this question in new ways have suggested that it is appropriate to see them as expressing an ideal of married love, toward which all should aim, but from which, perhaps inevitably, some will fall short. I would suggest that the texts that use these prohibitions do not offer an ideal of married love. Rather their real concern is the tension between the sexual asceticism that swept the early communities and marriage as a guarantee of sexual and social responsibility.

Context: Varieties of ascesis

In this third section of her article, Professor D'Angelo argues that the sayings are used in cases in the context of early Christian sexual asceticism and their aim is first to moderate and then enforce sexual asceticism. She summarizes her conclusion as follows:

In all the occurrences of prohibitions of divorce and remarriage in these primitive Christian texts, their context seems to be early Christian sexual asceticism. Paul and Mark exercise the prohibitions in order to moderate the force of early Christian asceticism by rejecting divorce for its sake; both are concerned to protect the ascetic call against practices which would bring it into ill repute. Luke rejects the prohibition of divorce; although the application of the prohibition of remarriage in Luke 16:18 appears to be metaphorical, the ascetic tenor of Luke makes it probable that it was applied literally in Luke's community. Matthew's greater righteousness includes a sexual ascesis that explicitly prohibits divorce in all circumstances except the 'fornication' of the wife; implicitly it demands divorce in these cases. The disciples express Matthew's view that these demands are the equivalent of celibacy. *Hermas* demands divorce in the interest of sexual purity if one's wife is discovered in adultery, but prohibits remarriage, in order to allow for the repentance of the divorced wife. The ascetic context of the sayings in these works is of importance to us in two ways. First, it confirms the prophetic origin of the sayings and of their variations; prophetic circles evince a particularly strong interest in sexual purity and asceticism.[69] Second, the context of sexual asceticism and the *ad hoc* character of the sayings themselves mean that they cannot be taken to be a determinative source of reflection and practice about marriage for the church communities of our times. They by no means express an ideal for marriage; rather, they deal with marriage in terms of what is expedient. The ideal toward which ancient Christianity aspired was sexual restraint. Freedom and the spirit were to be found in sexual asceticism.[70]

Thus while I do not believe that the observation that these sayings may come from the experience of early Christian prophecy necessarily undercuts their authority, the context from which they address divorce and remarriage does indeed raise profound problems about their use. They do not value remarriage because they cannot adequately value marriage.

For the most part these texts share the vision of their world that understood marriage as a social responsibility, but personal bondage. They offer freedom by sexual ascesis. But just as marriage in the world from which they come was a patriarchal institution, the freedom through sexual renunciation that the texts envisage was by no means equally available to all. There is a notable contrast between Paul and Mark on the one hand and Matthew and Luke on the other. Paul and Mark see the ascetic demand as addressed to women as well as to men, although it is not clear that women share equally in the ascetic call in the view of either. The Corinthians' ascetic principle is 'it is good for a man not to touch a woman.' In Matthew and Luke, on the other hand, the behaviour of women comes under scrutiny and is of concern to the formulation of the prohibitions. But women are not addressed in these sayings. The discipline that is described in both is addressed to the man. We know that early Christian asceticism as a call to freedom had an extremely strong appeal to women,[71] and the gospel of Luke makes some references to women who practise sexual asceticism. Yet in both Matthew and Luke the demands of sexual asceticism are articulated in an entirely androcentric fashion.[72]

It would be difficult to argue that the Church's tradition has overcome the inadequacy of the New Testament as source for a Christian vision of marriage. What is needed is a way of defining sexual mores in terms of relationship and responsibility rather than in terms of purity and pollution. Where will the resources for such a revisioning arise? I suggest that what is needed is a new exercise of the prophetic spirit.

New prophecies

The rising interest in the role of early Christian prophecy in the formation of the Christian scriptures has prompted scholars to look for elements in contemporary Christian community life that correspond to the functions of prophecy in the ancient churches. Two functions in particular have been singled out for special attention. One is the interpretation of scripture,[73] and the other the service of pastoral instruction in Christian living.[74] The office of pastoral instruction in this regard belongs in a special way to those who can speak with the voice of communal experience, to the tribunals, to organizations like Divorced and Separated Catholics, to the unheard voices of married and single parents, of battered women. This volume is addressed especially to such people, to those who can and must speak to and from these communal experiences; I look forward in hope to the instruction, the upbuilding that you will offer us. But such reflection and instruction is deeply intertwined with communal meditation on the scriptures. So before I close, I wish to point you toward an interpretation of scripture that might inform your task.

Most attempts to use the New Testament as a source for a theological vision of marriage and sexuality follow the lead of Mark 10:2–9 in attempting to base teaching on marriage in the intention of creation expressed in Genesis 1:27. But reaffirmations of creation can never address the history of oppression that is attached to marriage, Christian and otherwise. Instead I would suggest that to re-read, to re-member our communal arrangements of sex and gender in a way that hears and applies God's word to our living communities, we must begin from another use of the scripture in the New Testament. That use is the baptismal tradition of the new creation inherited and passed on by Paul:

> All you who have been baptized into Christ have put on Christ: there is among you neither Jew nor Greek, neither slave nor free, no 'male or female.'

This formula rejects the dispensation of Genesis 1:27 as the basis of Christian life. The unequal sexual arrangements of marriage and social intercourse are no longer appropriate for the communal life. Too often this verse has been cited as an affirmation of promordial or ultimate equality within the community. Galatians 3:28 should not be used as proof that the churches are OK, that they have at heart the best intentions toward women and the oppressed. Rather Galatians 3:28 must be seen as a call to the future. Remembering it should make and keep us profoundly aware of how badly the churches have behaved toward one member of each of these pairs. It is only very recently that we as members of the churches have begun to take account of the long sinful histories of our communities toward Jews, toward slaves, toward women. This text should not function in our thought as reassurance about our origins, but as a call to massive repentance.

(Mary Rose D'Angelo, 'Remarriage and the Divorce Sayings attributed to Jesus', in William P. Roberts (ed.), *Divorce and Remarriage: religious and psychological perspectives*, Sheed & Ward, Kansas City, 1990, pp. 78–106, abbrev. to only eight pages)

Notes

1. See, e.g., the commentary on canon 1056 in *The Code of Canon Law: A Text and Commentary* (Commissioned by the Canon Law Society of America: ed. James A. Coriden, Thomas J. Green, and Donald E. Heintschel; New York: Paulist, 1985), 742 and n. 11. The Apostolic Exhortation of John Paul II, *Familiaris Consortio,*, actually claims that the practice of excommunicating the remarried is based on scripture. See *On the Family* (Washington DC: United States Catholic Conference 1981), 83.
2. See e.g. Pheme Perkins, "Marriage in the New Testament and Its World," *Commitment to Partnership: Explorations of the Theology of Marriage* (ed. William P. Roberts; New York: Paulist, 1987), 5–33 esp. 15–16; also Joseph A. Fitzmyer S.J., "The Matthean Divorce Texts and Some New Palestinian Evidence," *Theological Studies* 37 (1976), 197–226; George MacRae S.J., "New Testament Perspectives on Marriage and Divorce," *Divorce and Remarriage in the Catholic Church* (ed.) Lawrence G. Wrenn; New York: Newman Press, 1973), 1–15.
3. These observations are made also by Joseph S. Fitzmyer, "Matthean Divorce Texts," 223–226.
4. Commentary on canon 1056 in *The Code of Canon Law*, 742.
19. Fitzmeyer, "Matthean Divorce Texts," 224.
20. MacRae "NT Perspectives," 9–10.
21. It should be noted that Fitzmyer and MacRae see, or at least focus upon, fewer variations than I have described. They focus upon 1 Cor. 7:12–16 and the exceptive clause in Matthew.
22. MacRae "NT Perspectives," 12.
69. See D.L. Balch, "Backgrounds of I Cor. VII: Sayings of the Lord in Q; Moses as an Ascetic *Theios Aner* in II Cor. III," *NTS* (1972) 351–364.
70. See on this Elaine Pagels, *Adam, Eve and the Serpent* (New York: Random House, 1988), esp. 3–77.
71. Kraemer, Ross, "The Conversion of Women to Ascetic Forms of Christianity," *Signs* 6 (1980–81), 298–307.
72. On the patriarchal character of asceticism for women, see Elizabeth Castelli, "Virginity and its Meaning for Women's Sexuality in Early Christianity," *Journal of Feminist Studies in Religion* 2 (1986), 61–88.
73. See e.g. Edouard Cothenet, "Les prophètes chrétiens comme exégètes charismatiques de l'écriture," *Prophetic Vocation* (ed. Johannes Panagopoulos), 77–107.
74. David Hill, "Christian Prophets as Teachers or Instructors in the Church," *Prophetic Vocation* (ed. Johannes Panagopoulos), 108–130.